Female
Circumcision

WOMEN FROM THE MARGINS

An Orbis Series Highlighting Women's Theological Voices

Women from the Margins introduces a series of books that present women's theological voices from around the world. As has long been recognized, women have shaped and continue to shape theology in distinctive ways that recognize both the particular challenges and the particular gifts that women bring to the world of theology and to ministry within the church. Their theological voices reflect the culture in which they live and the religious practices that permeate their lives.

Also in the Series:

Female Circumcision

The Interplay of Religion, Culture, and Gender in Kenya

Mary Nyangweso Wangila

ORBIS BOOKS

Maryknoll, New York 10545

Founded in 1970, Orbis Books endeavors to publish works that enlighten the mind, nourish the spirit, and challenge the conscience. The publishing arm of the Maryknoll Fathers and Brothers, Orbis seeks to explore the global dimensions of the Christian faith and mission, to invite dialogue with diverse cultures and religious traditions, and to serve the cause of reconciliation and peace. The books published reflect the views of their authors and do not represent the official position of the Maryknoll Society. To learn more about Maryknoll and Orbis Books, please visit our website at www.maryknoll.org.

Copyright © 2007 by Mary Nyangweso Wangila.

Published by Orbis Books, Maryknoll, New York 10545–0308.
Manufactured in the United States of America.
Manuscript editing and typesetting by Joan Weber Laflamme.

Library of Congress Cataloging-in-Publication Data

Wangila, Mary Nyangweso.
    Female circumcision : the interplay of religion, culture, and gender in Kenya / Mary Nyangweso Wangila.
        p. cm. — (Women from the margins series)
    Includes bibliographical references and index.
    ISBN-13: 978-1-57075-710-5 (pbk.)
    1. Female circumcision—Kenya. 2. Female circumcision—Kenya—Religious aspects. 3. Circumcision—Religious aspects—Christianity. 4. Circumcision—Religious aspects—Islam. 5. Indigenous peoples—Kenya—Religion. 6. Women—Kenya—Social conditions. 7. Women—Religious life—Kenya. 8. Sex role—Kenya. 9. Kenya—Religious life and customs. 10. Kenya—Social life and customs. I. Title.
    GN659.K4W34 2007
    392.1096762—dc22
                                                          2006030800

Contents

Foreword

Mercy Amba Oduyoye

On the map of Africa and the Arabic peninsula included in this book (p. xvi), I am situated in Ghana, in the zone marked "Infibulation"; yet I had no direct experience of the practice, nor did I know of its existence in Ghana until the debate sparked by the publication of *Gyn/Ecology: The Metaethics of Radical Feminism* (Mary Daly, 1978). That debate was intensified for me by *Possessing the Secret of Joy* (Alice Walker, 1992). But it took a television program in 1995 to jolt me into putting pen to paper to describe where I stood and still stand on this issue.

While thousands of women in Africa, the Arabic peninsula, and elsewhere have been circumcised, and many more are threatened by it, there are both women and men who ask, "Why all this fuss?" I dare say that I was not alone in my ignorance because in Africa the very telling itself has been taboo. Many Africans are irritated by the "fuss" because female circumcision is viewed as an issue of culture and religion, and not a sickness for which a cure is required.

Way back in the mid-1970s a woman from southeastern Nigeria— a student in the religious studies department of the University of Ibadan in Nigeria, where I was teaching at the time—described the circumcising of women to usher them into womanhood in an essay about initiation or transition rites among her people. When she was interrogated by the Ghanaian professor of the course, she proudly announced that she had been circumcised. I fell into a state of shock and disbelief. What could I say? This woman was an "insider." This led me to begin informal research, and I discovered how widespread and varied this practice was (and still is) among ethnic groups in Africa. Until then, in matters of culture and religion I had always upheld the principle of privileging the insider. Does not an Akan proverb say, It is the person sleeping by the fire who knows how much and where the heat hurts?

When I referred to the practice at public events, it was always in response to questions, and I named it female circumcision. Mary Wangila, the author of this book, who has greatly deepened my knowledge of the practice, also names the practice female circumcision, and that is what I shall use here, although I have joined both insiders and outsiders who have labeled it female genital mutilation. Eventually I shattered my self-imposed silence by writing and distributing a poem titled "When the Telling Itself Is a Taboo" to my friends, both insiders and outsiders. I wrote frankly, calling the practice "cruelty" and noting that surely the circumcising community does not set out to be cruel to its women. "Too simple," you might say, and I acknowledge this, but I used poetic license to name my gut response to excision and I wrote out of compassion rather than arrogance. Later I wrote a companion poem, "Leave Well Alone," that describes how men and women from different cultures and times have tortured or been tortured for the sake of beauty.

Since then I have been further educated by many women involved in both research and advocacy on the issue and also by debates on the practice, especially by women of the Circle of Concerned African Women Theologians. Included in this group are some Ethiopian and Kenyan women who have researched and written on this and other traditional practices that are harmful to women. Outstanding contributions have been made particularly by Nyambura J. Njoroge, a Kenyan, whose doctoral thesis from Princeton Theological Seminary explored "the cut." It was published under the title *Kiama Kia NGO: An African Christian Feminist Ethics of Resistance and Transformation* (Asempa Press, Accra, Ghana, 2000). In trying to render African words into English, she chose the term "the cut" to describe the variety of surgical procedures that are employed. Mary Wangila is clear about the need to be circumspect in choosing language for naming the practice and respectful to those engaged in the debate. I appreciate her particular emphasis that "any terminology adopted to label female circumcision must acknowledge the sociocultural and religious values that inform the practice, even while critiquing it."

Because a goal of African women is to bring life into their communities, it is a privilege for me to associate myself with this book by a Kenyan woman who is a sociologist, a theologian, and an insider. The tensions and challenges of being involved in the debate about female circumcision are very real. For some women it is a matter of life and death. The forces of colonialism, imperialism, European ethnocentrism, Christianization and Islamization, and the current globalizing of our world create crises of identity for many peoples of the world, especially for those who live in communities that are bound together by a particular ideology.

The insider/outsider debate raised by the author goes far beyond the immediate concern of this book. Should the United Nations, for example, ever "interfere" in a national crisis? However, read this book with care, because the theories used to examine female circumcision go beyond the subject but never subsume this matter of life and death for many women and girls. While a theoretical framework is essential, we must never lose sight of the fact that women and girls who have real names and expectations are dying because of female circumcision. Ponder the debate as stated in Chapter 3. Reflect on the questions raised at the beginning of that chapter and consider how they are answered by various persons and groups and from different social locations and advocacy stances.

I am personally drawn to this book because of its focus on the role of religion. Religion informs the attitudes and shapes the responsibilities of many Africans, whether they are practitioners of the Indigenous religions of Africa, of Christianity, or of Islam. Everywhere in Africa, although statistics differ, most Africans are influenced by African indigenous beliefs, even if they are members of families that have been Christian or Muslim for generations. Thus, pronouncing judgment or trying to transform a cultural practice without interrogating its social context has proved futile. This has been especially true with regard to the surgeries performed on the genitals of women and girls. Can we simply leave well enough alone? I maintain that we cannot, because female circumcision, as the author correctly spells out, is embroiled in patriarchy, which she describes as "a system that socializes everyone to accept normative social values and practices, even when such norms and values are oppressive."

One cannot isolate female circumcision from the general status and condition of women and certainly not from the overarching need to dismantle oppressive structures. Female circumcision is a health hazard, yes, but in dealing with it the inadequacy of the whole of Africa's health services should be brought into question. Female circumcision brings into focus the endemic material poverty that has become a lifestyle in Africa and the use of tradition and culture, religion, and belief as a pretext to "let things be." Raising the issue of female circumcision means asking all of these hard questions and examining many other gender-related issues.

The ambiguous statements, ambivalent attitudes, and double-talk present in religion point to the need for intense and careful study by religious leaders and by the rank and file of believers about what our religion really demands of us. We all need to learn more about the intricacies of our religious texts and the cultural hermeneutics necessary for their unraveling. Religion has the potential to bring about positive transformation, and religion should be brought into all searches for wholeness and liberation. While religious texts may be presented as two-edged swords, religions must demonstrate how they can be sources of empowerment through their social justice components and their insistence on the sacredness of all life.

That God does not will human beings to suffer cannot easily be contravened. This is where our work to transform unjust and harmful practices should begin. Surah 4:75, as quoted by the author, says in part, "Our Lord, take us out of this town, whose people are oppressors." Nevertheless, one of the most essential tasks of religious scholars is to admit the androcentric nature of religion, for it is this that has shaped much of what is oppressive to women, including female circumcision. Recognizing that religion is a human response to the "extraordinary" and a sense of "the beyond" that will free us all, men and women alike should work to dismantle harmful and oppressive systems, even those that may have been presented as divinely ordained.

Mary Wangila's approach to advocacy and the quest for transformation is not only fresh but also realistic. Transforming attitudes does not call for quick fixes. Stepping into the location of others is stepping onto sacred ground, and we must always tread softly but firmly. Read on, and you too may become an ally of those in circumcising communities who are straining to bring in the day when female circumcision will be a part of the past.

Preface

Even in this twenty-first century, African women continue to face challenges in the areas of health and human rights. These problems have been exacerbated by social change, interethnic and regional tensions and conflicts, a weak or nonexistent infrastructure, and the advent of HIV/AIDS. Today women in Africa struggle to provide for their families and to adapt to new values and ways of doing things while remaining true to their cultural traditions. At stake are their health, integrity, and rights as human beings.

The subject of social justice is not a purely academic topic for me. I am a feminist and a social activist. I am also a Kenyan woman who has lived in circumcising communities and counseled, taught, and interacted with girls and women in these communities who continue to live with the threat of being circumcised and the resulting health risks. I feel obligated to speak out about a practice that I find abhorrent, and my social and cultural context allows me to speak as an "insider" with firsthand knowledge of the effects of female circumcision and other social cultural practices experienced daily by women in Kenya. My academic training in sociology, ethics, and theology and my research and teaching experience in both Kenya and the United States have provided me with the tools to examine critically the practice within its social and cultural context. My goal is not purely academic; instead, it is to engage in social discourse to transform lives.

I am bringing my voice to bear on this issue in order to redirect the current debate, now international in scope, on female circumcision. This is my attempt to give women in circumcising communities a voice and to examine critically the social realities they face daily. Having spent most of my life in circumcising communities, I have witnessed the persistence of this practice in Kenya, even after its banning by the Kenyan government. I realize how deeply rooted and complex

the matter of female circumcision is, and how difficult it will be to
eradicate it altogether.

Any effective strategy to transform attitudes toward the practice of
female circumcision must be based on the needs of women in circumcising communities. I have chosen to emphasize the role of religion
and religious institutions because religion plays a primary role in shaping values and social behavior throughout Africa. Religion lies at the
heart of many myths and beliefs about female circumcision. Religion
can also play a major role in transforming attitudes because it per-
vades so much of African life. Religion, whether Christian, Muslim,
or Indigenous, is found at the grassroots level throughout all of Africa, and messages from religious leaders and teachings of religious
institutions have great authority in the African context.

As a sociologist and trained Christian theologian I strongly believe
that religion can play a role in transforming attitudes regarding female circumcision without summarily condemning all the rituals associated with it. Rituals are important throughout Africa and serve a
specific purpose, as they do in most cultures. While the persistence of
female circumcision among some Kenyans, even those with some education about the health risks involved, has been interpreted at times as a
willingness to continue this practice, it is more an indicator of the complexity of this social practice. And it illustrates a level of ignorance of
the gravity of health and human rights issues in these communities.

Although debates about female circumcision within Africa and internationally have highlighted significant issues, I am greatly concerned
with the generalizations, false assumptions, and misrepresentations that
have characterized these debates. Much of the discourse has obscured
the personal needs and realities lived by women in circumcising communities. I have been particularly concerned with the following points:

- Scholarly investigations of the practice of female circumcision
  often pay little attention to the larger sociocultural context.
- The continued outrage and cry for urgent change by some and
  the defense of the practice by others can lead to a lack of action
  and the persistence of female circumcision in spite of efforts to
  curb it.
- The inadequacy of strategies to curb the practice of female circumcision is primarily due to a lack of understanding of the social
  context.

- Advocates of eradicating female circumcision from the West and some from within Africa (who are often accused of being "Westernized") have been viewed as promoters of "cultural imperialism."
- Some Africans, or those who call themselves cultural relativists, use the practice of female circumcision to romanticize African culture; others use it for political gain at the expense of the social injustices women in circumcising communities continue to face.
- Many refuse to condemn the practice under the guise of religious freedom.

While all of these factors are important, I focus on the social dynamics within Kenyan communities and the significant role played by religion—two factors I feel are absolutely crucial. It is essential to understand the social context of a community before questioning any specific practice. Social practices do not arise from a void or a whim; rather, they serve a specific purpose. And in Kenya, as well as in other countries in Africa and other parts of the world, female circumcision is a social practice of believers in Indigenous religions, Christianity, and Islam.

I would like to acknowledge and thank the fifty Kenyan women informants for their willingness to share their views on such an intimate and controversial subject. To them I am deeply indebted. Although their names are concealed, their views represent the experience of many women in circumcising communities. It is my hope that many more women will emerge to voice their concerns about cultural practices that inhibit their human integrity.

The subject of female circumcision has also been taken up by a number of scholars whose works are most enlightening, and to them I am also indebted. Some of these authors are Fran Hosken, Alice Walker, Amede Obiora, Ellen Gruenbaum, Sami Aldeeb Abu-Sahlieh, and Anika Rahman and Nahid Toubia. Also most helpful are the reports of a number of organizations that have brought international attention to the issue of female circumcision, including the United Nations, the World Health Organization, the Maendeleo ya Wanawake Organization, the Convention on the Elimination of All Forms of

Discrimination against Women, the Research Action and Information Network for the Bodily Integrity of Women, and the Association of African Women for Research and Development.

I also want to acknowledge those who contributed to the final form of this manuscript by reading, editing, or opening my eyes to new insights. My deep appreciation goes to Susan Perry, Laurel Kearns, Traci West, Karen McCarthy Brown, Abena Busia, Katharine Brown, Maurice Amutabi, Shadrack Nasong'o, and Nikki Bado-Fralick. I am also grateful to friends and family, especially Melody Goodwin; my husband, Ptyberyous Wangila, for his love and support; and my children, Dennis, Brian, Tolbert, and Xylona, for their undeserved patience. You are my heroes. My parents, Esther and Michael Nyangweso, your role need not be emphasized.

This book is an invitation to reflect together on the realities affecting women in circumcising communities. It is also an invitation to extend love toward our daughters, wives, and mothers as we embrace our cultures and new ideas. It is an invitation to attend to the messages of Jesus, Muhammad, and our ancestors. And it is an invitation to live the fullest form of our cultures and to shun all that is inhumane, regardless of its origin.

Abbreviations and Acronyms

AAWORD	Association of African Women for Research and Development
AICs	African Independent Churches
CEDAW	Convention on the Elimination of All Forms of Discrimination against Women
FGC	female genital cutting
FGM	female genital mutilation
KISA	Kikuyu Independent Schools Association
MYWO	Maendeleo Ya Wanawake Organization
PATH	Program for Appropriate Technology in Health
RAINBO	Research, Action, and Information Network for the Bodily Integrity of Women
WHO	World Health Organization

Female Circumcision in Africa

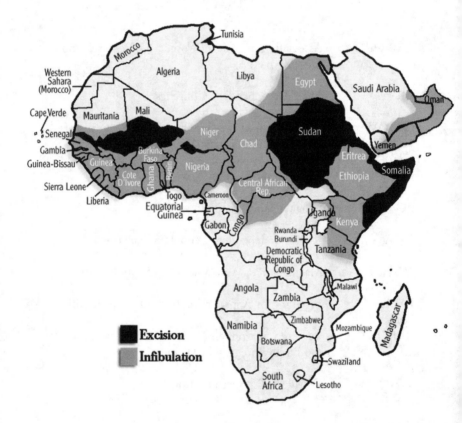

Data from Fran Hosken, *The Hosken Report: Genital and Sexual Mutilation of Females*, 4th ed. (Lexington, MA: Women's International Network News, 1993), 43.

1

The Controversy

It was the month of December in 2003 when I decided to visit Jane, a friend who lives in Kapsabet town in the Rift Valley Province of Kenya. I slept over to catch up on a whole year's news. The following morning the sleepy village of Kaptumo awoke to cries and loud wailing of women, accompanied by the sounds of *morswek*—a traditional horn—which sounds whenever a young woman has died.

I turned to my friend for an explanation. "Did someone die in the neighborhood?"

"A neighbor's daughter, Leah Yatich, a class seven pupil of Kaptumo primary school, died at the hand of a traditional circumciser," Jane explained. "The poor girl died from excessive bleeding. Her blood was strewn all over her father's house, chairs, tables, and everywhere."

"She must have died a painful death," I ventured.

"Sure," affirmed Jane. "Leah's parents could not take her to Kapsabet hospital because they risked arrest, since female circumcision was pronounced illegal in Kenya."

Poor girl! She paid with her life in an attempt to uphold tradition. All she wanted was to be a woman.

"What happened to the circumciser?" I asked Jane.

"Oh, you mean Nifa Chepkoech? She was killed by people who stormed her home. She had become notorious for killing young girls during circumcision."

In a single day a village had lost two women. How many women die every day in our villages in the name of tradition?

December is the month when circumcision rituals take place. The long holiday period before school resumes is conducive for the healing

1

process of those who have been circumcised. On my way back home I could not help wondering how many women were scheduled to be circumcised during this month and the misery that some of them would have to face in the name of tradition. I decided to catch up on the latest news. My eyes immediately fell on the following story:

> A 13-year-old girl who was admitted to hospital after being circumcised died yesterday. The girl was taken to Tenwek mission hospital last week when she bled profusely after the operation. She was said to have been diabetic and was one of the six girls who underwent the rite secretly at Kamundugi village in Singiroi Division, Bomet District.[1]

A year later another incident was reported in the *Daily Nation Newspaper*: "Twenty girls who were recently circumcised have developed complications and need specialized treatment. . . . The girls aged between 9 and 15 need reconstructive surgery because they 'have developed wounds.'"[2] Another article stated, "Two young girls are reported to have died last week after female genital mutilation."[3]

Stories like these continue to form the headlines of Kenya's daily newspapers in the month of December, even though female circumcision has been banned.[4] This is not to mention numerous cases of fatal circumcision that go unreported. Had I not visited Jane, I would not have known about Leah's case because it was not reported in the newspaper. It is unfortunate that as scholars continue to engage in the unending debate on female circumcision, innocent lives continue to be lost in circumcising communities, not to mention the painful health and marital complications that circumcised women experience. As advocates and critics of this practice continue to engage in controversial discussions on whether this practice should be abolished or not, hundreds of thousands of girls continue to spend nights in bushes and away from their homes in attempts to evade forced circumcision. The health risks to which Kenyan children and women continue to be subjected and the violation of the human rights of these significant members of the community in the name of tradition are tragedies that cannot escape moral judgment in our contemporary world. Concerns regarding the practice of female circumcision must be examined and addressed with regard to the welfare of all who live in these communities.

Table 1. Types of Female Circumcision

Mild *sunna*	Pricking, slitting, or removal of the prepuce of the clitoris. *Sunna* is an Arabic word meaning "tradition."
Modified *sunna*	Partial or total excision of the body of the clitoris.
Clitoridectomy/ excision	Removal of part or all of the clitoris and part or all of the labia minora. The vaginal opening is often occluded by the extensive scar tissue that results from the procedure. This makes sexual encounters painful.
Infibulation/pharaonic circumcision	Clitoridectomy and the excision of the labia minora and the inner layers of the labia majora. The raw edges are subsequently sewn together with catgut or made to adhere to each other by means of thorns. This causes the remaining skin of the labia majora to form a bridge of scar tissue over the vaginal opening. A small sliver of wood or straw inserted into the vagina prevents complete occlusion and thereby leaves a passage for urine and menstrual flow. The procedure is different when done in the hospital.
Introcusion	Enlargement of the vaginal opening by tearing it to allow intercourse.
Intermediate	Modified version of pharaonic circumcision consisting of removal of the clitoris and part of labia minora but leaving the labia majora intact. Suturing with catgut then narrows the virginal opening.
Recircumcision or refibulation	Performed on women who have given birth, or who are widowed or divorced to emulate a virginal vagina. The procedure is called *adla* (tightening) and is most frequently performed on women who have had previous pharaonic or intermediate circumcisions. The edges of the scar are sewn together, or the loose tissue is stitched. Refibulation is sometimes referred to as *adlat el raju*, meaning "men's circumcision," as it is designed to create greater sexual pleasure for the man.

Adapted from Angela Wasunna, "Towards Redirecting the Female Circumcision Debate: Legal, Ethical, and Cultural Considerations," *McGill Journal of Medicine* 5 (2002): 106.

Table 2. Female Circumcision in Africa

Country	Estimated prevalence	Number of women (in thousands)	Source
Benin*	50%	1,370	
Burkina Faso	70%	3,650	Report of the National Committee (1995).
Cameroon	20%	1,330	Study (1994) in the southwest and far north provinces by the Inter-African Committee, Cameroon section.
Central African Republic	43%	740	National Demographic and Health Survey (1994/1995).
Chad	60%	1,930	1990 and 1991 UNICEF-sponsored studies.
Cote d'Ivoire	43%	3,020	National Demographic and Health survey (1994); 80% of practitioners are Muslim.
Djibouti*	98%	290	UN ECOSOC report (1991).
Egypt*	80%	24,710	
Eritrea*	90%	1,600	
Ethiopia	85%	23,240	A 1995 UNICEF-sponsored survey in five regions and an Inter-African committee survey in twenty administrative regions.
Gambia	80%	450	A limited study by the Women's Bureau (1985).

Country	Estimated prevalence	Number of women (in thousands)	Source
Ghana	30%	2,640	Pilot studies in the Upper East Region (1986) and among migrant settlement in Accra (1987) by the Ghana Association of Women's Welfare.
Guinea*	50%	1,670	
Guinea-Bissau	50%	270	Limited 1990 survey by the Union Democratique des Femmes de la Guinée-Bissau.
Kenya	50%	7,050	A 1992 Maendeleo Ya Wanawake survey in four regions.
Liberia*	60%	900	
Mali*	75%	4,110	
Mauritania*	25%	290	
Niger	20%	930	
Nigeria	50%	28,170	A study by the Nigerian Association of Nurses and Nurse Mid-wives conducted in 1985-86.
Senegal	20%	830	Report of a national study by ENDA (1991).
Sierra Leone	90%	2,070	

Country	Estimated prevalence	Number of women (in thousands)	Source
Somalia	98%	4,580	
Sudan	89%	12,450	National Demographic and Health Survey (1989/90).
Togo*	50%	1,050	
Uganda*	5%	540	
United Republic of Tanzania*	10%	1,500	
Zaire	5%	1,110	
Total		**132,490**	

*Based on estimates; clear source unavailable. Totals may not add up due to rounding.

Source: Adapted from Dokumentation der Veranstaltung, *Weibliche Genital-iverstummelung* (FGM), 2001: 19–20. See also the WHO website; and Angela Wasunna, "Towards Redirecting the Female Circumcision Debate: Legal, Ethical, and Cultural Considerations," *McGill Journal of Medicine* 5 (2002): 106.

Table 3. Types of Female Circumcision by Country

Country	Type
Benin	Excision
Burkina Faso	Excision
Cameroon	Clitoridectomy and excision
Central African Republic	Clitoridectomy and excision
Chad	Excision and infibulation
Comoros	Excision
Cote d'Ivoire	Excision
Democratic Republic of Congo	Excision
Djibouti	Excision, infibulation
Egypt	Clitoridectomy, excision, infibulation
Eritrea	Clitoridectomy, excision, infibulation
Ethiopia	Clitoridectomy, excision, infibulation
Gambia	Excision and infibulation
Ghana	Excision
Guinea	Clitoridectomy, excision, infibulation
Guinea Bissau	Clitoridectomy, excision
Kenya	Clitoridectomy, excision, some infibulation
Liberia	Excision
Mali	Clitoridectomy, excision, infibulation
Mauritania	Clitoridectomy, excision
Niger	Excision
Nigeria	Clitoridectomy, excision, some infibulation
Senegal	Excision
Sierra Leone	Excision
Somalia	Infibulation
Sudan	Infibulation, excision
Tanzania	Excision, infibulation
Togo	Excision
Uganda	Clitoridectomy

Source: Excerpt from *Afrol News* at afrol.com, based on UN agencies; statistics from Amnesty International and the US government.

WHAT IS FEMALE CIRCUMCISION?

Female circumcision, referred to by its critics as female genital mutilation (FGM), is a sociocultural practice that involves the pricking, piercing, stretching, burning, or excision, clitoridectomy, and/or the removal of part of or all tissues around a woman's reproductive organs and in some cases infibulation (the stitching together of the vulva in order to narrow the vaginal opening).[5] A description of various practices is included in Table 1 above. This range of practices is commonly performed on girls between the ages of four and sixteen, among other reasons as an initiation rite into womanhood. In rural areas traditional experts, usually women known as circumcisers or excisers, perform female circumcision. In more urban areas the procedure is often performed in hospitals.

Although female circumcision is a worldwide practice,[6] it is particularly prevalent in Africa, where it occurs in approximately twenty-eight countries and is estimated to have affected about 132 million girls and women. Types of female circumcision differ from community to community in each country, as described in Tables 2 and 3.[7]

It is important to note that female circumcision is not found in all communities in Africa. Although statistics indicate that over 50 percent of the population in Kenya practice female circumcision, in some communities the percentage is as high as 90 percent.[8] Ethnic groups that do not practice female circumcision include the Luo, the Luyia, and the Turkana. The persistence of this practice in some communities in Kenya, even after the Kenyan government's ban of the practice, is an indicator of how deeply rooted and complex this practice is, and how difficult it will be to change unless more sophisticated strategies are adopted to address this issue effectively.

The debate over female circumcision is healthy because it highlights significant issues that must be understood with regard to this practice; any subject that interrogates the conflict between universalist and relativist values must be examined in context. However, some of the discourses on this issue have obscured critical questions that must be addressed with regard to the welfare of women in circumcising communities. For instance, while it is important to respect cultural values associated with this practice, a recurrent theme in debates over this practice, a critical examination of female circumcision in its social context is necessary in order to explore the implications of any position that negatively affects the welfare of women in these communities.

Although it is erroneous to assume that everyone in circumcising communities would like female circumcision to be eradicated, as claimed by some critics of this practice, it is similarly erroneous to claim that everyone in these communities wants the practice retained. Thus, even as cultural concerns informing the argument of defenders of this practice must be acknowledged, the health risks and violations of the rights of women and children in circumcising communities must also be acknowledged.

In considering these critical questions, several issues have come to my attention:

- The scholarly investigation of the practice of female circumcision often neglects giving close attention to the larger social and cultural contexts.
- The continued outrage and cry for an urgent change in this practice by some and the defense of this practice by others can lead to a lack of action and the persistence of this practice in spite of efforts to curb it.
- The inadequacy or simplicity of strategies employed to curb the practice of female circumcision is due to a lack of consideration of the sociocultural contexts.
- Some advocates of the need to eradicate female circumcision, mostly from the West, are accused of being "Westernized" Africans who use this practice to promote a consciousness of imperialism.
- Some Africans or those who call themselves cultural relativists have used this terminology not only to romanticize the culture of circumcising communities but also to hide behind the cloak of culture or to bargain for political policies.
- The politicization of this practice often serves self-interests at the expense of social injustices that women in circumcising communities continue to face.
- Many refuse to condemn the practice under the guise of freedom of religious practice.

While all of these aspects are important, it is the last, the role of religion, which is central in this book. There is an absence of scholarly work that explores the role of religion in the dynamics of this practice and the usually ineffective efforts to curb it. Yet religion is not only fundamental to the practice and persistence of female circumcision but also has the potential to transform attitudes toward it. In Kenya female circumcision is practiced by Christians, Muslims, and believers in Indigenous religions, and religious reasons are often given to justify the practice.

In my opinion, two critical questions in the debate over the practice of female circumcision should be:

1. Should female circumcision be retained in circumcising communities regardless of the health hazards and the violations of the rights of children and women that this practice compromises?
2. For those who advocate the need to eradicate female circumcision, what strategies should be adopted in order to address this issue appropriately within its sociocultural context, given the realities that shape the continuation of this practice?

Religion must be integrated in investigations of female circumcision, including efforts to curb this practice.

WHAT IS AT STAKE?

In responding to the question about the need to retain or eradicate female circumcision, some feminist scholars, such as L. Amede Obiora[9] and Fuambai Ahmadu,[10] have argued for the need for this practice to be interrogated in terms of its cultural, religious, and social significance. They have questioned exaggerated, stereotypical, misplaced, and imperialistic attitudes that have informed some of the critics of this practice. Also critiqued is the notion of human rights as a Western imposition of foreign epistemological categories and conceptual systems on "the body of the other reality"—that of African traditional worlds.[11] Central to this argument is the fact that female circumcision is a practice with social and cultural meaning in the communities where it is performed and should not be condemned or eradicated on the basis of foreign values and "disputable health effects."[12] Underlying this critique is an endorsement of the clinicalization of the practice for hygienic reasons.

Yet scholars who argue for the eradication of female circumcision, such as Kenyan feminist Micere Githae Mugo, cite the reality of health hazards associated with this practice and the inability to guarantee safe medical procedures. The reality of social change that is taking place in African communities and the adoption of new values that include new understandings of the human person and the rights that person deserves are highlighted as facts that must be acknowledged in these communities. Mugo summarizes her argument thus:

> Given the possibility of health risks associated with circumcision, especially in this day and age of the HIV epidemic, any unnecessary laceration or puncturing of the body is negatively adventuristic. . . . Androcentrically constructed sexuality is definitely an issue here, especially given the fact that circumcision is interlinked with an "education" that socializes initiates to view womanhood in patriarchal terms. . . . on the eve of the twenty-first century, I do not see physical initiation as a necessary rite of passage, even if it is in the form of "ritualized marking of female genitalia . . . where the clitoris is barely nicked or pricked to shed a few drops of blood." . . . Realistically speaking, for most of Africa the availability of basic health services and facilities, let alone reliable ones, is a critical problem. For this reason, talk of using medically safe ways to conduct circumcision is an abstraction for the majority of poor people on the continent who observe the practice. . . . It is time we drew a decisive line between liberating cultural practice and outdated traditions, beliefs and rituals.[13]

Whatever position one takes on this subject, it is important that a critical evaluation inform a given position in order to assess the implication of a particular stance to the realities and welfare of women in these communities. It is true that female circumcision is a cultural practice with deep-rooted significance for those who practice it, and this should be acknowledged in any given discourse on this subject. However, to dismiss the notion of human rights simply because it is based on individualism, a foreign value to African communities, which traditionally embrace collective rights, is an oversight of the social reality that most African communities are experiencing today. Even if the critique of individualism is valid, one fails to understand why women and children in circumcising communities are not perceived as groups of people with inalienable rights, beings who should be able to live healthy lives in terms of personal dignity or group rights that ought to be acknowledged and respected in these communities.

The issue about strategies to be adopted in order to address female circumcision has featured in the debate with regard to the appropriateness and effectiveness of the strategies most often employed to date. Some strategies employed have been critiqued for criminalizing and victimizing those who embrace this deeply rooted cultural practice, often because of misconceived assumptions about communities that practice female circumcision. As a result, many of these strategies have been short lived and have led to an inevitable escalation of underground resistance and to the persistence of the practice. For instance, discussing the failure of the attempt by missionaries and the colonial government to ban this practice in Kenya, Lynn Thomas points out how "in three years following the ban more than 2,400 girls, men, and women were charged in African courts with defying the Njuri's order."[14] Thomas also discusses instances where some Meru girls circumcised themselves in defiance of the ban, leading to a slogan popularly known among the Meru community as *ngaitana*, literally translated, "I will circumcise myself."[15]

Whenever a strategy intended to offer a solution ends up exacerbating the problem, it is necessary to examine it and consider new strategies. Although I acknowledge the range of positions on this subject and the significant issues articulated in the debate on female circumcision, I am opposed to the practice of female circumcision just as I am opposed to traditional practices such as the sacrifice of virgins to gods to invoke rain, female infanticide, foot binding, slavery, genocide, widow burning, and other culturally justified practices that compromise the welfare of any individual or group of individuals in a given community. I recognize that the controversy that surrounds the subject of female circumcision is fundamental to a free understanding of the body, self, sexuality, family, and morality—aspects that bring into focus tensions relating to cultural differences.

However, what is pertinent in this debate is the question about our contemporary world and social transformations that draw from new sources of knowledge and experience. In other words, as important as it is to acknowledge the larger social cultural contexts that shape both the efforts to change this practice and resistance to such change, it is also important to acknowledge the fact that rituals involving the practice of female circumcision have not only developed and changed over time but that attitudes toward this practice have similarly changed among some of the people.

In some Kenyan communities, for instance, Christine J. Walley observes how the initiation of young girls has been transformed from the pre-colonial to the colonial and postcolonial era and how the agency of the individual is becoming accepted in Kenyan communities as a way of resisting social norms.[16] Claire C. Robertson also reports on instances of resistance to female circumcision by women in Kenya during the colonial era, when some Kikuyu women took advantage of mission stations in their attempts to escape forced marriages and circumcision.[17] Mugo clearly points out these changing attitudes toward aspects of culture such as female circumcision: "On the eve of the twenty-first century, I do not see physical initiation as a necessary rite of passage, even if it is in the form of 'ritualized marking of female genitalia.' . . . There are other forms of self-assertion that are more relevant to current day needs in which women engage."[18] Social change, therefore, comes with the social critique of values and structures that have outlived their meaning.

It is important, therefore, that, although a cultural relativist position that embraces the need to respect cultural views should be respected for its contribution to the need to acknowledge and respect difference, caution must be taken not to allow strategies of dismissal to be selectively used in the name of cultural relativism to resist valuable change or obstruct such interrogation. It is a fact that the colonial encounter with our cultures has resulted in problematic understandings of both Western and indigenous cultures of our communities, and it is also true that imperialism is still a reality. However, as Indian feminist Uma Narayan observes with validity, the word *Westernization* has sometimes been used as "a rhetorical device, predicated on double-standards and bad faith, used to smear selectively only those changes, those breaks with tradition, that those with authority to define 'tradition' deplore."[19] Sometimes little attention is paid to how the word *Westernization* is used to resist even constructive changes. For instance, the critique of indigenous culture by some African women is sometimes simply dismissed as a "symptom of 'westernization,' the 'incarnation of a colonized consciousness,' a betrayal of 'our traditional ways of life,'" or as "the views of 'privileged native women in whiteface' seeking to attack their 'non-western culture' on the basis of 'western' values."[20]

Dismissing all cultural criticism as Western amounts to portraying contemporary communities in Africa as having unchanging traditions, which is not only unrealistic but also a deviation of the discourse in question. Such accusations also ignore the genuine concern expressed by African women for their sisters and portray critics as unable to think for themselves. Instead of simply dismissing criticism as Western, it is important that we pay attention to change within our social contexts in order to challenge dismissal strategies used by some in our communities to "defer the articulation of issues affecting women."[21] Culture, as a set of interpretive understandings and aggregate consciousness, is always under construction and therefore always changing. As it evolves, so too humans evolve, making human conceptions or original rationale about what is right and good or wrong and bad fluid. Cultural practices change over time, given the ongoing adaptation of new values—both secular and religious.

Without appearing to suggest that all change is for the better, or advocating that those who defend cultures are conveying the notion that change is bad and tradition is good, I appeal for the need to interrogate critically cultural elements in order to identify those elements that have lost value in our contemporary communities. It is a fact that some changes that have taken place in our communities have improved the lives of women while others have worsened their situation. To defend a cultural practice under the guise of rejecting Westernization is what Narayan refers to as "an attempt to curtail and cut short political dialogue about particular practices, institutions, and changes and to preserve a misguided sense of 'cultural pride' that equates respect for culture with blindness to its problems."[22]

In light of this argument, it is important that Kenyans as well as other African communities come to realize that our communities with their distinct cultures, like other cultures, have genuinely morally objectionable features of their own, that is, features that must be subject to critical scrutiny. In interrogating a cultural subject such as female circumcision, it is therefore important to distinguish misrepresentations and cultural imperialism from normatively justifiable criticisms of sociocultural institutions and values that promote this practice, a task I attempt to accomplish in this book.

THE CENTRALITY OF RELIGION

In this book I examine female circumcision as a sociocultural practice that is shaped by the values of a given community. Religious values, explicitly or implicitly, overt or covert, help define social attitudes and behavior in a community. Drawing upon sociological theories of religion, I explore the role of religion in defining attitudes of Kenyans toward women's sexuality with specific reference to female circumcision. While I engage some of the issues in the debate on female circumcision, my main objective is to explore the role of religion in promoting this practice. I cite examples from the belief systems in Kenya—Indigenous religions, Islam, and Christianity—not only to illustrate how female circumcision is legitimated by these religions but also to argue that the liberative role of these belief systems can be of potential use in transforming the values, attitudes, and social behavior associated with this practice.

The centrality of religion in the dynamics of female circumcision is my main concern for two reasons. First, religion is one of the main factors that define the social behavior of Kenyan people. Second, in my interviews with Kenyan women, religion is one of the reasons consistently cited, not only for performing this practice, but also as a strategy for addressing the issue. Of the fifty women interviewed, 90 percent cited religion (Christianity, Islam, and Indigenous beliefs) as one of the reasons for performing female circumcision. Fifteen of twenty-two uncircumcised women (68 percent) cited religion as influencing their decision not to be circumcised. For instance, a 45-year-old Meru woman, Gitobu, stated that girls in her community are taught that "it is taboo not to be circumcised" and that "the clitoris of an uncircumcised woman will grow too big." She explains how this practice is further justified by some Christians who argue that "even Abraham and Jesus were circumcised." Gitobu explains further how she escaped circumcision because her father was Christian. In contrast, a 48-year-old Samburu Muslim woman, Maisha, believes that female circumcision is "a religious ritual for serious Muslim women since cleanliness is a virtue among Muslims."

Forty-three of the fifty women interviewed (86 percent) believe that religion has the potential to transform attitudes toward female circumcision. For instance, a Kalenjin woman, Wanyama, a nurse, argues, "Once girls/people understand that it [female circumcision] is not biblical, then, it will be easy to stop the practice. . . . Religious leaders should preach to people and give them the biblical truth about female genital mutilation." Similarly, Butaki, an Elgon Maasai woman, argues:

> There is no biblical documentation of female circumcision. . . . The church has been in the forefront in discouraging the practice and many girls have benefited in as far as education and well-being is concerned from church organizations and non-governmental organizations [NGOs]. People who are entrenched in Christianity have shunned it.

A Muslim woman, Maisha, also argues that religious leaders should support efforts to educate circumcising communities.

The story of Isnino Shuriye, a Muslim exciser, which appeared in *The New York Times,* confirms these women's views. Shuriye, who used to infibulate girls in the Garissa town of northeastern Kenya, recounts how proud she was of her work. She explains, "I felt like I was doing the right thing in the eyes of God. I was preparing them for marriage by sealing their vaginas." It took visits by religious leaders *(imams)* opposed to the practice to get her to abandon her profession. After being sensitized to the fact that female circumcision was harmful and inconsistent with the teachings of the Qur'an, Shuriye was left with regrets about the harm she had done to girls in her community. Unfortunately, she now has to face castigation from other Muslims who lack the knowledge that she now possesses.[23] Details about responses concerning the place of religion in the practice of female circumcision are illustrated in tables 4 to 8 referred to in subsequent chapters.

The significance of religion in the practice of female circumcision is also affirmed in the film *The Day I Will Never Forget,* which concerns the practice of female circumcision among Kenyans.[24] In this film a British film maker, Kim Longinotto, documents the experience of a number of women and girls, including an eight-year-old Muslim girl, Fouzia Hassan, of the town of Eldoret in western Kenya. She is shown begging her mother not to circumcise her sister Fardhosa. In this film Islam and Indigenous belief systems are cited as reasons for the practice of female circumcision among Kenyans. The role and importance of religion[25] in female circumcision has also been discussed briefly by Efua Dorkenoo,[26] L. Amede Obiora,[27] John S. Mbiti,[28] Sami Awad Aldeeb Abu-Sahlieh,[29] and Jomo Kenyatta.[30]

My motivation for examining the subject of female circumcision evolves from (1) the persistence of this practice in many Kenyan communities in spite of numerous attempts to curb it; (2) the resistance to

the practice by some Kenyan women due to health hazards and violations of the rights of women and children, as illustrated by the grow-
ing number of children who resist the practice and run away from
their families; (3) my disapproval of the practice; (4) my personal knowledge as a Kenyan woman of the effects of these practices on the daily
experiences of these women; and (5) my firm conviction as a trained
Christian theologian that religion can play a role in transforming attitudes regarding this practice without necessarily condemning rituals
associated with it.

The persistence of female circumcision among some Kenyans, even
among those with basic education on the health consequences, is an
indicator, on the one hand, of how complex this practice is, especially
given the numerous efforts by feminist activists, women's groups, health
organizations, governments, human rights activists, early missionaries, and some Christian and Muslim leaders to change attitudes toward this practice.[31] On the other hand, its persistence also illustrates
the ignorance that continues to prevail in circumcising communities
about the health and human rights issues that arise from this practice.[32] And yet, it is immoral to overlook the cries of those women and
children who want nothing to do with the practice and especially those
who are unable to make an informed choice, due to their ignorance of
the potential risks associated with this practice.

As a Kenyan woman who has lived in circumcising communities,
counseling, interacting, interviewing, and teaching girls and women
in these communities, witnessing their struggles with the health consequences of this practice and the threat of being circumcised on a
daily basis, I feel obliged to speak out on this issue. Furthermore, the
conversations I have had with other Kenyan women allow me to speak
as an "insider," representing one of the significant voices that has been
lacking in this debate. As a researcher schooled in sociological and
theological theories, and having researched and taught both in Kenya
and in the United States on issues related to this subject, I bring my
voice to bear on this issue as a way of redirecting the current debate to
examine critically the social realities that Kenyan women face daily.
Since this book results from interviews over a period of time with a
broad range of women and religious leaders from varied communities
in Kenya, I attempt to describe social patterns observed in their stories and behavior to illustrate how these patterns shape social behavior such as attitudes toward the practice of female circumcision.

ORGANIZATION OF THE BOOK

This book is divided into six main chapters. In the first two chapters I introduce the task of the book and the socioreligious setting within which the practice of female circumcision is performed in Kenya. I explore the relationship between social practices and values in Kenyan communities to elucidate how these influence each other in the realization of the social needs of a given community. I describe the religious context of Kenyan communities to illustrate how belief systems define social behavior such as the practice of female circumcision in Kenya.

In the third chapter, I explore, in detail, some of the significant issues arising in the debate on female circumcision in order to highlight the reasons and assumptions behind the furor over female circumcision, such as the health consequences, human rights violations, issues of relativism and universalism, and strategies adopted in curbing the practice. While critiquing assumptions in the debate, my objective is to draw attention to critical issues in this debate and illuminate how real concerns about the practice of female circumcision and the situation of women in Kenya are inevitably obscured by assumptions. Most important, I argue for the need to integrate the religious dimension in all discussions of this practice, especially where attempts to curb this practice are concerned.

In Chapter 4 I examine the relationship among religion, gender, and sexuality as a backdrop for understanding how gender constructs and attitudes toward sexuality are legitimated by religion. Citing cultural and religious attitudes toward women and their sexuality, I illustrate how notions about virginity, initiation rites, early marriage, dowry fidelity, widowhood, and polygamy interrelate with notions of family, community, and religion to influence practices such as female circumcision. Drawing from belief systems in Kenya, I illustrate how attitudes toward women and gender roles have reinforced traditional attitudes toward women's sexuality and consequently the practice of female circumcision.

Building on this argument Chapter 5 is an illustration of how religion promotes the practice of female circumcision among Kenyans. In this chapter I present some of the views of Kenyan women regarding the practice of female circumcision, highlighting the reasons for the practice and attempts to curb the practice. Thereafter I present a detailed account of how Indigenous religion(s), Islam, and Christianity, directly or indirectly, contribute to the persistence of female circumcision among Kenyans. In my analysis I note in part that whereas religious systems such as Christianity and Islam do not necessarily advocate the practice of female circumcision, this practice was, and continues to be, given a religious justification in various Muslim and Christian communities, although these justifications differ across communities and across time. This, as I point out, should concern religious leaders of these belief systems.

In my sixth chapter I draw from concerns highlighted in my discussion about this practice to propose strategies to address this issue. I adopt a feminist advocacy position that draws from the notion of religion as liberative to propound the argument that religion has significant potential for social transformation. As a sociologist and a feminist theologian I draw not only upon the sociological understanding of religion as an ideology that can also promote social change, but also upon my theological training. I advocate a critical evaluation of our cultures, traditions, and belief systems (indigenous or adopted) in order to raise questions, as necessary, in an attempt to embrace only those aspects in indigenous cultures and belief systems that promote human development in its fullest sense. Although I recommend the need to incorporate religious perspectives and principles in attempts to conscientize and transform attitudes and behavior toward female circumcision, I emphasize a critical evaluation of the process of social transformation to ensure that what is selected is an enhancement of the status of women in Kenya. I conclude the book with a brief discussion of how religious institutions can participate in efforts to transform attitudes toward female circumcision and other cultural practices that pose questions of social injustice for women throughout the world, but particularly in Kenya.

2

Religion and the Social Behavior of Kenyans

Social attitudes and the behavior of individuals are deeply embedded in a community's value system. As a significant social institution, religion influences social behavior because it is a source of shared values and rituals drawn from a given community's world view and ethos.[1] To understand attitudes that inform a practice such as female circumcision, one must interrogate the role of religion in shaping these attitudes. This chapter briefly describes the social structure of Kenya, emphasizing the social status of women. It provides an overview of the practice of female circumcision in Kenya and then explores the influence of religion on the behavior of Kenyans.

THE SOCIAL STRUCTURE OF KENYAN COMMUNITIES

Social behavior is constructed by our societies. Any social institution has its values, norms, and basic needs. These are drawn from and reinforced by the community's world view and ethos, what Clifford Geertz refers to as "the cognitive, existential aspects" and "the moral (and aesthetic) aspects of a given culture."[2] Through their interactions, social institutions provide mechanisms that inform members about appropriate behavior while they sanction or reward conformity and punish any deviation from the established social norms. Through socialization, that is, the learning of values, norms, and skills necessary to participate in social life, individuals are shaped.

Most ethnic groups of Kenya share modes of social organization based on their ancestry, kinship by blood or marriage, seniority, and geographical location. The common elements in Kenyan ethnic communities are those of patrilineage and sub-clans.[3] A patrilineage consists of males and females descending along the male line from a common male ancestor. Within patrilineages, clans are established with common membership traced to a common ancestor on the father's side. Most communities practice exogamy, a practice wherein members are not allowed to marry within the same clan or lineage: members of the same lineage are considered kin whether through blood or marriage. The relationship between kin is very important because it provides the basis of support and interdependence. Often members of a clan act as "the unit of sociability and cooperation" by working together in the fields or herding.[4]

The family, the most fundamental institution in every society, ensures reproduction and the proper care of both children and its members. As the smallest cultural unit it also participates in the responsibility of imparting cultural values to the younger generations. In the Kenyan context *family* refers to both the nuclear family and the extended family. While *family* can refer to the couple and their children, it is also applicable to polygamous families, grandparents, cousins, nephews, aunts, uncles, and their children because one is expected to provide for them as if they were immediate family. *Family* also includes departed relatives who are referred to as the "living dead" because they are believed to be alive not only in the memories of their surviving families but also in the spirit world. They are thought to be still "interested in the affairs of the family to which they once belonged in their physical life."[5]

In most traditional communities the family is a great source of pride. Organized hierarchically, the man is the head of most family units. Since polygamy is common in such communities, the number of wives and children a man has demonstrates his status and success. In rural areas where extended families are common, clan members often live together in a village in an expression of unity. This lifestyle, however, is changing as families tend to become smaller and communal responsibility diminishes, especially in urban areas due to modernization, Christianity, and Westernization. However, in most areas, rural communities continue to adhere to traditional systems.

Gender roles within families are based on each community's understandings of femininity or masculinity, and chores are distributed according to gender. Sometimes one ethnic community's perception of gender roles may be the opposite of another ethnic community's understanding. For instance, while it is normal for a woman to thatch a house among the Kikuyu of Kenya, a woman found thatching a house among the Luyia or the Luo communities of western Kenya is breaking a serious taboo. This is not to say that some gender roles are not similar in most communities. An example is the role of women as family nurturers and caregivers, which is common to most communities.

It is not surprising that traditional family structures were disrupted by the colonial system, whose alternative sources of income and power pulled people into the colonial economic system as laborers. Ethnic leaders or chiefs were regarded as potential sources of power to exploit by the colonial administrators. Eventually social structures and lifestyles grew to be defined by Westernized education, often run by missionaries, and culture. Some Kenyans who took jobs in the government moved to urban areas where industries were located, thus disrupting long-established social structures based on familial associations. Traditional lifestyles are not completely diminished, however. Rural areas continue to adhere to traditional ways.

THE SOCIAL STATUS OF WOMEN

Every culture makes distinctions between the two genders through socialization. Socialization patterns are different for males and females, and in Kenya transition or initiation rites, which form part of this socializing pattern, often dramatize gender attributes of young members of the community, who are expected to assume a new social status as adults. Even though women make up more than half of the population in the world, their status in most societies is far lower than that of men due to culturally specified gender attributes and responsibilities. Their low status is due to social factors such as patriarchy, sexism, cultural stereotypes, illiteracy, and religion, to mention but a few. According to feminist scholar Susan Okin, the status of women in most societies remains lower than that of men because "modes of thought and attitudes about them [women] continue to form the education and values imparted to our younger generations."[6]

Yet, it is important to acknowledge that power relations in any given society are complex. This is not only because of extraordinary cultural diversities that affect the division of female and male roles and activities, but also, as Lance Morrow explains, because of the cultural biases and methodological problems involved in social science research.[7] Commenting on this subject, L. Amede Obiora explains how perceiving patriarchy, or the total control by males over the construction of social life, can obscure the variable ways in which men and women are bound together in social units, institutions, and categories that interact and crisscross gender divisions.[8] Because of this, social relations in a particular social structure should not be assumed to be identical to those in another social situation. Similarities can exist in different social structures, but the social structures and values of a given society must be understood within the framework of that culture in order to appreciate the complexities that inform them.

Kenya is a patriarchal society. First, in most communities one's ancestry is traced through a male figure and based on patrilineage. Second, power and property are also male identified. Men own most of the property, and in most communities women and children are considered the property of men. Practices such as polygamy, domestic violence, "widow inheritance" (remarriage of a widow by a brother or relative of her deceased husband, also called levirate marriage), early and arranged marriages (betrothal of girls as young as ten), and female circumcision are common ways of establishing male power and the subsequent subordination of women in society.

Widow inheritance draws from the cultural belief that the widow of a deceased man, his children, and his property should all be transferred for protection to a male relative of the deceased because a woman cannot handle such high-ranking affairs as property management. This practice assumes that women are also the property of men. The practice of widow inheritance is also one of the many practices to which women in Kenya are exposed in order to control their sexuality and to maintain their place in society. Among the Rendile, for instance, when a man marries he "takes control" of his wife. According to one Rendile woman, "You must follow his rules. . . . If you make a mistake—if he thinks that you have gone to another man, or that you did not care for the goats—he can leave you without animals and without food and water, and he can beat you."[9]

Although a few communities, such as the Kikuyu, claim to be matrilineal, similar male/female power dynamics are found. In other words, matrilineal descent does not necessarily equal power for women. The Kikuyu claim to be matrilineal because their lineages are traced to the first woman ancestor, Mumbi. Unlike most Kenyan communities in which children are believed to belong to the father, the children of a Kikuyu couple are believed to belong to the mother. In case of divorce, for instance, a Kikuyu woman takes custody of the children, unlike in most patrilineal communities.[10] However, matrilineality does not imply significant power, since such systems continue to practice polygamy, early and arranged marriages, and wife battering, and they affirm the expectation that a woman submits to her husband. As feminist anthropologist Ellen Gruenbaum observes, "Matrilineal societies in which women's important roles in kinship systems are easily recognized nevertheless usually have men in important power roles as political leaders. Matrilineal kinship systems do not prevent women's subordination or female circumcision."[11]

Patriarchal values are instilled in children through songs, initiation ceremonies, and stories.[12] Although in some communities women of a certain age and status are granted significant positions in the patriarchal hierarchy, these positions still operate within the patriarchal structure. For instance, women who have passed childbearing age are given positions previously held by men because they are believed to have relinquished their femininity. In addition, because of their age and status, they are believed to have accumulated wisdom useful to the society. Such women are consulted on social matters as well, and in some cases they are allowed to join decision-making committees. There are also times when these women may assert some power; in matters of marriage and initiation of the youth into adulthood, for example, such women serve as instructors. In circumcising communities these women take on the role of the circumciser and enforce the need for circumcision. The significant social roles of these women, however, do not negate patriarchy in any way.

Patriarchy is a complex system. Gruenbaum defines it as follows:

> Patriarchy is not simply a system of rule by males over females, but a more complex set of relationships that result in domination by older men over both younger men and females. But there is other domination and authority here as well: females over children, older women over younger women, older children over younger children, boys as they grow up increasingly asserting themselves over girls, even older sisters who used to have authority, and so on.[13]

In other words, while men occupy the highest place in the patriarchal hierarchy, the relationships in this hierarchy are categorized not only by gender but also by the age and social status of the community members. It is misleading to assume that patriarchy is only about male dominance and female subjugation.

Cultural values that promote patriarchy are responsible for the low status of women in society. Among the indicators for Kenyan women are their levels of illiteracy and education, types of occupation, age at first marriage, economic status, property ownership rights, legal status, roles in decision making, and representation in political and administration positions, to name but a few. Among the Nandi, for example, men are viewed as physically, intellectually, and morally superior to women. Girls are referred to as *lagok ab got*, "children of the house," while boys are referred to as *lagok ab sang*, "children of the outside." Men are also associated with the right—the stronger side—while women are associated with the left—the weaker side.[14] The symbolic identification of women with domestic duties and men with public concerns instills attitudes that promote male dominance and female subordination. In most ethnic communities in Kenya women are considered dependents of men; women are expected to be obedient to their husbands and male relatives.

Girls are socialized to accept their roles as weaker than and subordinate to men. In most communities girls are socialized in the family through initiation rites as well as the religious and educational systems. These institutions are responsible for instilling into girls the belief that they are weaker than men and that their rightful role in society is in the domestic sphere. Traditional stories that portray women as the weaker sex are told to girls and boys, passing on such stereotypes. Some of these stories negatively portray women who have held traditional male positions as power hungry, conceited, and immoral, while others reinforce the rewards of domesticity.

The Kikuyu, for example, have a myth about male dominance and women's subjugation. According to this myth the Kikuyu had a tyrannical matriarchy in the past that was passed down through the female descendants. During this time women ruled with an iron hand while men were forced to do most of the domestic tasks, including cultivating, planting, harvesting, food preparation, care of children, hunting, and protection of the community. The women, who did not do much, ordered men around and imposed all kinds of punishments on them.

The men conspired to end this tyranny by impregnating the women, thus making them weak in order to take control and create a new world order. This myth, which is still popular among the Kikuyu, is intended to demonstrate that motherhood and power are incompatible.

To discount women's dominance further, a second myth is told. Wangu Wa Makeri, a female colonial chief, fell from power because she became so intoxicated with conceit and crazed for power that she danced naked before a crowd, shaming her community. She was promptly removed from power. This myth not only offers a negative message about women's sexuality, but it also socializes girls and women to believe that women cannot be trusted as rulers.[15]

During initiation rites girls are taught to desire early marriage and to be submissive to their husbands or face physical discipline (wife battering). They are encouraged to be good homemakers and to persevere even in difficult situations. Among the Kikuyu, a *mutumia*—a woman who perseveres, does not answer back, expresses no opinion, and is seen but not heard[16]—is described as a good wife. This message is emphasized to brides in songs during the wedding ceremony. Such an ideal ensures that women do not complain about their treatment. Men are encouraged to discipline disobedient wives by beating them "at least once," because if they die without beating their wives, "the curse" of their ancestors will catch up with them.[17]

As a result of these stereotypes and attitudes, women have developed low self-esteem with regard to participation in the so-called public sphere. Because of the internalized belief that they will be unsuccessful in these roles, very few women are willing to be educated, to engage in politics, or to take part in decision-making forums in the community. Most see themselves as the property of men and never strive to own property of their own. Some cannot even imagine the possibility of challenging social structures that marginalize them because they believe those structures are normal and natural.[18]

Because of the perception that women's roles should be confined to the domestic sphere, most communities do not value education for girls. Boys need to be educated to fulfill their roles as heads of households, providers, protectors of the family, and as agents in the public sphere. Girls are encouraged to perfect their skills as wives, mothers, and housekeepers. A Kikuyu woman, Watoro, explained how education for girls was discouraged: "The one who puts on a dress and goes to school is a prostitute. My father refused to let me go to school because he said I would become a prostitute. I never felt sad about not going to school. I was happy going to dances, because I was not alone."[19] And it is true that religious beliefs, Indigenous as well as those of Christianity and Islam, have reinforced these attitudes toward women by portraying women as submissive agents whose roles are to be found in the domestic sphere. For example, whenever the place of women in society is under discussion, Christian ministers commonly refer to Pauline texts from the New Testament about women as subservient.[20]

In communities where initiation rites are practiced, girls are encouraged to marry immediately after seclusion. Virginity, a basis for honor and a handsome dowry, is seen as an important gift a girl can grant her parents. In some communities girls are betrothed as early as ten years of age, and immediately after initiation rites they move in with their husbands. Because girls are married so young in many Kenyan communities, the literacy rate among men is approximately 91 percent, while that of women is only 80 percent.[21] Many girls who are attending school drop out after their initiation rites because they are either pregnant or because they believe that their education is valueless. Among the Maasai, for example, one of my informants explained that a girl can get married after her circumcision wounds have healed, even at the age of fifteen.

In Kenyan politics women are equally disempowered, especially in leadership roles. Even though Kenya achieved independence in 1963, the first female cabinet member, Winifred Nyiva Mwendwa, was appointed only in 1995, following pressure from women's groups. Other than Mwendwa, women such as Julia Ojiambo, Marere wa Mwachai, and Agnes Ndetei, among others, served only as assistant ministers. Only with the 2002 general elections in Kenya was there an increase in the number of women at the parliamentary level, with women's representation rising to 8.1 percent.[22] Currently, Kenya has a parliament of 222 members, with 210 elected and 12 appointed. Of these, 17 are women (7.6 percent). The last parliament had only 9 women members (4 percent).[23] The absence of women at the policy-making level is a primary reason why women's issues and rights continue to be overlooked or inadequately addressed.

Because women in most communities have been led to believe that they are a form of property, and given the Kenyan legal system's indifference to their needs, women are the poorest of the Kenyan population.[24] Most communities do not expect women to inherit property from their husbands, and a woman lives on any piece of land only as a guest of male relatives by blood or marriage. In cases where women are allowed to own property, they can use it only in consultation with male members of the household, clan, or village. While land-tenure legislation in Kenya asserts that everyone is allowed to own land, in reality women lack the same rights as men. Although the land control boards require the consent of the wife before land is sold, quite often this requirement is overlooked by village elders who strongly believe in male ownership privileges. As Mary Omosa observes, even when crops are cultivated, "women are required to present written authority from their husbands to be able to receive payments for proceeds from marketed cash crops."[25]

When a husband dies, widow inheritance is practiced in many communities. Even though the law provides for equal consideration of male and female children, in practice most inheritance problems do not come before the courts and most often women are excluded from inheritance settlements or given smaller shares than male claimants. Moreover, in most communities a widow cannot be the sole administrator of her husband's estate unless she has the consent of her male children, implying that she is less able to make a sound decision than either her husband or her male children.

Commenting on this treatment of Kenyan women, Omosa observes how negative stereotypes about women continue to hinder government efforts to eliminate discrimination against women. The marginalization of women in social institutions and the legitimation of biased sexist practices lead to "isolation, economic and emotional deprivation, threats, desertion and harassment; common ways in which women's self-confidence is undermined."[26] Women who resist traditional bonds are categorized as dissidents, divorcees, frustrated, single, and domineering, common weapons of ridicule intended to stigmatize those who disagree with the cultural expectation of women as submissive, dependent, and passive.

In spite of this, significant efforts are being exerted at various levels to eliminate obstacles that promote the low status of women in Kenya. The need to improve the status of women is coupled with the government's realization that women's productive and reproductive roles are closely linked to other social, cultural, legal, and religious conditions. The proclamation of 1975 as the International Women's Year by the 1972 UN General Assembly Resolution 3010, the UN General Assembly's 1976 proclamation of the UN's Decade for Women

(1976–85) (Resolution 3520), and the 1985 Nairobi Forward Looking Strategy, among other policies, have inspired efforts to advance the status of women in Kenya.

Building on this and other international principles of equality espoused by the UN Charter (1948), such as the Universal Declaration of Human Rights, the 1966 International Covenant on Civil and Political Rights, the 1979 CEDAW, and the Declaration on the Participation of Women in the Promotion of International Peace and Cooperation, Kenya has made some significant efforts by creating women's departments in key ministries such as education, agriculture, health, appropriate technology, technical training and culture, and social services. Various women's organizations, both secular and religious, have emerged in Kenya, an indicator of serious concern about the development of services for women. These movements, which include the Association of African Women for Research and Development (AAWORD), are contributing to awareness of the need to improve the welfare of women.

It is also important to note, however, that although Kenyan women seem to have low status in society, attitudes toward women are more complex than this, especially where Indigenous religions are concerned. Women play a significant role in the religious activities of communities as priests, prophets, diviners, mediums, and healers. They offer prayers for their families, heal the sick, and officiate at ritual ceremonies. Most often it is women practitioners who handle rites of passage associated with children. Among the Luyia, for instance, it is the duty of women to bury children. In most communities that circumcise girls, women are the circumcisers. Women are also believed to possess mystical powers. Rosalind Hackett lists a number of ways in which East African women have achieved higher status as mediums, symbolized by their use of male sitting stools, male ceremonial dress, and spears. Using this authority they are able to exert power over women's and sometimes men's affairs in the community.[27] Because of this elevated status of women in Indigenous communities, Christianity and Islam are criticized for worsening the status of African women. These religions undermine the ceremonial leadership roles women take on in Indigenous communities. Additional well-organized efforts, however, are necessary in order to address persistent stereotypes that promote the marginalization of women and attitudes toward practices such as female circumcision.

FEMALE CIRCUMCISION IN KENYA:
AN OVERVIEW

Kenya has more than forty recognized ethnic groups that range in size from a few hundred to more than three million people. Some of the largest ethnic groups in Kenya are the Kikuyu, or Agikuyu (about 22 percent), the Luyia (14 percent), the Luo (13 percent), the Kalenjin (12 percent), the Kamba (11 percent), the Kisii (6 percent), and the Meru (6 percent), with the Samburu, the Somali, the Maasai, the Giriama, and others collectively composing about 15 percent.[28]

Although statistics indicate that over 50 percent of Kenya's population practices female circumcision, in some communities, such as the Maasai, the Kisii, the Somali, and the Borana, the percentage is as high as 90 percent.[29] Most Kenyan communities that practice female circumcision also practice male circumcision. In these communities both male and female circumcisions are perceived as initiation rites into adulthood. However, some ethnic groups, such as the sub-ethnic groups of the Luyia, practice only male circumcision. Some, including the Luo and the Turkana, practice neither. Such communities, however, have their own equally painful ways of initiating their members into adulthood, such as the removal of the six front teeth among the Luo, and scarification and the piercing and pulling of ear lobes and lower lips among the Turkana and the Pokot, although these are also changing with time.[30]

The types of female circumcision commonly found in Kenya are clitoridectomy and excision, with about 10 percent practicing infibulation.[31] Types of circumcision vary from community to community, and sometimes from clan to clan, as do the ages at which the procedure is performed. While the age range is generally from six to fifteen, girls may be circumcised before they reach the age of six or even when they are older than eighteen.

Since the 1920s several governments of Kenya have sought to curb female circumcision without much success. The difficulty results from controversies surrounding the practice, but also from colonial, missionary, and general assumptions about the African people and their cultures, in general, as well as the strategies used to condemn this practice.[32] Given how deeply rooted the practice is and especially because it is considered as a way of defining womanhood and observing religious and social obligations in Kenya, it is difficult to fight female circumcision.

The controversy over female circumcision in Kenya began in 1906 with the coming of Christian missionaries, who denounced the practice. These missionaries allied with the colonial government to curb female circumcision through criminalizing the practice and excommunicating Christian converts who insisted on performing it. Opposition took the form of resistance, rebellion, and the formation of nationalistic movements, which eventually led to the struggle for independence from colonial rule. For instance, the 1913 Protestant mission's conference on female circumcision led to the Church of Scotland's mission campaign to expel and excommunicate circumcised girls and their parents from the church for eighteen months. This increased pressure to abandon the practice.[33]

While renouncing female circumcision was considered a way of declaring loyalty to Christianity, some Christian converts did not agree. Their resentment would probably have been minimal if the missionaries had not sought help from the colonial government. This resentment was deepened further when the 1926 conference of East Africa governors, of which Kenya was a member, banned brutal forms of this practice. The resulting rebellion prompted the government to reconsider its position and relax the ban.[34]

The politicization of female circumcision worsened the situation, since the nationalistic movements that struggled for independence adopted this practice as a method of resisting colonial rule and missionary criticism of traditional culture. For instance, in the 1950s female circumcision was aligned with nationalist movements such as the Kikuyu Central Association and the Mau Mau struggle for political independence.

It is important at this point to mention the role of Jomo Kenyatta, the first president of Kenya. Kenyatta, who had been identified by his Kikuyu community as an icon of independence and a potential leader of nationalistic movements, was approached to help his community defend the country from colonial control and imperialism. To show his commitment to nationalism, he took an oath vowing to defend his country and his culture, including the practice of female circumcision. Kenyatta, who had initially despised female circumcision because of his missionary upbringing, ended up supporting this practice to fulfill his political ambitions. His book *Facing Mount Kenya* (1938), which became a classic in defense of the practice, was a pledge of loyalty to his tribesmen. Kenyatta used an anthropological argument to articulate an essentialist view of female circumcision in order to secure political power and the supremacy of men.

The name *Kenya*, an elision of the Kikuyu word *Kiri-nyaga* meaning "the abode of the gods," provided symbolic support for the eventual success of the nationalist struggle. As Emmanuel Babatunde observes, "The gods were in charge and so long as the living kept to the traditions of their ancestors, victory over the foreigners was assured."[35] Kenyatta succeeded in rallying men and women in Kenya to stand effectively against the British colonial administration. Most important, as Hosken observes, "he managed to strike a basic chord of the universal male brotherhood over the issue of sexual control of females and thus enlist the tacit yet strong support by the vast majority of men which the ruling patriarchy regards as their untouchable right."[36] As an icon of independent Kenya and the first president of Kenya, Kenyatta's position greatly strengthened resistance to attempts to curb this practice among Kenyans. Abandoning this practice was and is still equated with Europeanization and deculturation. This has led most Kenyans who claim to be patriotic to embrace this practice.[37] Both the tension and the complexity of this issue are clearly articulated by Lynn Thomas, who explains that some girls ran to the bush and circumcised one another in defiance of the government's ban of the practice and of their own parents, who feared breaking the law.[38]

Because of the controversy, attempts to curb the practice were met with mixed responses, with some communities abandoning the practice while in other communities secret and forced circumcision of unwilling girls continues. The Kenyan government has tried numerous times to outlaw the practice to no avail. President Moi's condemnations of the practice in 1982 and 1989 seemed to fall on deaf ears, and in response the practice went underground.[39] In 1996 a proposal to criminalize female circumcision was defeated in Parliament with some members, including some women, arguing that the practice should be continued because "it reduces women's sexual drive and therefore promiscuity, premarital sex, and adultery."[40]

Attempts to curb the practice have also been made by activist organizations such as the Family Planning Association of Kenya; the Kenyan chapter of the International Federation of Women Lawyers; the African Women's Development and Communication Network; MYWO; and other human rights organizations.[41] For instance, the MYWO, a

Kenyan women's political organization, in conjunction with the Program for Appropriate Technology in Health (PATH), introduced an alternative rite-of-passage program *(Ntaanira na Mugambo)*, popularly known as "circumcision through words." This program, which requires girls to be initiated without being physically circumcised, is barely accepted in some communities.[42]

The controversy over female circumcision has led to the current debate, with advocates referring to its condemnation by those who are neither Africans nor from circumcising communities as an example of interference by outsiders.[43] Although this attitude is justified to some extent, given the imperialist assumptions of some opponents of female circumcision, it is nonetheless important that a number of issues be placed in perspective. For instance, it should be asked if this condemnation by outsiders is simply interference in our Kenyan culture or if these outsiders have a licit argument that is obscured by dismissing them as outsiders. I will take up this issue in the following chapter.

It is important to note that although this brief historical review of female circumcision and efforts to curb the practice in Kenya points to the complexity of the situation, it is inaccurate and misleading to assume that everyone in Kenya supports female circumcision. Since the 1980s an increasingly intense dialogue has emerged between Kenyans who seek to eradicate female circumcision and those who seek to preserve it as an integral part of Kenyan culture. Some Kenyan women perpetuate this practice and other Kenyan women oppose it. According to Micere Githae Mugo, women like Rebecca Njau, Charity Wachiuma, and even Mugo's own mother resisted female circumcision long before current opposition emerged publicly.[44] In 2002 two schoolgirls took their father to court and won the right not to be circumcised.[45] The movie *The Day I Will Never Forget* follows a large group of girls who ran away from their homes and in the end filed a law suit against their parents in order to be protected from circumcision.[46] Some men also oppose the practice. In 1999 Meru elders in the Nyambene District rejected female circumcision and suggested that an alternative rite of passage replace it.[47] It is important that differing voices on the practice of female circumcision be both articulated and heard.

RELIGION AND SOCIAL BEHAVIOR

Because religion informs general behavior and specific practices such as female circumcision, it is important to understand the religious

landscape of Kenya with its roots in Indigenous beliefs and missionary and colonial attitudes toward Indigenous systems. Kenya's social
values and attitudes have also been influenced by the nationalist movements, Islam, and the Christian independent churches. Understanding how religious systems affect social behavior is fundamental to understanding the shaping of attitudes toward gender and women's
sexuality.

Religion is a complex system that functions in relation to the norms,
customs, and ethics of a given society; it is also part and parcel of the
social fabric of any given community. Religion can sanction social order and also challenge it. This social order, such as gender roles, the
family, or the clan, is maintained by grounding answers to questions
about the "why" of institutional arrangements and what "ought to be"
in legal or sacred sources. The social practices, in turn, function to
justify and maintain the social order and harmony. It is not easy to
question or challenge them.

Religion is a powerful source to justify reality because it draws on
sacred or divine sources, sources that are not human and are deemed
more powerful.[48] Religious references to *something* beyond human society—which may be called the supernatural, God, divinities, or ancestors—create fear, awe, and reverence. In the context of Kenya, to
change the social order is to challenge God, the gods, or the ancestors. The fear of challenging such powerful beings prevents many from
trying to do so, a powerful factor in maintaining the social order.

Because religion reflects upon the ultimate—who we are, why we
are here, and how we should act—religious systems always address
issues of gender roles and sexuality. As a social institution, religion has
its own ideology about sexuality and its place in human life. Drawing
from this ideology and those of other social institutions, religion, interacting with the social institutions, produces social controls over
gender and sexual expressions. It provides moral codes and taboos
that delineate appropriate sexual behavior, and sanctions, rewards, or
punishes as appropriate. Although the range of permissible sexual practices varies greatly among cultures, their justification or condemnation usually has religious underpinnings. Gender identity is likewise
core to any social order, and the proscription of gender-based permissible sexual behavior is key in defining sexuality and related practices.[49]

Specific social institutions and practices are determined by the social structure and needs of a given community. Dorothy Smith uses
the concept of "ruling relations" to illustrate how social relations are

tailored to fit the objectives of those dominant in society. These relations, which form administrative, management, professional, and organizational units in a given society, regulate, organize, govern, and control people's behavior. They are objectified, normalized, and made into systems of communication, knowledge, information, regulation, and control, making them complex and dependent upon one another.[50] For instance, a patriarchal society has ruling relations that define male and female attitudes and consequent behavior in favor of male dominance. Although all participate in the ruling relations, not all benefit equally from them.

To understand how religion shapes Kenyan norms and modes of ethical conduct, it is important to be aware of how it seeks to promote certain structures and values. Unlike modern Western world views that distinguish the sacred from the profane, Kenyans tend to seek religious explanations for everything that happens to them. It is this that John Mbiti refers to when he describes Africans as "notoriously religious."[51] Indigenous religions permeate all aspects of life with no formal distinction between the sacred and the secular, the religious and the nonreligious, or the spiritual and the material. Mbiti explains:

> Wherever the African is, there is his religion: he carries it to the fields where he is sowing seeds or harvesting a new crop; he takes it with him to the beer party or to attend a funeral ceremony; and if he is educated, he takes religion with him to the examination room at school or in the university; if he is a politician, he takes it to the house of parliament.[52]

It is important that any practice of the Kenyan people be perceived in this context. In addition, when examining any practice such as female circumcision, the interconnectedness of several variables, such as religion, social status, or economic dependence, needs to be acknowledged outright to gain a true picture of a given community's perceptions.

It is also crucial to understand the concept of the individual, because the Kenyan understanding differs from most Western definitions. Kenyans do not think in the binary forms of either/or but rather in both/and categories. As Mbiti observes, "An individual does not and cannot exist alone except corporately."[53] Individuals owe their existence to other people, including those of the past generation, the family, the clan, and their contemporaries. An individual's life is a part of the whole and is mutually interdependent on others. Corporate existence in a continuum gives the community the responsibility to "make, create, or produce" an individual through rites of incorporation. When an individual is born, the community organizes the birth ceremony to initiate the new being into the physical world. Later, he or she is initiated by the community into adulthood in order to assume adult responsibilities. With marriage, an individual is expected to procreate in order to continue the existence of the family, clan, and community. At death, the individual is initiated into the spirit world. Through these rites an individual passes from one stage of corporate existence to another.[54] These fully symbolic rites of incorporation include the unborn as well as the spirits of the departed.

Mbiti accurately summarizes this understanding of the human person, "I am, because we are, and since we are therefore I am."[55] The strong sense of community interwoven in the social values and practices of any given community in Kenya is fundamental in discerning the communities' norms and ethical conduct.[56] Ultimately, the practice and continuation of cultural practices are of primary importance to all members of the community. This is particularly clear in African Indigenous religion, in which the notion of individual salvation does not make sense apart from the larger social unit. One pleases the ancestors not just for one's own good but for the sake of social balance and harmony.

Kenyatta explains: "In the Kikuyu community there is no really individual affair, for everything has a moral and social reference. The habit of corporate effort is but the other side of corporate ownership and corporate responsibility is illustrated in corporate work no less than in corporate sacrifice and prayer."[57] Consequently, a practice such as female circumcision is considered everyone's responsibility. Kenyatta argues that "the moral code of the tribe is bound up with this custom and that it symbolizes the unification of the whole tribal organization."[58] Thus, in Kenya, the process of socialization itself is deeply religious, and every member of the community takes as a personal responsibility the correction and disciplining of any child for the well-being of the community.

An important aspect of communal identity closely connected to the understanding of the individual is the concept of relatedness. When Kenyans attempt to rationalize a behavior, they consider how it will affect those around them, including the unborn and the spirits of the departed. In other words, for Kenyans, the concept of relatedness goes beyond biological and rational understanding to embrace invisible and supernatural knowledge. It is a system of ethics that acknowledges the inability of human beings to comprehend all truths in the world, and it acknowledges the reality of mystery. As Bénézet Bujo validly observes, this ethics of relatedness rejects the Western idea that rationality alone determines one's humanity and responsibility, because an isolated individual cannot exist.[59] However, non-reliance on absolute rationality does not necessarily imply irrationality; rather, it acknowledges the fact that knowledge is too complex to be limited to only one aspect of knowing.

It is not surprising, therefore, that in most Kenyan communities the establishment of norms for ethical conduct cannot be justified by reason alone. Human beings are holistic beings surrounded by some form of mystery that cannot be grasped by reason alone. For this reason, some things are taken as facts even though they cannot be rationally explained. This perception is particularly key in understanding health and healing in the African context, and it is why suffering, misfortune, disease, accidents, or calamities may be attributed to mystical forces.[60] Any form of suffering, however naturally it is explained, is perceived as having a mysterious cause that must be speculated upon before one can settle down to normal life. Possible actions of witches, sorcerers, ancestral spirits, or gods must be eliminated before normal life can resume.[61] Because reason alone cannot encompass every aspect of the truth, arguments about practices such as female circumcision that maintain they are unnecessary or unnatural are doomed to fail.

The role of religion in the social behavior of Kenyans must be understood as revolving around ideas of community and relatedness and it must be accepted that social practices are often indistinguishable from religious beliefs. The roles of God and the ancestors must be acknowledged and respected. Social actions and practices continue these all-important relationships, and abandoning practices such as female circumcision may threaten key social relationships in all directions.

In summary, then, the social behavior and practices of most Kenyans have a *religious justification*, and most social practices are linked to or derive from *the need for social harmony* as determined by the community's world view. However, it should be noted that the desired social harmony may be disrupted by disagreements on certain social practices. For instance, practices such as polygamy, widow inheritance, female circumcision, and even forced marriages have long been sources of conflict in Kenyan society. As Mugo correctly observes, female circumcision encountered resistance in Kenya well before Western scholars attempted to condemn it.[62]

RELIGIONS IN KENYA

Even though almost 90 percent of Kenyans claim to be either Christian or Muslim, Indigenous religions are still significant in understanding the religious world view of Kenyans. In fact, Indigenous religions form the backdrop against which these newer identities were established, and most rural populations continue to engage in activities categorized as Indigenous. Thus, Indigenous religions may have greater importance than the statistics indicate. For many Christians (78 percent of the population) and Muslims (10 percent), the basis of moral values still derives from their Indigenous cosmology.[63] In addition, in recent years a number of new religious movements that draw to a certain extent on Indigenous religion have developed in Kenya, attesting to the continuing appeal of traditional religions.

Indigenous World Views

Those who profess Indigenous religions make up about 10 percent of the population.[64] Indigenous world views are mystical but at the same time very real to members of the community. The nature and structure of indigenous religions are usually characterized by belief in a Supreme Being, divinities, ancestral spirits, and other mystical powers that manifest themselves in witchcraft, sorcery, and misfortunes.

The Gods

The Supreme Being, who is usually associated with the creation of the universe, holds a superior position. Although rarely appealed to directly, the Supreme Being is the ultimate source of power. For instance, the Akamba believe in Mumbi, the creator of the universe; the Kikuyu, in Ngai, the creator, ruler, and distributor of gifts to the rich and the poor; the Meru, in Murungu, the provider of rain; the Luyia, in Nyasaye Khakaba, the distributor of wealth; the Dorobo, in Araua, the supplier of their needs; the Kipsigis, in Cheptalil, their sustainer; and the Sabeis, in Oiki, the creator of the universe.[65]

In communities where divinities or lesser gods exist, they are perceived to be related to the Supreme Being in one way or another. Divinities are delegated particular responsibilities such as fertility, good harvests, rain, and health. In communities where divinities are found, they serve as intermediaries. For instance, among the Dorobo of Kenya, Araua is believed to be a moon goddess, sister of the sun god, The sun god is the Supreme Being. The Keiyo believe in Ilat, the rain god. The Suk believe in Ilat, the son of the Supreme Being, Tororut. Ilat is said to fetch the water that is used by Tororut to make rain.[66]

The Supreme Being and divinities are guardians of morality. In cases of moral decay, such as breakage of taboos, the Supreme Being can cause affliction to victims or the whole community. The Supreme Being is sometimes believed to be responsible for epidemics, drought, famine, mental disturbance, infertility among women, and loss of livestock and fields. In some cases the Supreme Being or divinities are believed to use spiritual beings such as ancestors to bring affliction.[67] Sacrifices must be offered to appease the Supreme Being or ancestors in case of such afflictions. Among the Turkana, for instance, the Supreme Being is believed to punish those individuals who commit incest or violate the requirements of important rituals having to do with illness or death.[68] The Suk interpret calamities and cattle diseases as the Supreme Being's punishment for misdoings. The Kikuyu believe that the Supreme Being—Ngai—and divinities are responsible for certain misfortunes, such as punishment of those who disobey the Supreme Being. The Supreme Being may punish disobedience by famine or even death.[69] Given this belief in the punishment for disobedience by the Supreme Being and divinities, most people seek to adhere to all moral and social expectations of their communities to avoid disobeying the Supreme Being and to avoid punishment in the form of misfortune.

Ancestral Spirits

The belief in ancestral spirits is also central to Kenyan Indigenous religions and African world views. Most African communities believe that death is not the end of life. Ancestral spirits exist as custodians of a community's family affairs, traditions, ethics, and moral activities.

Any offense in these matters is an offense against the ancestors.[70] Ancestors are dreaded, because, if offended, they may cause misfortunes such as incurable diseases. They are said to get offended by the nonperformance of certain rituals, the violation of taboos, lack of respect to the elderly, and even burial of the dead in a nontraditional way. Diseases are often viewed as punishment for wrongdoing. A cleansing ceremony must be performed in order to avert the anger of the ancestors. Various rites are observed in respect of the ancestors in order to maintain harmony.[71] When happy, ancestors are believed to be a source of blessings such as fertility, healthy life, good harvest, and social stability. They are said to be conduits through which morality is instilled and new ideas are received, interpreted, understood, and accepted. This is a strong source of social legitimation of cultural norms.

Spirit possession is a common practice in Indigenous religions because this practice is viewed as a medium of communication through which the ancestors get in touch with the living. Mbiti explains this phenomenon:

> Spirit possession occurs in one form or another in practically every African society. Yet, spirit possession is not always to be feared, and there are times when it is not only desirable but people induce it through special dancing and through drumming until the person concerned experiences spirit possession during which he may collapse. When the person is thus possessed, the spirit may speak through him, the role of a medium, and the messages he relays are received with expectation by those to whom they are addressed.[72]

Although these spirits are concerned with community welfare, they may punish any member for misbehavior. They are said to possess an individual who has offended them, causing mental illness. Or they may destroy the person completely.[73] Among the Luyia, ancestral spirits may caution the community against impending danger. When angry, ancestors are said to punish the offender with misfortune or even death. To appease their anger, a sacrifice must be offered.[74]

Belief in curses, oaths, and taboos continues to be part of Kenyans' lifestyle. Curses, oaths, and taboos draw their power from the mystical world. Most Kenyan communities believe that anyone who offends the elderly could incur a curse. In most communities a curse is effective only when pronounced by an elderly person. It is believed in principle that the Supreme Being or an ancestor will execute the curse if it is justifiable. Curses are feared mostly when pronounced by close relatives. A curse by parents to their children, or uncles and aunts to their nieces and nephews, are feared most because of their potency.[75] Although in some cases curses are believed to be effective even if the victim is unknown, most curses are within family circles.

Oaths bind people mystically together. Through an oath two people who are unrelated undergo a ritual, which usually involves an exchange of blood by drinking it or rubbing it into the body. This ritual is believed to transform them into *blood brothers*, a term used to connote their closeness. From then on, the two individuals relate to each other as siblings. For instance, their children cannot marry; to do so would be considered incest, a taboo. During oaths, the Supreme Being, divinities, or ancestors are called upon to make the oath binding.[76] The violation of a taboo is believed to bring misfortunes. Among the Kikuyu, for instance, a taboo is called *megiro*. Violation of *megiro* causes *thahu*, an illness that is associated with bad luck, a curse, or anger of the ancestors. *Thahu* emaciates the victim's body, and its symptoms may include boils. If precaution is not taken in good time, *thahu* may lead to death. In order for a curse or ancestral anger to be averted, a purification ceremony *(tahika)* must be held.

Because of this belief in the mystical world, diviners continue to be important in Kenyan communities. A diviner is believed to possess the appropriate power to cure both the bewitched and the possessed. Diviners may combine roles such as prophet, medium, medicine person, spiritual healer, arbitrator, and rainmaker.[77] Since disease is considered more than a physical symptom, apart from Western medical diagnosis of a health problem, the diviner is usually visited by some Kenyans to establish whether there is any mystical cause of the illness.[78] In communities where life is associated with mystical power and beings such as ancestors, to dismiss the validity of a diviner is to alienate individuals in these communities from their social realities.

Christianity

The arrival of Christianity in Kenya led to massive conversions. Currently, about 78 percent of the Kenyan population claims to be Christian. Christianity introduced a lifestyle based on the teachings of Jesus Christ. For Christians, a believer must take seriously the example of Jesus as written in the Bible and preached by religious leaders.

Whereas these sources of Christianity are valid in defining a Christian life, there are discrepancies that arise from misunderstandings and differing perceptions of certain lifestyles. These misconceptions result from individual interpretations of Christian texts and the influence of culture on one's perceptions. For instance, whereas the message of Christ seemed to be acceptable to Kenyans, the attitude of missionaries toward Africans and their cultures seemed to raise much suspicion and resentment among Africans. This is largely due to the fact that, from the beginning, Christianity was presented by missionary leaders as highly critical of African cultures and values. Drawing from Western missionary assumptions that Africans were without any religion, education, or culture, and that Africa provided a virgin field for sowing the seeds of western Christianity and civilization, missionaries considered Africans to be pagans, heathens, and denounced their cultures and behavior as being of the devil.

Missionary Christians initiated a new way of worship as well as a new lifestyle including new systems of music, education, health, medical clinics, and burial of the dead. Mission centers consisting of churches, schools, hospitals, mission residences, orphanages, and gardens became centers that disseminated a Eurocentric world view. Locals were encouraged to strive for superior values. Transformation of the individual was at the level of the mind, which began with conversion. Churches sought government support and encouragement to stamp out Indigenous practices such as belief in ancestors, polygamy, and female circumcision.[79] Such actions brought about conflict between the Indigenous values and the values of the West, triggering resentment among Kenyans who felt that they were being stripped of their way of life. By opposing ancestor veneration, the foundation of religion in Africa was being opposed since it provides a link between the present and the past. Further, the role the ancestors as custodians of morality was undermined as the missionary church "raised havoc with the mores existing in African societies" like Kenya.[80]

In reaction to the missionary attitude African Initiated Churches (AICs) emerged. AICs began as African expressions of resistance to an intrusive and disruptive colonial presence. They represent efforts to Africanize the Christian faith and the message brought by Western missionaries. They originated mostly out of African efforts to salvage some sense of self-worth and dignity amid the daily struggle for survival as menial laborers in a capitalist economy, especially during the colonial period.[81] AICs also encourage the revelation, spiritual possession, and healing aspects of the Holy Spirit, all of which resonate with Indigenous religious forms of healing through exorcism. The Bible is interpreted literally in order to accommodate traditional practices such as exorcism.[82]

The preoccupation with exorcism and the power of the Holy Spirit and messianism built around messianic leaders in some of the AICs serves as compensation for the thwarted social aspirations for positions of leadership yearned for by African men and women in mission churches. In spite of the resistance of Africans to the missionary enterprises in Kenya and in Africa in general, a sense of brotherhood and sisterhood cutting across denominational, tribal, and racial lines, as well as other social differences, is a significant value that can be attributed to the Christianity brought by the missionaries.

Islam

Muslims make up about 10 percent of Kenya's population.[83] The highest population of Muslims is found along the Kenyan coast among the ethnic groups such as the Swahili, the Digo, the Bajun, the Pokomo, the Somali, and Asian Kenyan communities. More than half of the Muslims in Kenya are Somalis, with many others belonging to the Swahili, Bajun, and Wajun groups.[84] Although Kenya has a very diverse Muslim population, most Muslims in Kenya live along the coast; some are located in the northeastern province. Most communities are found chiefly in towns though there are a few communities in rural areas.[85]

Islam introduced values based on the teachings of Muhammad as found in the Qur'an and Hadith. Islam was acceptable to Kenyans because it fits easily into the African cultural framework. Islam adapted Indigenous religious practices where necessary and integrated them into canonical social ethics. In some cases Islam introduced or reinforced new practices. For instance, the Islamic concept of the family system and accompanying regulations correspond to the African code. This includes notions of polygamy, the dowry, and one's responsibility to relatives. Islam did not demand that converts disdain or reject their native traditions. Traditional African practices such as funeral and death rites, child-naming ceremonies, dowry, and circumcision were sanctioned by Islam. Practices such as female circumcision were introduced or reinforced among female-circumcising communities such as the Swahili, the Somali, and the Borana along the coast. Indigenous beliefs seem to be stronger among Muslim women because, customarily, they are less involved in the more formal observances of Islam such as attendance at noon prayers in the mosque. As Isa S. Wali observes, "'Africanized' Islam contented itself with offering immediate values without trying to displace the old ones."[86]

To understand the social behavior of Kenyans, it is imperative that matrices of values embedded in their sociocultural context be examined. A practice such as female circumcision must be understood in its complex social context. The role of religion on women's sexuality and female circumcision is examined in Chapters 4 and 5.

3

The Debate
over Female Circumcision

The subject of female circumcision has been examined by a number of scholars who have described the prevalence of female circumcision in African communities as well as in African communities of the Diaspora. These works have highlighted the different types of female circumcision as well as the health consequences and injustices associated with this practice. These voices have drawn international attention to this practice and have frequently engaged in the debate as to whether or not female circumcision should be eradicated.[1] The conversation regarding female circumcision features a wide spectrum of perspectives and responses from the various disciplines and social locations of those participating in the debate. It is not surprising that positions of both moral universalism and cultural relativism feature prominently in this debate.

In this chapter I (1) explore the basic issues emerging in the debate, (2) identify some of the differing positions, and (3) distinguish among certain assumptions about this practice and the reality faced by women in circumcising communities. I am often disturbed by both assumptions and misconceptions about the practice of female circumcision and concerned that discussions of it be properly located within its social context. Some key questions are the following: What is the appropriate terminology? What factors promote female circumcision? Is female circumcision a violation of human rights? Is female circumcision a crucial problem faced by Africans? Are there sufficient grounds to eradicate this practice? If so, what strategies should be adopted to curb it? An exhaustive discussion of all the issues involved goes far beyond the scope of this book, so I have highlighted a few issues to illustrate the need to interrogate the social context and in particular the role of religion that inform attitudes toward this practice.

THE DEBATE OVER TERMINOLOGY

The debate often begins with the term used to refer to genital surgeries performed on girls as part of their initiation into adulthood. The use of the term *female circumcision*, used in most African communities, is a source of significant controversy among critics of the practice because it is viewed as an inappropriate description of the more extreme forms of female genital surgery, especially infibulation and clitoridectomy. Use of *female circumcision* is critiqued for de-emphasizing the severity of most forms of the practice by alluding too easily to male circumcision, in which only the foreskin of the penis is cut.[2]

Critics have argued that while both male circumcision and female circumcision violate a child's right to physical integrity, the two practices must be understood as distinct. In male circumcision the removal of the foreskin does not damage the male reproductive organ; the cutting in female circumcision is anatomically much more extensive. As Rahman and Toubia observe:

> The male equivalent of clitoridectomy, in which all or part of the clitoris is removed would be the amputation of most of the penis. The male equivalent of infibulation—which involves not only clitoridectomy, but the removal or closing off of the sensitive tissue around the vagina—would be the removal of all the penis, its roots of soft tissue and part of the scrotal skin.[3]

Furthermore, critics continue, while male circumcision affirms manhood and virility, female circumcision is explicitly intended to show a woman's confined role in society and to restrain her sexual desires.[4] These critics prefer the term *female genital mutilation* (FGM) to describe all forms of genital surgeries insisting that "any definitive and irremediable removal of a healthy organ or tissue is inherently mutilation."[5] The term FGM is generally used by a wide range of women's health and human rights activists and by representatives of anti-circumcision organizations such as the Foundation for Women's Health Research and Development, the World Health Organization (WHO), the Inter-African Committee on Traditional Practices Affecting the Health of Women and Children, the United Nations, and the Research, Action, and Information Network for the Bodily Integrity of Women (RAINBO). FGM is preferred by such organizations because it is technically accurate in describing the practice, it gives a clear indication of the harm caused by it, and its emphasis on the harm makes it a very effective advocacy tool.

The term *genital mutilation* has, however, also been rejected by some who find it offensive, alienating, criminalizing, psychically mutilating, and even shocking to the communities that perform female circumcision because it implies excessive judgment and insensitivity toward individuals who have undergone the procedure. The term connotes intentional harm and implies an evil intent, which is contrary to the intention of family members who circumcise their daughters.[6] According to Micere Githae Mugo, the term *mutilation* imposes an external definition on Africans while it negates or displaces their self-definition; these scholars believe the indigenous definition should be left intact even if one disagrees with it.[7] Critics of the term *genital mutilation* stress the need to underscore the positive reasons behind the practice and to avoid being judgmental. In addition, they maintain, mild forms of the practice, such as the symbolic pricking of the clitoris or the excision of its prepuce, fall short of mutilation. According to L. Amede Obiora, even the term *circumcision*, which simply means "cutting around," accurately describes excision and overstates symbolic pricking.[8]

The term *genital mutilation* is rejected by others because of the bias associated with it. Western feminists, who have generally preferred the term *genital mutilation*, are critiqued for projecting double standards by condemning female circumcision without being critical of the many bodily practices that prevail in the West, such as the piercing of tongues, ears, noses, labia minora, belly buttons; breast implants; face lifts and nose or lip reconstructions; and the self-imposed destruction caused by bulimia and anorexia. Such critics maintain that all mutilations in every culture should be similarly critiqued without making one appear more severe than another.[9]

To avoid the connotations and inadequacies associated with the use of the terms *female circumcision* and *female genital mutilation*, new terminologies have been proposed. These include *female genital surgery*, *ritual genital surgery*, and *sex mutilation*. The Uganda-based initiative Reproductive Education and Community Health Program proposed the term *female genital cutting* (FGC), arguing that it is a more precise and less value-laden term. The term *genital surgeries* has been proposed by scholars such as Isabelle Gunning, Hope Lewis, and C. M. Obermeyer as a value-neutral alternative. However, terms that refer to female circumcision as surgeries have been critiqued for lending the practice "an air of legitimacy," which can be problematic.[10]

Those who use the term *female circumcision*, as I do, tend to do so in order to avoid the connotation of evil intentions associated with mutilation and also out of respect and sensitivity to the communities concerned. Female circumcision is practiced by most Kenyans as a traditional value intended to foster traditional understandings of adulthood. Most communities perceive this practice as an inherent good and not intended as harm. Whereas it is important that a term describing any action be an accurate description, a term that is offensive or ridden with misconceived assumptions should be avoided. It is also important that critique always be self-critical to avoid misjudgment and disingenuousness. Leila Ahmed, a Muslim feminist, points out that genuine feminism is "vigilantly self-critical and aware of its historical and political situatedness to avoid becoming unwittingly collaborators in racist ideologies whose costs to humanity have been no less brutal than those of sexism."[11] It is important, therefore, that any terminology adopted to label female circumcision must acknowledge the sociocultural and religious values that inform the practice, even while critiquing it.

REASONS FOR FEMALE CIRCUMCISION

Inaccurate assumptions and misrepresentations infuse the controversy over female circumcision. Most opponents of female circumcision have linked it to patriarchal social structures and practices. Patriarchy is viewed as a social structure that is reinforced by practices such as female circumcision and polygamy in order to promote male dominance and female subjugation and, more especially, to constrain women's agency, sexuality, and behavior. This control of female sexuality is meant to ensure fidelity and to ascertain that any child born to a circumcised woman is a legitimate child of her husband. Discussing this understanding, Nancy Bonvillain, a feminist, explains how female genital mutilation is consistent with "men's fear of and therefore wish to control women's sexual behavior."[12] In other words, female circumcision reinforces male dominance, which is a precondition of a patriarchal community.

Western Criticisms Based on Male Domination

Related to the notion of patriarchy is the argument that female circumcision is performed in order to control women by weakening their sexual desire. Feminists such as Mary Daly, Alice Walker, and Nancy Bonvillain have argued that female circumcision is a rite designed by men to control women's sexual pleasure and thus is purely sexist and oppressive. Alice Walker and her colleague Pratibha Parmar call female circumcision "the sexual blinding of women" to convey the notion that sexuality is literally destroyed.[13] Daly labels female circumcision an "unspeakable atrocity," torturous, and mutilative, that is aimed at depriving African women of their femininity, sexual sensitivity, and pleasure.[14]

In fact, the removal of the clitoris and labia manora destroys sensitive parts of the reproductive organ. The narrowing of the vaginal opening leads to painful intercourse, and the pain experienced during the procedure leads to the association of sexual intercourse with pain, which brings about frigidity and the dislike of sex among circumcised women. Explaining the effects of female circumcision on sexuality, Bonvillain argues:

> Women who are subjected to the procedure have reduced sexual desire, both because of the loss of part of their sexual organs and because of their fear of the pain involved with intercourse. They therefore are unlikely to engage in premarital or extramarital sexual activity that evidently so threatens the patriarchal social systems that male-dominated ideologies legitimate. In addition to the control exerted over women . . . infibulation is thought to increase a man's sexual pleasure while obviously causing pain to his partner.[15]

The Hite Report, frequently cited by feminists, explains what is denied to women who have been circumcised: "Clitoral stimulation evokes female orgasm, which takes place deeper in the body, around the vagina and other structures, just as stimulation of the tip of the male penis evokes male orgasm, which takes place in the lower body of the male."[16] In other words, many feel that the removal of the clitoris during circumcision automatically reduces women's sexual pleasure. Some men are also said to suffer from the lack of sexual fulfillment of their wives. This is illustrated by Dr. M. Mahran's observation: "Excision is one of the causes of the ever increasing use of hashish among men who believe, albeit wrongly, that smoking it delays ejaculation, giving men their orgasms at the same time as their excised wives; 16 percent of excised women admit that their husbands smoke hashish for sexual reasons."[17]

This notion of sexual control is informed by ideas of purity, premarital chastity, and passive sexual experiences intended to restrain women's sexual activities. During the initiation process, circumcised women are taught not to initiate sex, even in marriage, and not to show that they are enjoying intercourse or they will be labeled prostitutes.[18]

African Responses

These arguments based on patriarchal and sexual control have been criticized as unfounded by some scholars because they do not take into account the social contexts of female circumcision. For example, it has been argued by scholars such as Ahmadu and Obiora that perceptions of female circumcision as a form of a patriarchal control of female sexuality can be shallow, uninformed, and misrepresent reality. Obiora maintains that female circumcision is practiced because of sociocultural values other than patriarchy and the sexual control of women, including values and attitudes about sexuality, fertility, procreation, public recognition of life-cycle changes, solidarity among women and clan members, and social continuity. These attitudes and values should not be ignored.[19]

Whereas Ahmadu and Obiora do not contest that patriarchy and sexual control are possible reasons behind the practice of female circumcision, they consider radical Western feminists' insistence on associating this practice with gender politics to misrepresent the sociocultural meaning of the practice. As Ahmadu argues, they are based on the "universalized assumption" that "human bodies are 'complete' and that sex is 'given' at birth."[20] For Western feminists the clitoris represents an integral aspect of feminine sexuality and erotic function.

The Western paradigm of male control is also criticized by some African scholars because it contradicts the variety of ways in which men and women are bound together in social units and categories that cut across gender divisions such as those in Africa.[21] Obiora argues that patriarchal social institutions exist far beyond circumcising societies and that some polyandrous and matrilineal societies also practice female circumcision. In addition, girls and women are often the most ardent defenders of clitoridectomy, which is performed by women with the apparent consent of the circumcised or her proxy.[22] According to some African scholars, criticizing the practice on the grounds of patriarchy also ignores the complex notions of gender; initiation rites intricately mesh gender and ranks such as age, hierarchy, and physical hardship that young men and women endure to ensure cohesion and social harmony within the community.

African scholars also critique the allegation that women blindly and wholeheartedly accept patriarchy, including mutilation, an assumption that disregards African women's efforts to resist the practice. The critique that African women are subjugated and thus devoid of agency demonstrates misunderstandings of the realities of the African social context. Mugo, for example, explains how female circumcision has been resisted by some Kenyan women prior to the current international campaign against this practice. Critiquing Walker and Parmar, Mugo explains:

> One wonders whether Parmar ever reads African women's works, for this is an area in which much work and writing have seen daylight and moonlight. From Kenya alone, Parmar should have heard of Rebeka Njau and Charity Wachiuma, but then she does not even know that Ngugi wa Thiong'o, famous as he is, comes from Kenya! What about the work of scholars, researchers, professionals, and activists, such as Nawal El Saadawi, Nahid Toubia, Zelda Salimo, Awa Thiam, Shehida Elbaz, Asthma A'Haleem, and many more? Having imagined a void in the arena where anti-circumcision activities are supposed to take place, Parmar concludes, "This reluctance to interfere with other cultures leaves African children at risk of mutilation." Parmar might blush to learn that my own mother, now in her eighties, was active in this work long before she and Walker walked the earth.[23]

The assumptions of some Western feminists about the control of women's sexuality are offensive to the African understanding of women's bodies and sexuality.[24] Alice Walker is accused further of being preoccupied with sexuality when she defines women as "genital carriers," a term that can be very offensive to African women, for whom the very mention of genitalia is taboo and disrespectful. By defining African women as "genital carriers," Walker ignores the African perception of humanity as holistic.[25] Her insensitivity to the feelings of African women is demonstrated further when she compares female circumcision to AIDS, an incurable epidemic with devastating effects on African women. Such a position is highly offensive to circumcising communities.[26]

THE FUNCTIONING OF PATRIARCHAL SYSTEMS

Although valid issues are being raised by the debate about female circumcision, certain assumptions need to be clarified. For example, as previously mentioned, other patriarchal social institutions exist outside of circumcising societies and some polyandrous and matrilineal societies also observe this practice. This does not in any way dissociate female circumcision from patriarchy, but it must be noted that female circumcision is one among many practices found in patriarchal communities. Also, patriarchal societies that do not practice female circumcision have their own means of controlling women and their sexuality. In Kenya, for instance, in non-circumcising communities such as the Luo, the Luyia, and the Turkana, virginity, widow inheritance, taboos, and curses are used to control the sexuality of women. Polygamy and wife battering are cultural values in these communities. Among the Turkana the piercing of the earlobes and the lip is a very painful way of initiating children into adulthood. During initiation, the Turkana educate their initiates on matters of masculinity, femininity, and sexuality. Traditionally, Luo boys and girls are expected to remove their six lower teeth at puberty, and girls are trained to remain virgins until marriage and to be good and chaste wives to their husbands.[27] The difference is that such initiation rites do not damage sexual function. Any unnecessary bodily harm must be condemned.

Similarly, to argue that female circumcision is not patriarchal because it is defended and performed by women does not take into account how patriarchal systems operate. According to Gruenbaum, men are not necessarily the only ones who support sexism or women's oppression in patriarchal communities. Patriarchy is a system that socializes everyone to accept normative social values and practices, even when such norms and values are oppressive. Dorothy Smith's concept of "ruling relations" describes how social relations operate in a patriarchal society to promote the interests of social structures such as patriarchy. As she observes, both men and women are socialized to internalize patriarchal norms as "right" or tradition, without question, regardless of apparent injustices that such a structure may promote.[28] Women's actions as defenders of practices such as female circumcision must be understood within this social context. As Bonvillain explains: "The fact that it is women as midwives who perform female genital mutilation and women as mothers who arrange the procedure for their daughters demonstrates the power of social and religious ideology and the paralyzing self-negating effects of patriarchal discrimination."[29] Men are equally socialized into patriarchy and, just as some women actively advocate or participate in female circumcision, there are men who object to such practices because of the injustices they inflict.

Furthermore, arguing that female circumcision is practiced among some matrilineal communities does not necessarily make it any less patriarchal. As mentioned earlier, matrilineal descent does not always imply women's power. Matrilineal communities can still have patriarchal characteristics. Even if women possess some power in matrilineal communities, it does not always follow that issues such as women's health and human rights are considered. In other words, the matrilineal nature of a community is not a sufficient reason to defend a practice with serious health consequences for its female members.

WOMEN'S SEXUALITY AND FEMALE CIRCUMCISION

Although African critics of Walker and Parmar claim that female circumcision as "the sexual blinding of women's sexuality" is based on Western assumptions of femininity and the erotic functions of women's sexuality, it is an equally sweeping generalization to assume that Kenyan women have no need for sexual pleasure and satisfaction. To be socialized to accept a certain lifestyle does not necessarily mean that an alternative lifestyle is not desired. Ignorance of a different lifestyle should not be a reason to reject it. If a practice such as female circumcision interferes with women's sexual satisfaction, then perhaps there is a need to reexamine the meaning of sexual satisfaction. It is generally agreed that sexual fulfillment is part of a biological and social need that is transcultural and, like culture itself, dynamic. What should be considered are the wishes of African women: Do they want to maintain or to change cultural norms or practices that may deny them sexual fulfillment?

Since Kenyans have embraced a variety of other Western ideas ranging from political and economic systems to agricultural practices and technology and have been exposed to new ideas, including understandings of sexuality, it is illogical for cultural apologists to insist on traditional cultural ideas and practices that may be outdated, particularly if social injustice is involved. If Kenyan women perceive that a practice such as female circumcision interferes with the happiness of Kenyan girls today, this should be acknowledged and efforts should be made to educate circumcising communities to accept this social transformation. This is not to say that all Western influences or ideas are good; they must be carefully examined, as is true of Kenyan cultural concepts, for their benefits or potential harm.

Arguments for female circumcision in the name of beauty or "technology of the body" are complex because, as Martha Nussbaum observes, cultures differ in what is regarded as beautiful.[30] In some patriarchal communities women's bodies are commodified and physically modified to meet certain "beauty" practices; such physical modifications are symptoms of misogyny aimed at maiming, crippling, and weakening women. As Mary Jackman observes, a culture that promotes such forms of beautification portrays "animosity towards women."[31] (It should be noted that some Western practices, such as dieting for the "perfect" body, can be equally and validly criticized.) In such cultures it seems a basic requirement that one should suffer to be beautiful. This ideology is internalized so that women and men admire those who excel in meeting the beauty standards of their day, which compounds the social pressure to conform. Women in circumcising communities experience this kind of pressure, forcing them to accept female circumcision in order to fit in their communities. This kind of pressure has resulted in numerous deaths in the name of tradition.

The film *The Day I Will Never Forget* illustrates clearly how social pressure works. The viewer sees a woman talking to girls, purportedly asking them to make their own choice about circumcision. Yet she threatens them with misfortunes that will result for being uncircumcised. Out of fear of ridicule or misfortune, an uncircumcised girl accepts the operation. The film shows how the intricate network of beliefs that bolster or repudiate specific forms of violence are shaped by the social structures and values of a community.[32] While individuals who endorse practices such as female circumcision may not necessarily be driven by misogyny, the value placed on controlling women's bodies may indeed be motivated by patriarchal values ingrained in that culture. It is difficult, if not impossible, to isolate the practice of female circumcision from the patriarchal social system of which it is a part. Understanding the larger sociocultural context of a social practice such as female circumcision enables one to direct criticism to the actual problem, if indeed one exists, rather than to make incorrect or baseless assumptions.

OPPOSITION TO FEMALE CIRCUMCISION

It is clear that in some communities female circumcision is an integral part of the social and cultural system. Yet the practice is invariably associated with injustices to women that include health risks, early marriage, gender oppression, and limited educational opportunities.

Potential Health Risks

Although female circumcision is not the most dangerous practice affecting women's health globally, its adverse effects are undeniable, even though these effects are difficult to measure, especially where the practice is illegal and performed in secrecy. Female circumcision is associated with both short-term and long-term health risks. Short-term complications include hemorrhages from the rupture of the blood vessels of the clitoris, severe pain, shock from acute pain and blood loss, risk of infections such as tetanus, HIV/AIDS, hepatitis B and C, and potential death due to excessive bleeding. In most cases there is limited access to immediate medical attention.[33] In some cases the urethra, anal sphincter, vaginal walls, or bartholin glands are permanently damaged, and acute pain or fear may lead to the dangerous retention of urine. In cases where infibulation is performed, sexual organs may be damaged further when the vulva is reopened after marriage, then sewed together again, and possibly later reopened after a death or divorce.[34]

Long-term complications associated with infibulation include genito-urinary problems such as difficulties with menstruation and urination as a result of the "nearly complete sealing off of the vagina and urethra."[35] In some cases pelvic infections result in sterility or prolonged labor with the risk of fetal brain damage and fetal death, back pain, and painful menstruation.[36] Untreated lower-urinary-tract infections can also lead to bladder and kidney infections resulting in renal failure, septicemia, and death.

Female circumcision is also said to diminish sexual pleasure and in certain cases leads to an inability to experience a clitoral orgasm. As Shell-Duncan and Hernlund observe, "Infibulated women may experience painful intercourse and often have to be cut open for penetration to occur."[37] Infibulations may also prevent vaginal intercourse, resulting in anal intercourse as an alternative, which may lead to more tissue damage.[38] Obstetrical complications include obstructed labor and excessive bleeding from tearing and de-infibulation during childbirth, which can result in vesico-vaginal and rector-vaginal fistulae (openings between the vagina and the urethra or rectum, allowing the unstoppable flow of urine and the passage of feces through the vagina).[39] Some African women live with abscesses and cysts caused by the practice. Vaginitis, sterility, and the frequent need for episiotomies during childbirth continue to be part of their lives.[40]

Health risks that result from female circumcision arise because this practice is usually performed in unhygienic circumstances with very limited access afterward to medical care. Most often unsterilized instruments are used, including knives, razor blades, scissors, thorns, and pieces of glass. Because circumcision takes place in a group setting, these instruments are used on more than one person, increasing the risk of infection.[41] Some of these health risks are validated both by responses of the fifty women I interviewed and also in the film *The Day I Will Never Forget*, which follows the attempts of an infibulated woman to be de-fibulated after her wedding in order to consummate her marriage.

Wanyama, one of my informants who is also a nurse, had this to say about the health risks experienced by circumcised women:

> I have met and interacted with these women who are circumcised and their experience is pathetic and painful. I am a nurse and so I have tried to assist those who are circumcised, during delivery, for instance, and it is not easy either for the mother or the midwife. There are more complications such as perineal tears,

bleeding, delayed second stage leading to still births, infections, et cetera.[42]

Other studies on health risks associated with female circumcision include that of Dr. Mark Besley for the Division of Family Health of the World Health Organization in Geneva. In a 1993 documentary interview he remarked, "There is no single practice which has such a dramatic negative effect on health in the broadest sense as female genital mutilation."[43] Similarly, Dr. Rosemary Mburu, a Kenyan gynecologist, has estimated that 15 percent of all circumcised females die from bleeding or infections.[44] Other reports estimate that out of every one thousand females who undergo female circumcision, seventy die.[45] In just the month of October 2001, twenty-one girls were hospitalized in Kenya due to serious infections after they were forced to undergo the practice. The girls, aged nine to fourteen years, were removed from school by their parents, who wanted to make sure that the government, which has banned the practice, would not interfere.[46]

Due to the secrecy that shrouds the practice, many serious injuries go unreported, often with tragic results. Chepkorir, another of my informants, recounts:

> Even though the government has banned this practice, it is still prevalent. Most people do it in secrecy. What I don't like about this is the fact that whenever a problem arises in the process, most of us will fear to take our daughters to the hospital for fear of being apprehended. . . . That is what happened to my neighbor.[47]

Chepkorir's neighbor failed to take her daughter to the hospital when she hemorrhaged, and the girl died. Attempts to interview the neighbor were fruitless; she was not willing to talk about it. It is impossible to estimate accurately the number of infections and deaths caused by female circumcision. This is true because of the secrecy involved, but also because the majority of these procedures take place in rural areas where such records are not kept. In addition, because of the nature of the operation, unsuccessful procedures are concealed from outsiders and the authorities. Only a very small proportion of such cases reach the hospitals. Women with excessive bleeding often are taken for medical care only at the last minute when their condition is critical or hopeless. Severely limited transportation in rural areas compounds the problem.

The government seems unable to prevent deaths resulting from female circumcision because of its failure to develop sensitive strategies to eliminate the practice and also because of its lack of commitment. As argued by Gruenbaum, this lack of commitment may be attributed to the fact that the laws enacted to criminalize this practice "were the by-products of external pressure and did not reflect the desire of the local people to suppress the tradition."[48]

Among the organizations that have condemned the practice of female circumcision is WHO. According to Chronicle 31 (1986) of WHO, female circumcision is a traditional practice whose adverse effects are undeniably dangerous and even life threatening. In August 1982 WHO formally opposed female circumcision in a formal statement of its position to the UN Commission on Human Rights. The statement condemns the practice as dangerous and life threatening and opposes any "medicalization of this operation, advising that under no circumstances should this practice ever be performed by health professionals or in health establishments."[49]

The condemnation of female circumcision on the basis of health risks has raised questions as to whether the practice should be eradicated on this basis or whether it should be retained in a less dangerous form, popularly known as *sunna*, and performed under sanitary conditions. Some African scholars, including Obiora and Ahmadu, have argued that the health risks attributed to this practice are not valid reasons to eradicate it. First, they maintain that the cultural value of the practice overrides the health consequences. Second, they state that the health hazards associated with this practice have been exaggerated by its opponents, noting that the health risks associated with female circumcision vary according to the type of circumcision performed and that mild forms, especially *sunna* and symbolic pricking, do not pose health threats.

Third, these scholars claim that even where the most harmful type of circumcision is performed not all women suffer from these consequences. Normal sexual function and enjoyment of sex have been observed in some clitoridectomized African women, discounting the argument that female circumcision adversely affects the sexual fulfillment of women.[50] Fourth, they maintain that female circumcision is no longer performed in the traditional manner, which reduces possible health risks. In its modern forms only a drop of blood or the prepuce is extracted from the clitoris.[51] These scholars argue that supervision by trained physicians and the use of modern medical procedures and technology can eliminate the danger of medical complications.[52]

Whereas some of these arguments are valid, they are based on misleading and sweeping generalizations about African women. While health risks associated with female circumcision do not necessarily affect all circumcised women, these risks are a reality, due to the unhealthy conditions and manner in which the practice is traditionally performed. This fact cannot be ignored as long as some women in these communities continue to suffer from these risks and as long as some individuals continue to live in fear, as illustrated in frequent escapes of many girls to prevent circumcision. In many communities in Kenya, especially in rural areas, medical services are scarce. Female circumcision is done secretly for fear of arrest. Further, social ridicule inhibits seeking medical care.

The Question of Human Rights

Female circumcision is also opposed as a violation of the human rights of children and women: bodily integrity, self-determination, freedom of choice, and sexual fulfillment. Children are coerced, often "kidnapped" from reluctant mothers or fathers and exposed to unnecessary and excruciating pain in a procedure that is irrevocable and is carried out in the name of culture and religion.[53] Female circumcision, which is usually performed on girls between the ages of four and sixteen, violates their freedom of choice. No effort is made to inform them about the health risks involved, nor is their consent sought. They have no real choice in the matter. Therefore, female circumcision is an irrevocable operation to which children, who are totally vulnerable and have no power, should not be subjected. Their future as women with rights to sexual fulfillment is also denied.

Those who object to female circumcision as a human rights violation bring the weight of the United Nations to their argument. Opponents assert that the practice violates the human rights articulated in Article 5 of the Universal Declaration of Human Rights. This article cautions against the subjection of any person "to torture, or to cruel, inhuman or degrading treatment or punishment." Female circumcision, therefore, which violates the rights of women and children to good health and bodily integrity and freedom from torture, is viewed as a denial of this right.[54]

Female circumcision is also seen as an example of the general sub-jugation of women. It is considered a form of violence against women because it violates CEDAW, enacted by the United Nations in 1981. CEDAW calls for an end to all gender discrimination and requires that nation-states modify their cultural and social patterns of conduct of both men and women with a view to eliminating prejudice and all practices based on gender inequality and stereotyped roles.[55]

In addition, female circumcision is considered a violation of Article 24 (3) of the UN Convention on the Rights of the Child (1990), which protects children's rights to good health, because it exposes them to cruel and exploitative tendencies that endanger their health. Most important, the enforcement of this practice through coercion and kid-napping unwilling children is cruel.[56] The UN Declaration of the Rights of the Child adopted in 1959 stipulates that each child should be given the opportunity "to develop physically, mentally, morally, spiritually and socially in a healthy and normal manner and in condi-tions of freedom and dignity" (Principle 2) and should be "protected against all forms of neglect, cruelty, and exploitation." (Principle 9).

Female circumcision is also considered a form of torture and, there-fore, a violation of the 1984 United Nations Convention against Tor-ture and Other Cruel, Inhuman or Degrading Treatment or Punish-ment. According to this convention, "torture means any act by which severe pain or suffering, whether physical or mental, is intentionally inflicted on a person for . . . any reason based on discrimination of any kind" (Article 1). According to the Minority Rights Group Interna-tional, female circumcision is comparable to torture, given the avail-able description of "the reactions of children—panic and shock from extreme pain, biting through the tongue, convulsions, necessity for six adults to hold down an eight-year-old, and death."[57] This practice is also considered a violation of the right to health and bodily integ-rity of women and children because, as Shell-Duncan explains, it "in-tegrates the issue of physical, mental, sexual health and child develop-ment."[58]

The international commitment to protect human rights began early in 1948,[59] when the UN Commission on Human Rights adopted a draft declaration that, in turn, was adopted by the General Assembly that year as the Universal Declaration of Human Rights.[60] In this char-ter the United Nations proclaimed that its purpose was to "achieve in-ternational co-operation . . . in promoting and encouraging respect for human rights and for fundamental freedoms for all without distinction as to race, sex, language, or religion" (Article 1(3)).[61] Under Articles 55 and 56, all signatory members pledged "to take joint and separate action in cooperation with the organization for the achievement of the purposes of the United Nations, including the promotion of a universal respect for, and observance of, human rights and fundamental freedoms for all" (Article 55(c)).[62] According to the Preamble of the Universal Declaration of Human Rights, human rights are based on the "recognition of the inherent dignity and of the equal and inalienable rights of all members of the human family" as the "foundation of freedom, justice and peace in the world."

The condemnation of female circumcision as a violation of human rights has led to the establishment of laws in a number of countries and states. In the United States, for example, section 116 of the Illegal Immigration Reform and Immigrant Responsibility Act of 1996 reads:

(a) Except as provided in subsection (b), whoever knowingly circumcises, excises, or infibulates the whole or any part of the labia majora or labia minora or clitoris of another person who has not attained the age of 18 years shall be fined under this title or imprisoned not more than 5 years, or both.

(b) A surgical operation is not a violation of this section if the operation is:

(1) necessary to the health of the person on whom it is performed, and is performed by a licensed person in the place of its performance as a medical practitioner, or

(2) performed on a person in labor or who has just given birth and is performed for medical purposes connected with that labor or birth by a person licensed in the place it is performed as a medical practitioner, midwife or a person in training to become such a practitioner or midwife.

The Constitution of Kenya provides that "every person is entitled to fundamental rights and freedoms of the individual . . . whatever his sex" (Section 70). Campaigns and strategies to eradicate female circumcision as a health risk and a violation of human rights, such as those in Kenya, are based on the UN Universal Declaration of Human Rights.

The association of female circumcision with human rights triggers the irreconcilable debate of universalism and culturalism, a debate in the human rights movement involving the "universal" (or absolute) and "relative" (or contingent) character of the rights declared. Advocates of human rights claim universality, which stipulates that international human rights such as equal protection, physical security, free speech, religion, and association are and must be the same everywhere in the world. In other words, human beings are entitled to certain universal rights by virtue of being human, regardless of their cultural contexts. Advocates of cultural relativism, on the contrary, claim that rights and rules about morality are encoded in and dependent on cultural contexts. The term *culture* is often used in a broad and diffuse way to encompass not only indigenous traditional and customary practices but also political and religious ideologies and institutional structures. In other words, notions of right and wrong differ throughout the world because cultures differ. Therefore, no culture should impose its ideas on another culture. In essence, it can be said that cultural relativism contradicts the basic premise of the human rights movement.[63]

Scholars engaging in this debate include Obiora, Ahmadu, Sylvia Wynter, and Nussbaum. According to Obiora, the human rights argument is propounded by universalists who invoke "monolithic categories and constructions of dignity, integrity, and empowerment to condemn genital surgeries, and relativists who argue for locally autonomous and culturally sensitive reformatory strategies."[64] Obiora faults universalists for disregarding other people's cultures and perceptions of humanity. She questions the universalist interpretation of Article 5 of the Universal Declaration of Human Rights because, in her view, cultural standards and values are specific, and human beings have a tendency "to generalize from their situated perspectives and realities that are influenced by assumptions." She explains:

Article 5 . . . stipulates: "No one shall be subjected to torture, or to cruel, inhuman, or degrading treatment or punishment." The meaning of this provision, though, is not self-evident. Conceptions of human dignity tend to be indeterminate and contingent, and what may appear to one school as torture, may be absolved or approved of by another as culture. An act one may condemn as depreciative of human dignity may have been enacted by its practitioners as an enhancement of human dignity. The very act that one may construe as cruel and violative of Article 5 may be embraced in cultures where it is practiced as a "technology of the body."[65]

Feminists such as Obiora equate the United Nations' position on human rights with the Western assumption that Western cultural values are superior and should be used as a yardstick to judge other cultures, regardless of the incommensurability between and among the various cultures.[66] They feel that the use of human rights to condemn female circumcision is unjustifiable because it is based on Western conceptions of the human as a "purely biologized being based on the model of a 'natural organism,'" which is, itself, "culture specific."[67] This is contrary to African conceptions of the human person rooted in collective rather than individual rights. Obiora considers this attitude to contradict claims of sovereignty, domestic jurisdiction, and cultural autonomy, especially within postcolonial regimes such as those in Africa.

African scholars such as Ahmadu and Obiora have even claimed that African women define themselves as whole people through female circumcision and that eradicating this practice would deny this human right to women. Obiora and Wynter advocate the need for a transcultural system of human rights that is sensitive to cultural ambiguities and differences among cultures and that can serve as a middle course between conflicting positions. This, it is believed, will balance advocating a change in attitude toward female circumcision and protecting the interests of women.[68]

Although the argument that some Western scholars have tended to apply imperialist assumptions to other cultures, not to mention the complexities surrounding the practice of female circumcision, both those who condemn female circumcision and those who seek to defend it have overlooked certain essential insights. These include (1) an understanding of the complex social contexts within which female circumcision is practiced, (2) how culture and especially religion influence attitudes toward female circumcision, and (3) that critical analyses of social practices must not be blind to issues of social justice.

Certain significant facts need to be established in the debate over female circumcision. First, as Wynter observes, instead of dismissing the idea of human rights as foreign and thus inapplicable in Africa, it is important to remember that cultural meanings are human inventions that arise over time and are internalized by people through the process of socialization.[69] Even though some practices are culturally approved, it is important to question whether they compromise the welfare of members of the community. Since human beings are "socialized beings," as Wynter argues, it is important to question the social and governing codes they embrace to determine if they are fair to the humanity of everyone who embraces them.[70] In other words, we need to evaluate critically what we, as Kenyan women, believe. Culture should not be embraced merely because it is dictated by our elders but because it fosters our individual and social welfare.

That human beings should be protected from social injustice, as stipulated in the UN Universal Declaration of Human Rights, even if such actions are culturally justified, should not be dismissed lightly. It is important to recognize that respect for cultural differences and a commitment to studying them in context do not necessarily mean being blind to cultural universals, such as the need to acknowledge the human worth of every individual.[71] There are universal norms that can make intercultural communication possible.

Do Universal Human Rights Exist?

The concept of human rights springs from modern Western thought about the nature of justice and not from an anthropologically based consensus about the values, needs, and desires of all human beings. To seek an anthropologically based consensus on human rights by examining human cultures is to confuse the important concepts of rights, dignity, and justice. Human rights apply to the human being or groups of individuals by virtue of their being human. As Wynter argues, since human rights values are trans-cultural, they are not necessarily foreign, although they have been lost in the constructed cultural inequalities in which individuals have been socialized.

> Both the origins of the why of this practice [female circumcision], as well as of the why of the western cultural practices of stigmatization and criminalization (which define these practices as "genital mutilation" and "torture" and thereby as practices defined by their ostensibly inhuman otherness), are to be found only in the context of a parallel quest for another and even more centrally lost origin—that of the human itself.[72]

According to Steiner and Alston, scholars of international law, human rights represent "a radical departure from the many status-based, non-egalitarian, and hierarchical societies of the past and present; therefore these rights are a moral good that should be accepted on an ethical basis."[73] This interpretation of Steiner and Alston can provide great hope to women and children who belong to circumcising communities but are resisting a cultural practice that they believe is harmful to their personal well-being.

Steiner and Alston maintain that human rights are universally applicable in principle, not only because of the social evolution of the entire world toward state societies, but also because there are affinities, analogues, and precedents for the actual content of internationally accepted human rights in many cultural traditions. Furthermore, given our modern state-centric world, all human beings ought to subscribe to a basic understanding of human rights. Indeed, the current tendency toward globalization and the need to pursue social justice make human rights relevant throughout the world.[74] It is a moral imperative to look for universal "roots" of human rights in different areas of the world and in different traditions. As Kwasi Wiredu argues, "Any custom which violates a moral rule is *ipso facto* condemnable as bad, not *for* this reason or that society but *simpliciter*."[75]

Even though human beings have both common and conflicting interests, the basis for universal norms lies in the biological nature of human beings. In order to coexist in society, some adjustment or reconciliation of these interests must be made.[76] The possibility of such an adjustment rests on the fact that human beings have a basic natural sympathy for their kind. Unfortunately, as Wiredu observes, this sympathy is in some cases sparse and in other cases easily extinguished by a variety of causes.[77] To avoid conflict, individuals must adopt a moral code of impartial sympathy, enabling them to treat others as they would expect to be treated in a similar situation. As Wiredu suggests, this behavior is the basis for universal care for one another.

The Dangers of Cultural Relativism

This argument is not meant to downplay the relevance of cultural difference as advocated in cultural relativism. Rather, it cautions against adopting a relativist position that would inhibit one's ability to evaluate critically social situations and thus overlook injustice in a given cultural context. According to ethicists Francis Beckwith and Gregory Koukl, extreme relativism leads to "a world in which justice and fairness are meaningless concepts, in which there would be no accountability, no possibility of moral improvement, no moral discourse, and no tolerance."[78] In other words, while it is important to admit that female circumcision, for example, can be a culturally justified practice, the practice itself, like any social practice, should not escape interrogation in terms of ethical justice, human rights, human integrity, freedom of choice, and modernity.

Cultural relativism that seeks to romanticize culture must be avoided because there is no "perfect" culture. As Micere Githae Mugo observes, the romanticization of fossilized cultural values, such as female circumcision, "absolves neo-colonial governments of the many responsibilities" owed to their citizens. It also implies a defense of the practice, an attitude that may allow feminist proponents of female circumcision to dictate to "their less privileged sisters."[79] Any social critique must avoid baseless assumptions and biases, and it must also avoid drifting into an overdeveloped ethnocentricism that turns a blind eye to social injustice.[80]

Since customs often rest upon beliefs about the world, beliefs rooted in social structures that are radically different, they should be open to cross-cultural evaluation based on cognitive standards that transcend cultures. Certain cultural practices such as infanticide in pre-Islamic Arabia, foot binding in Asia, widow burning in India, and sacrifice of virgin girls to invoke rain in some indigenous communities of Africa should be critiqued. Ethical human beings have a responsibility to take a stance regarding the implications of such practices for humanity. Anthropologist Julian Steward poses a fundamental question when he asks if, as human beings, "we unanimously oppose the brutal treatment of Jews in Hitler Germany," why should we be silent about "other kinds of racial and cultural discrimination, unfair practices, and inconsiderate attitudes found throughout the world?"[81] Would cultural relativists argue that such treatment was culturally legitimate? As human beings we have the moral responsibility to reflect upon and criticize historical events, whether we are directly involved in them or not.

The Role of Justice

Customs vary greatly from one society to another and even within the same society from one era to another. This must be acknowledged by scholars and members of all communities. Kenyans have their understandings of human rights and their ways of doing things. However, if some of these beliefs or practices are unfair to some members of the community, they must be critiqued. Wiredu suggests that the "failure on the part of some benefactors of Africa to make or observe the distinction *between cultural rights and social justice* in all its subtlety has not served the continent well."[82] And it is important to acknowledge that Africa is not alone in this failure.

When critically analyzing issues of justice, a distinction must be made between culture and morality. Inattention to this distinction can result in what Wiredu refers to as "authoritarian moralism."[83] Wiredu maintains that when analyzing rules of conduct it is essential to separate culture from morality, and that even within culture, a distinction should be made between the rationally explicable elements and what a given community considers normative. Individuals are thus able to recognize in their own culture ethical norms of universal applicability that make possible dialogue and interaction among different peoples, groups, or individuals. At the same time, they are able to understand the norms by which they live.

It follows, then, that indifference should not be shown to social practices that are injurious to health and dignity just because they are approved cultural practices. Injuries sustained in pursuit of beauty can range from minor to severe, from physical restriction to physical immobility. Practices can result in physical pain or discomfort and even humiliation before one attains a certain standard of "beauty." Such practices should be discouraged. In the same way, female circumcision should be critiqued on the basis of the associated health risks and human rights violations; it should not be necessary to point to examples of serious mistakes that resulted in serious injury or death. Similarly, the value of this practice within a given community should not be overemphasized, given that the practice is no longer valued to the extent that some scholars would claim.

Commenting on the issue of justice and cultural uniqueness, ethicist Marion Iris Young reminds us that while difference can be a source of power, recognition, identity, and emancipation, it can also be an instrument of exploitation, marginalization, violence, and, especially, cultural imperialism.[84] In other words, while nonrecognition of difference may lead to misunderstanding and neglect of important cultural differences, extreme focus on culture can lead to overlooking social injustices perpetuated by that culture. It is crucial, therefore, to define justice, even in the midst of cultural values and claims of uniqueness.

It is, however, important to acknowledge that modern human rights standards lack international cultural legitimacy. This is not only because the idea of human rights as formulated by the United Nations violates many societies' more fundamental beliefs about the way social life should be ordered, but also because some of these countries did not participate in formulating these rights. African and Asian countries did not participate in formulating the Universal Declaration of Human Rights in 1948 because, as victims of colonization, they were not yet members of the United Nations.[85] Thus, some resistance to these rights as binding on these countries is not surprising. Even when some countries participated in preparing such documents, they may have done so based on differing world views and philosophical assumptions. As Muslim scholar Abdullahi Ahmed An-Na'im candidly observes, "The preexisting framework and assumptions favored individual civil and political rights over collective solidarity rights, such as a right to development," values subscribed to by African and Asian communities.[86]

This raises the question of whether Western notions of human dignity are inherently different from non-Western notions of dignity, a question often at the center of the debate over practices such as female circumcision. For instance, most African societies do not consider a non-socialized individual as a self-reflective being, but rather as an individual in the process of absorbing the community's culture faithfully and following the rules and customs expected of a person of his or her station. The human group takes precedence over the human person.

It is important to emphasize, however, that, to be effective, human rights advocates must work within the framework of a cultural context. An-Na'im observes that, insofar as human rights are "perceived to be alien to or at variance with values and institutions of a people, they are unlikely to elicit commitment or compliance."[87] Human rights must be examined, understood, and accepted in communities that adopt them. Cultural legitimacy is a significant factor in gaining compliance with human rights standards. Outlawing a practice such as female circumcision without appraising the social factors that influence it can lead to misunderstandings that eventually affect the response of these communities, as is seen in the history of Kenya's outlawing of the practice.

Religious beliefs are also a significant factor in identifying universal norms of morality and justice. Essential to any religion is a respect of human worth and a sense of moral uprightness; these are basic principles of social justice. Obviously, belief systems can be misused to justify social practices that are contrary to transcultural norms of morality, and there is a need to be cautious of moral precepts in religions that can be used to justify inequality and deny fundamental human rights. In terms of female circumcision, religion plays a significant role in explaining the value placed on this practice, but it can also be a significant factor in transforming attitudes about the practice. This will be discussed in subsequent chapters.

THE INSIDER/OUTSIDER CONFLICT

Another issue in the debate on female circumcision is who should be involved. Those who are not from communities that perform female circumcision are regarded as *outsiders*, a term that becomes ambiguous because it is also used to refer to uncircumcised individuals, even if they are Africans or members of circumcising communities, as well as early missionaries to Africa, members of colonial governments, and Western feminists. According to Fuambai Ahmadu, an African feminist, a number of scholars who have written on female circumcision come from ethnic groups where female circumcision is not practiced or they themselves have never undergone the procedure.[88] The crucial question is what right, if any, do outsiders have to interfere in other people's cultures. Outsiders engaging in the debate on female circumcision have been criticized for interfering in the internal affairs of circumcising communities. They are also criticized for lacking the ability to comprehend female circumcision in the same way as an insider, one who has lived the experience. As a result, it is claimed that outsiders have no way to appreciate the good or evil of this practice, let alone to understand its complexity within circumcising communities. Thus, an outsider will surely face the problems of misinformation, misrepresentation, and misinterpretation, coupled with certain assumptions and biases.

Drawing on this argument, Western feminists such as Walker and Daly have been critiqued for their involvement in condemning the practice of female circumcision. They have been accused of being outsiders and also of propounding universal assumptions rooted in Western ideologies. Their critique of female circumcision is based on the underlying assumption that Western culture is a "dominating culture self-appointed to be the barometer of morality and ethical standards," and that they are the instruments of salvation for African people.[89]

Walker is specifically accused of assuming a messianic attitude in addressing African women on female circumcision by the way she depicts these women through Tashi, a character in her novel *Possessing the Secret of Joy*. Mugo maintains that Tashi is presented as a dependent invalid, a victim who never recovers from her mutilation and betrayal by her own mother and waits for Westerners to rescue her.[90] Even when she is "rescued to America," Tashi is portrayed as savage and animalistic while adoring America and its culture. America and Europe become lands of salvation. In the end, African women are seen as incapable of agency or self-liberation.

African scholars such as Obiora, Mugo, and Ahmadu, on the other hand, advocate that feminists condemn all forms of oppression without adding or duplicating other oppressive notions. There is always a need to acknowledge the agency, experiences, and values of the oppressed if any form of genuine social transformation is to take place. The intent of feminists should be to empower the voices of women. They should resist being clouded by racism and other forms of prejudices, which betray the very principles they purport to defend.

Nonetheless, it is important to recognize that while the role of the insider is very significant in articulating issues that affect one's experience, the role of the outsider cannot be completely dismissed because of errors made by a few misguided scholars. An outsider who understands and interrogates the sociocultural context of a particular community can inform and instruct. This requires education of the outsider in the social conditions and life experiences of the community and in the way the community's social structures operate, especially if oppression of some members exists. Positive examples of the work of outsider scholars include Jean Davison's *Voices from Mutira* and Janice Boddy's *Wombs and Alien Spirits*.[91] These projects attempt to represent accurately the practice of female circumcision in given communities without making judgments. Davison's work gives a voice to Kenyan women as she records verbatim their experience of this practice, the reasons behind female circumcision, and how efforts to eradicate this practice have transformed their lives. Boddy presents a similar account among the Hofriyati of Sudan and acknowledges how meaningful the practice is perceived within the contexts in which it is practiced.

Although an insider can adequately and accurately describe the practice of female circumcision, she must also have the analytical tools to analyze critically and to reflect on the dynamics in her situation. In some cases critical analysis can be offered only by an outsider with expertise in the field because judgments based purely on social location can lead to errors. It is my belief that both outsiders and insiders can make significant contributions to social analysis: the efforts of outsiders can supplement or be integrated with insiders' contributions in order to discern more clearly the issues in a given context. My intention is not to overlook the assumptions of Western scholars about Kenyan communities or the debate on female circumcision, as they do raise important issues, but rather to acknowledge that both outsiders and insiders have significant roles in reflecting upon social injustices in any community, as long as they are willing to seek a deeper understanding of the issues at hand.

STRATEGIES TO COMBAT FEMALE CIRCUMCISION

Opponents of female circumcision—outsiders and insiders alike—have attempted to curb this practice. Some of the strategies adopted have generated much controversy for a number of reasons. First, some strategies are critiqued for ignoring both the social context within which female circumcision is practiced and its relevant sociocultural values and what eradication of the practice would mean for individuals in circumcising communities.

Second, some strategies that criminalize these rituals are critiqued for propagating imperialistic assumptions, for negating the identity and agency of female circumcising communities, and for overlooking local efforts to end the practice. Nor have such strategies included attempts to educate women on why female circumcision should be discouraged or to empower women themselves to end the practice. Instead, circumcised women and their communities are simply blamed for perpetuating the practice. Mugo explores this aspect in her critique of Walker's portrayal of the character Tashi.[92]

Third, some strategies are also critiqued because of their coercive nature, an approach that is unworkable with a culturally rooted practice. Without educational programs that explain why a practice that was an accepted and valued norm is suddenly criminal, the criminalization, arrest, and prosecution of practitioners of female circumcision can lead to serious resistance. As noted earlier, this has certainly been true in Kenya. The persistence of female circumcision clearly indicates resistance, as does the increasingly clandestine performance of this practice. The unsanitary conditions connected with the latter lead to a substantial increase in health risks.[93]

Teresia Hinga, a Kenya feminist, explains how the daughters of Christian converts in Kenya who denounced female circumcision faced ridicule and derision within their communities for failing to undergo the rite that would culturally define them as women. She also reports that because uncircumcised Protestant girls could not withstand the resulting psychological torture, abuse, and social ostracizing, they sought secret circumcision so they could fit into their communities.[94] Instead of curbing the practice, coercive strategies have often led to the clandestine practice and resurgence of this practice, as in Kenya.

Western feminist approaches to female circumcision are also criticized for advocating confrontation and the immediate abandonment of the practice. Such a strategy does not account for the multiple factors at play in communities that perform female circumcision, including the relationship between men and women and the role of the community in enforcing social values. These difficulties are further compounded by high rates of poverty, illiteracy, and unemployment, particularly in rural areas. As Hinga wisely observes, a strategy that seeks a collision course with men in society cannot yield desired fruits for African women because most of them are dependent on these men for survival. Hinga explains, "While African women acknowledge the oppression by men, they do not use the direct method of throwing stones, reasoning that this would pose a threat to women's solidarity."[95] Confrontation is only possible if an individual is assured of protection, support, and self-sustenance, an impossible situation for most African women.

The debate has provided suggestions for strategies to curb female circumcision. First, all strategies should work to address the social and cultural experiences and needs of female-circumcising communities. Second, these strategies should be avenues through which women at risk can cultivate agency and become active participants in the transformation of their oppressive reality. Finally, these strategies must ensure the clinicalization of female circumcision where it persists. Strategies suggested by most scholars include (1) circumcision through words, (2) clinicalization of the practice, and (3) conscientization through education.

Circumcision through Words

Popularly known in Kenya as *ntaanira na mugambo*, this practice encourages the observance of rituals associated with female circumcision without physical circumcision. Circumcision through words grew out of the collaborative efforts of two Kenyan women's groups, MYWO and PATH, to acknowledge the value associated with female circumcision for some communities. Initiates attend a week-long program of counseling, training, and instruction about womanhood. They learn about anatomy and physiology, sexual and reproductive health, hygiene, gender issues, respect for adults, and the importance of self-esteem.[96] On the last day a ceremony performed in the presence of the entire community signals the girls' passage into womanhood.

Efforts made by MYWO and PATH to introduce this practice have yielded some positive responses. Among the Meru, it is reported that "in six years of operation, the project has prevented just over 1,000 genital cuttings."[97] The slow acceptance of the program in some circumcising communities is probably due to the fact that it leaves out traditional goals of the practice such as the repression of sexuality or beautification. As Hernlund observes, some critics of female circumcision still oppose circumcision through words because "what is taught to the girls during seclusion is based on 'patriarchal values' and geared at 'turning them into submissive wives and mothers.'"[98] In other words, circumcision through words does not promote the ideals of social justice that are essentially in question. Other concerns not addressed include the need to foster women's agency and the right to sexual and corporal integrity.

Clinicalization of Female Circumcision

The clinicalization of female circumcision has been suggested by some scholars, including Obiora, in order to provide a harmless form of surgery while accommodating the cultural needs of circumcising communities. Clinicalization will certainly render the practice more sanitary and limit adverse health consequences for women and children.[99] According to Obiora, one Seattle hospital proposed accommodating cultural needs of Somali families by conducting "a symbolic blood-letting" on the hood of the flesh above the clitoris—a "small nick on the prepuce"—without the removal of any tissue.[100]

While the clinicalization of female circumcision seems to be a viable solution, constraints must be acknowledged. First, medical services in general are very scarce in Kenyan communities, especially in rural areas. Like most African governments, Kenya is more concerned with basic needs and survival than with a specific issue such as the clinicalization of female circumcision. The gross economic, social, and political inequalities prevalent throughout Kenya, and many other African countries, restrict the availability of clinical services to upper-class members of the society, leaving others at risk. Second, this method can work only if bans on the practice are lifted. For example, in Kenya, where female circumcision is banned, it is performed in secrecy and most parents are afraid to take their daughters for medical care, which increases exposure to health risks. Third, the clinicalization of female circumcision addresses only one concern, namely, health consequences. Issues about women's and children's rights to choose, sexual fulfillment, and sexism remain unaddressed. Fourth, opponents of circumcision argue that "no action will entrench female genital mutilation more than legitimating it through the medical profession," a reason why the Seattle proposal was abandoned by WHO.[101] Furthermore, as Obiora observes, the notion of a mild circumcision is ambiguous, as it can encompass a wide range of operations and does not preclude the risk of serious infection or injury.[102] While clinicalization may be a good short-term solution, it should be supplemented with the conscientization of communities about the need to transform their attitudes.

Conscientization through Education

Conscientization though education is a strategy of educating and sensitizing circumcising communities about the possible consequences of female circumcision. Because it addresses issues of cultural dynamism and the need to abandon outdated values and practices, this strategy seems most effective in changing attitudes toward the practice and eventually leading to its abandonment. It has been shown that individuals who are aware of the consequences associated with female circumcision or are more educated are less likely to have their daughters circumcised.[103]

Obiora points out that meaningful education "eschews vanguard politics and seeks to nurture a self-conscious interaction between the subject, possessed of a fresh sense of ability, and her context." She explains further:

> This process celebrates the realities of women's experiences as the starting point for individual and social change. Its ultimate strength lies in its capacity to simultaneously afford the structure for substantive appreciation of the exact conditions of social relations, while fostering understandings of local predilections and theories of change.[104]

Mugo observes that this position counters approaches that use coercion and punishment, especially when these approaches happen to be situated within the oppressive institutions of capitalist and neocolonial states.[105]

Certain factors do need to be taken into consideration to enable the effectiveness of this strategy. First, although education is a good method of conscientization, all forms of education do not necessarily conscientize: education can be a source of both domination and liberation. Education that indoctrinates the individual to accept the oppressor's ideology is not conscientizing because it simply transfers "neatly wrapped knowledge" that is uncritical.[106] That is why claims about educated people practicing female circumcision must be evaluated as to the kind of education they have received. According to Paulo Freire, conscientization can be compared to a painful birth because it involves "an excruciating moment, a rebirth, an awakening to the realization that one has to abandon convictions" once held because of new principles the person now embraces, such as the principle of justice.[107] The need to promote education that conscientizes is therefore crucial.

In addition, if the educational program is not tailored to empowering circumcising communities about female circumcision, the oppression of women, and other social injustices, the long-term goal may prove difficult to attain. Feminist Ifi Amadiume indicates that the content must be clearly defined and tailored to specific objectives. For example, does it address only issues of health hazards associated with this practice or will it also address issues of social justice such as human dignity, freedom of choice, and how these values are compromised in given social cultural settings?[108] There is also a fundamental need to integrate religious values in the conscientization process: religious ideals promoting female circumcision can be countered only by the use of religious ideals that demystify any religious links associated with this practice.

In summary, any method may gain very little ground if it does not cater to the needs of the whole community and include the conscientization of every member of the community about the health risks and other injustices associated with female circumcision. An effective method must be well thought out, carefully planned, and sensitively implemented.

4

Sexuality, Gender, and Religion in Kenya

To understand any experience one must examine the social and cultural patterns that shape, structure, and constrain it. Similarly, an analysis of a *woman's* experience must understand the cultural definitions of gender in her particular community. Most cultures have at least two gender subcultures, with clear cultural distinctions between the two, and each with its own patterns of socialization. Generally, transition rites or initiations, in some form, are an integral part of socialization into the community. These rites, often with a focus on gender, dramatize the attributes expected of an individual. These culturally specific features of gender then become reference points for personal gender identity.

Efforts to understand a practice such as female circumcision must strive to interrogate and understand all aspects of sexuality within a specific society. Since understandings of sexuality in most societies are rooted in religious beliefs, religion should be included in the variables to be examined.

GENDER AND SEXUALITY

Gender and sexuality are fundamental aspects of every individual's identity that define the experience of being male or female. As a cultural construction, gender takes on socially and historically specific forms within a given society. Whereas all cultures create social categories from the observable differences between men and women, it should be acknowledged that cultural notions of maleness and female-ness can vary greatly.[1] Similarly, although men and women may share understandings of what constitutes gender or sexuality, their positions will vary according to their gender, race, and social location. Thus, a man's understanding of masculinity or maleness may differ from that of a woman, even though they belong to the same community.

The relationship between gender and sexuality also points to the complexity inherent in understanding how social experience and rela-tionships function in specific historical-cultural conditions. As soci-ologist John H. Gagnon has noted, "the patterns of gender roles and erotic development that we observe in Western European societies and their descendants are only a few of the potential designs available for humans."[2] Thus, what constitutes maleness or femaleness, and the related practices, should be interrogated within a matrix of social mean-ings.

Sexuality as a concept is more complex to define than gender be-cause it is highly dependent on a specific historical-cultural context. While both concepts have a biological explanation, usually referred to as an essentialist view, most cultures assume that sexuality is hidden and that gender is visible.[3] Even though gender identity and sexual behavior have their roots in biological and even psychological factors, they cannot be completely understood apart from the social environ-ment that shapes the ways in which members of a particular society behave sexually. Gagnon observes that gender and sexual expressions unfold and can make sense only when viewed through the lens of their respective social contexts.[4] The social understanding of sexuality, usu-ally referred to as a social-constructionist view, underscores this real-ity. Considering both views of sexuality and gender—essentialist and social constructionist—provides a clearer understanding of sexuality and related topics.[5]

Gender relations should be understood in terms of power relations because, like power, gender does not exist outside relationships, and gender relations are usually based on power dynamics.[6] Feminist theo-ries of sexuality generally locate sexuality within the theory of gender inequality and treat sexuality as a construct of male power. Because of the dominance of male power, male interests construct the meaning of sexuality and set the standards for what is allowed, expressed, and experienced. According to feminist Catharine MacKinnon, sexuality is "a dimension along which gender pervasively occurs."[7] It is where "dominance eroticized defines the imperatives of masculinity," and "submission eroticized defines femininity."[8] Sexuality, then, is an area that clearly manifests the inequality of the sexes.[9] Since men's interests constitute how sexuality is articulated in a society, what is considered to be female sexuality is essentially the male-objectified expectations of what sexuality ought to be. Thus a thorough examination of a social cultural practice such as female circumcision demands an interrogation of the conceptions of gender and sexuality that inform such an experience.

THE CONTROL OF SEXUALITY

Gender and sexuality are significant instruments of social organization. Apart from masking powerful dimensions of human life, sexuality is also a primary ground on which human relationships are sanctioned as natural and good or unnatural and wrong. Given most societies' concern with well-defined structures in order to maintain social order, sexuality is often viewed as a potentially disruptive force to be controlled.[10] Many societies, therefore, are organized to steer members toward what is defined as a "good" sex life so that social harmony is maintained, and their social systems contain rules and regulations linking sex and gender roles in order to restrict and control sexual behavior.[11] Included are rules about age, legitimacy, and appropriate expressions of sexuality; attitudes and behavior are then categorized into moral, normal, and natural, or unnatural, abnormal, and immoral. The latter terms carry heavy stigmas. Every society has its own definition of what constitutes normal or moral behavior. Its rules and regulations help to shape appropriate expressions of sexuality and to punish those who do not conform.

The norm in most Kenyan communities confines sexuality to marriage. In addition, the function of sexuality is to ensure that children are born and cared for properly. Heterosexual unions are thus considered the norm and any deviation is stigmatized and severely punished. In most Kenyan communities homosexual behavior and/or bisexual behavior are considered inappropriate and other forms of sexuality that threaten the social order, such as fornication, adultery, and incest, are strongly discouraged.

The policing of sexuality in Kenya and other societies tends to be common in communities where a family's name and reputation are the key to power and status, including the inheriting of property.[12]

Under such conditions total respectability and confidence in paternity are considered essential, and the behavior of one member of the family reflects on all. Such regulation of sexuality often makes use of various myths about the negative consequences of disapproved sex acts. Control also takes the form of penalties for premarital and extramarital sex or cohabitation, and in some cases, control is expressed through comprehensive sex and family education.[13]

The Control of Women's Sexuality

Women's sexuality has been a target of control in most societies because it is viewed as threatening to the male culture.[14] According to Ortner, the universal devaluation of women is based on the assumed hierarchy of culture over nature. Culture, which is viewed as within the sphere of human control, is equated to the male sphere, while nature is equated to the women's sphere.[15] As theologian Rosemary Radford Ruether observes, women are equated to nature because their "physiological processes are viewed" not only as "dangerous and polluting to the higher (male) culture," but also because their "social roles are regarded as inferior to those of males, falling lower on the nature-culture hierarchy."[16]

But this cultural view of woman is inconsistent. Whereas femaleness is perceived as "the devalued parts of the self," as Ruether explains, "woman as mother, as original source of life, primary mediator of nature and culture," is seen as possessing "powers of life and all that supports and inspires the human (male)."[17] Her despised sexuality, which equates woman with nature, is also portrayed as powerful and as a symbol of the divine, therefore dangerous. It is a force that can "tempt and distract men from their duties."[18] In some communities women's sexual desires are considered insatiable, and a woman's presence is thus considered too seductive for even the most disciplined of men to resist.

Another theory about the need to control women's sexuality draws from women's ability to reproduce life and to produce blood that is not related to a wound. This is viewed as a threat to men's power because women are said to possess the power to create the next generation, a power unavailable to men. Ruether explains:

> The first subjugation of woman is the subjugation of her womb, the subjugation of access to her body, so that she should not

choose her own beloved or explore the pleasures of her own body but that her body and its fruits should belong first to her father, who would sell or trade her to her husband. She must be delivered as undamaged goods, duly inspected, any signs of previous use punished by death. Only the male to whom she has been legally handed over may put his seed in her body, so that he can be sure that the children that emerge from her body belong to him, pass on his name, inherit his property.[19]

Because of this attitude, women in most societies are not allowed to explore and express their sexuality freely and openly. Because of this association with the flesh, which symbolizes sin, they are prohibited from performing certain duties, such as holding priestly offices, due to the alleged impurity of their bodies.[20] Some form of physical or psychological control is enforced in order that women conform to these prohibitions. Control is exerted over both unmarried and married women, but in different ways.

It is not surprising that the stricter the patriarchal system is, the stricter will be restrictions on the expressions of female sexuality. Since most patriarchal societies perceive the honor of men to reside in the purity of their kinswomen and wives, control of their sexuality serves to enhance this honor.[21] Usually societies enforce the premarital chastity and postmarital fidelity of women in part by emphasizing beliefs about the weaknesses and sexual susceptibility of females and the rampant sexual aggressiveness of males.[22]

Sexuality is a vital topic for feminist social theorists because it is integral to women's oppression. Feminist theorists understand that the control of women's sexuality reflects higher forms of power—power usually drawn from patriarchal notions of male power and dominance and of female powerlessness and submission.[23] Feminists generally consider sexual pleasure—the cycle of arousal, desire, and orgasm—as a basic natural and pre-social need that should not be denied to anybody. Rape, sexual harassment, abuse of girls, prostitution, pornography, and other degrading acts are viewed as acts of domination expressed through sexuality and should be condemned.[24]

In the 1960s and 1970s a number of books were published on how women's bodies work, including the *Hite Report: A Nationwide Study of Female Sexuality* and *My Secret Garden*.[25] These treatises urged women to move beyond virginity as a badge of honor. During this time Western feminism began to challenge sexual ideals such as virginity, early marriage for women, confinement of women to the home, belief in the goodness of marriage for all women, and belief that sexual experience is incompatible with a woman's marriageability. Such ideals were perceived as ways of controlling women's sexual freedom and infringing on their integrity as rational people. It was suggested that women embrace their rights in order to control their own bodies, sexually and reproductively, both in and out of marriage, including the right to withhold (or give) sexual consent without fear and the right to decide if they would or would not bear children.[26] Although these views were developed first by Western feminists, they do have some bearing on critiques of female circumcision in other locations.

Control of Women's Sexuality in Kenya

Kenyan norms and modes of ethical conduct are based on an African world view that perceives the individual primarily in terms of the community. The same is true of sexuality. It is understood in relation to an individual's marital relations but also in relation to the role of marriage, social status, spiritual matters, and social ideologies. This is necessary in order to maintain order in the community. This means that the sexuality of a Kenyan woman is understood, first and foremost, in terms of her identity as a social person. Referring to the experience of most African communities, which also holds true for Kenya, Elizabeth Amoah, a Ghanaian feminist, explains that because a woman's sexuality is part of her identity, it is intertwined with not only biological, physical, and socioeconomic aspects but also with the religious and spiritual dimensions of life.[27] Attitudes toward women's sexuality are based on the attitude of the community toward femaleness and maleness, puberty and fertility rites, marriage, and widowhood, especially as they relate to the welfare of the community. In contrast, Western views of sexuality tend to focus on the individual. Although this concept is generally alien to the African understanding of the human being in relation to the community, it is increasingly being examined and probed in contemporary Kenya.

In most Kenyan communities femaleness is associated with reproduction, caretaking, generosity, modesty, and the dignity of perseverance, obedience, submissiveness, conformity, and dependence. Maleness, on the other hand, is associated with virility, strength, authority, power, leadership, and the ability to bear physical pain, to offer protection, and to provide economic sustenance. These values are generally inculcated in the individual from early childhood; boys are taught not to cry because "men do not cry," and girls are told not to insult boys or be forceful or they will be considered "female males." Gender roles in most Kenyan communities are determined by these restrictive characteristics. Attitudes toward a man's strength and a woman's weakness are usually translated into all parts of a marriage, including sexual relations. The woman's sexual role is to be more or less marginal or passive, and she is not expected to take the initiative in sexual activities such as courtship, to show desire for sexual intercourse, or even to indicate that she is enjoying sex—at risk of being labeled a prostitute.

Gender expectations begin at birth. Among the Kikuyu, for instance, when a girl is born, the mother screams four times and the father cuts four stalks of sugar cane. If a boy is born, the mother screams five times and the father cuts five stalks of sugar cane. This is a symbol of the boy's higher role in society.[28] From then on, the child belongs to the entire community and is nurtured and disciplined by every member of the community. From birth, the parents and the community at large instill gender expectations in children. In most cases girls are brought up to embrace household duties such as cleaning the house and fetching water and firewood; they are also taught to treat boys and men as superior beings. On the other hand, boys are taught to embrace duties such as hunting and sitting with elderly men to learn about leadership, wisdom, and how to protect their families.

At puberty an individual is considered ready for the responsibilities of adulthood. A sharp distinction between maleness and femaleness is made at this time. While men enter into the world of power, girls are instructed in matters of womanhood, such as sexual games, menstruation taboos, and the "secret" of childbirth. A girl is taught the moral values of the sanctity and purity of her body and how to remain clean and undefiled sexually until marriage. Great emphasis is placed on maintaining her virginity. Although some communities such as the Kikuyu and the Akamba allow premarital sexual activities, penetration is not allowed because virginity must be maintained. Sexual activities allowed before marriage include only the fondling of each other's genitals as a means of instilling self-control in the youth.[29] As Davison observes, "Newly initiated youth of both sexes were allowed to sleep together and engage in sexual play and experimentation without intercourse under a strict code of behavior in a communally controlled environment designed to prohibit premarital pregnancy."[30] As part of the rite of female circumcision, an exciser must ensure that the initiates are virgins. Girls who are not virgins are considered a disgrace to their families and face embarrassment by being excluded from important initiation rituals.

During puberty, girls are also advised on how to become good wives. A good wife cooks well, prepares meals quickly for her husband and the whole household, is obedient to her husband in all matters, follows his dictates, and respects and obeys her in-laws. The initiates into adulthood are introduced to matters of sexuality through blunt references to sexual organs and sexual activities. This is usually done through admonitions and ridicule and in songs sung during puberty rituals. The initiate is also introduced to themes of subordination, power, authority, and challenge.

After marriage, chastity is expected from married women, with infidelity demanding severe punishment, including divorce. Most women fear to be divorced not only because of the stigma attached, but also because a divorced woman and her parents are often required to go through the painful ordeal of returning the dowry, which has usually already been used by members of the extended family.

Menstruation is another important subject at puberty because it is considered unclean and dangerous. In most communities a menstruating woman is taught to avoid certain people or places so she won't contaminate them. Contact with certain people is believed to render all their powers impotent and inactive, a sign of the power associated with the ability to bleed. A woman in this state, for example, is not allowed to fetch water in certain rivers, greet or talk to the chief, address her husband directly, or visit shrines. In some Kenyan communities a girl who has not had her first menstrual period is forbidden to have intercourse because such an act is believed to bring misfortune on the whole community.[31] In such cases a purification rite must be performed because infertility may result.[32] Infertility and childlessness are dreaded in most Kenyan communities as they can lead to the dissolution of marriages.[33]

The Role of Marriage

The role of women in marriage and the importance of marriage are also stressed during initiation because this is the path to procreation. In most communities begetting children is a way of attaining personal and communal immortality.[34] As the giver of life, a woman is considered to be the intermediary between existence and nonexistence.[35]

Marriage strengthens and reestablishes the community as it unites not only the two individuals but also the extensive kinship groups to which they belong. In other words, marriage is viewed as a community contract. It signifies solidarity with the ancestors and implies fertility and the transmission of life that ensures the survival of the community. Finally, marriage establishes a fellowship with the living, the dead, and the unborn. As Bénézet Bujo argues, marriage is the "narration of one's ancestors, one's biography, and the writing of one's autobiography."[36] The transmission of life through procreation is a fundamental responsibility of all.

Since most communities circumcise girls at an early age, early marriages are encouraged so that girls maintain their virginity until their wedding night. Among the Maasai, for instance, marriages are arranged for daughters as young as twelve. In Kenya, generally, if a girl becomes pregnant before marriage, the man responsible is obliged to marry her.[37]

Marriage gives a man exclusive rights over his wife's body and sexuality. Regretfully, some men take advantage of this privilege, and wife battering and other violent acts are justified in terms of such rights. In most communities it is the responsibility and privilege of a man to "discipline his wife or wives" in order to subdue them. Kikuyu men encourage one another to beat their wives at least once, otherwise the curse of their "ancestors would catch up" with them.[38] This behavior is found in other communities as well, including the Luyia, the Luo, and the Kisii. Rape in marriage is unheard of, simply because husbands always have the right to sexual intercourse. Men enforce this privilege through a variety of means, and, in some communities, denying sex to a husband is a valid reason for wife beating. It is believed that sexual intercourse contributes to a happy and successful marriage, and young brides are usually advised not to deny their husbands sex under any circumstances.

In most communities sex is allowed only within the institution of marriage. Uncontrolled sex outside of marriage can contaminate one's lineage, clan, and the community at large with "bad" blood. Although adultery is prohibited, married men are allowed to seduce unmarried women with the intention of marrying them, since polygamy is allowed. A woman may be allowed to have sex outside marriage but only with her husband's consent. This culturally acceptable practice is usually secretive and rare. Among the Maasai, however, such a union is considered a sign of hospitality or is intended to provide children for an impotent man. The children of such a union belong to the woman's husband. Mbiti explains:

> There are areas where sex is used as an expression of hospitality. This means that when a man visits another, the custom is for the host to give his wife (or daughter or sister) to the guest so that the two can sleep together. In other societies, brothers have sexual rights to the wives of their brothers. . . . Among the Maasai, members of one group who were initiated in the same batch, are entitled to have sexual relations with the wives of fellow members.[39]

If a husband dies, a widow is usually not allowed to have sexual intercourse for a prescribed period, which can be as long as a year, after which she can remarry (be "inherited"). A widow who violates this rule brings misfortune on herself and on the community at large. Although widow inheritance ensures that a woman's sexual needs are satisfied, this practice is intended to control the sexual freedom of a widow. Her remarriage to the brother of her deceased husband prevents the possibility that the family or clan will be contaminated by outside blood. It also ensures that any inheritance stays in the family. Children born of such remarriages belong to the deceased husband.

It is interesting to note that during the rites of initiation, married women express pride in their sexuality and in their womanhood, which they see as something that men desire and that cannot be taken away from them. This is one time when they are at liberty to express their displeasure with men. In the Marakwet community, for example, women take this opportunity to ridicule men's selfish sexual desire and consequent dependence on women. Sometimes they also criticize men's inability to satisfy women's sexual needs.[40] There are also instances when women come together to chastise a man who has been mistreating his wife. Such power dynamics on the part of women are very rare in patriarchal communities.

When female circumcision is practiced, it is usually part of the initiation rites and is intended to control excessive sexual desire and to ensure that a girl remains a virgin until she is betrothed. Muturi, a fifty-four-year-old Kenyan immigrant to the United States, commented: "Female circumcision is our tradition. If we want our girls to remain clean, undefiled, and pure, we must continue this practice. We do not want our girls to be promiscuous like American women who have no values."[41]

RELIGION AND FEMALE SEXUALITY

Human attitudes toward sexuality are embedded in the value systems of society, which, in turn, are expressed in religious beliefs. All religions have teachings about sexual behavior that reflect a larger understanding of the sexual nature of humans and of procreation. Attitudes toward sexuality and the symbolism of sexuality vary widely from one society to another and also from one religious tradition to another. Among the Maasai of Kenya, for instance, while sex outside marriage is allowed as a sign of hospitality to a male guest, such an action would be frowned upon in other communities and considered an act of infidelity by religions such as Christianity and Islam. However, most religions generally tie sexuality to the production of children and condemn "deviant" sexual practices as threats to the social order.

In Kenya, as in most African communities, women's sexuality and fertility have a place at the core of religion. Like Christianity and Islam, Indigenous African religions have distinct ways of defining women's sexuality, although it should be noted that encounters with "foreign" religions have had a certain influence.

Indigenous Religions and Women's Sexuality

The control of female sexuality in Indigenous religions is transmitted, in part, through religious stories. Myths, folktales, and songs are used to tell of the consequences of not honoring a community's sexual norms, including infertility, barrenness, and the death of siblings, husbands, oneself, or close relatives. Such storytelling also reinforces stereotypes about the need for women's fidelity in marriage (and widowhood), passivity during intercourse, and courage during initiation, especially where female circumcision takes place. One Kikuyu myth, for instance, tells of a woman's need to be protected from herself and from self-destructive activities "for her own good."[42] Wanjiku Mukabi Kabira narrates one of these stories:

> Wandang'otho . . . gets married and he is very good to his wife. He decides to go on a journey. He spends eight days building a fence around his home to protect his wife and then tells his wife not to answer if anybody calls. The woman is therefore left safely

protected. When the man goes, an ogre comes and calls, "Wandang'otho!"

"Wandang'otho is not in," says the woman.

"Where is he?"

"He has gone to make spears."

"To do what with the spears?"

"To kill the ogres."

The ogre in the meantime removes one of the branches of the fence. He comes every day and repeats the same thing. Eventually the hole is big enough and the ogre enters and eats the woman.[43]

Another story, entitled *Wagaciairi*, tells of wives who run away from their husbands and marry men who turn out to be ogres. Their "dedicated" husbands realize the sufferings their wives undergo and save them, taking them back home where the women live happily ever after under their "protection."[44] The message of these stories is that women need to be protected from themselves because of their irresponsible, stupid, and senseless nature. Unless controlled, women can be disloyal and easily engage in infidelity. They also need discipline to remind them that they need to stay in their traditionally designated place.

Religious stories among the Kalenjin describe women's sexuality as defiling; they are considered unclean and unfit to be in close proximity to the gods. Ironically, virgins were used as objects of sacrifice in traditional communities because the body of a virginal woman was regarded as the best gift a community could offer to a god or a monster.[45] This seeming contradiction can be explained in two ways. First, the sacrifice of virgins is based on the common attitude that women are sex objects. Thus, the best gift a community can offer a god or a monster is the body of a woman with whom no man has slept; hence, the insistence on virginity in most communities. Second, only the powerless in society are unable to resist a ritual that ultimately involves their death, which indicates the low social status of women in these communities. Narratives of virgin girls being sacrificed for rain are quite prevalent in most Kenyan communities.[46] Stereotypes about women's place in society and attitudes toward sexuality are therefore perpetuated by indigenous stories that are still prevalent in most communities.

Christianity and Women's Sexuality in Kenya

Judaism and Christianity have helped to shape Christian attitudes on sexual engagement throughout the world. Most Judeo-Christian attitudes toward sexuality were influenced by the Greek notion of dualism, which emphasized a distinction between the world of the spirit and that of the body, with the former viewed as good and the latter as evil. Life was perceived as a conflict between good and evil, between the desires of the soul and the pleasures of the body. Sexuality was equated with the body and thus considered bad because it was pleasurable and could result in procreation and the "imprisonment" of other souls.[47] This dualism identified masculinity with transcendence, rationality, and logos, and femininity with immanence, emotionality, and eros.[48] It was believed that the higher or male reality must dominate and control the lower female reality. Dualism, incorporated in Christian thought through the interpretations of the early Christian church fathers, many of whom had been raised in dualistic scholarly traditions, was thus incorporated in the Christian scriptures. This dualistic context should be kept in mind when reading Christian scriptures.

Christian teachers and missionaries in Africa, as in other areas, have used scripture to illustrate how sexuality can derail human beings from the ways of God, often emphasizing that women's sexuality is dangerous and needs to be dominated and controlled. Their general emphasis has been that God permits sex only for procreation and that it is essentially a necessary evil. Texts that were interpreted in this way are found in both testaments, with prime examples being the stories of creation and the "fall" in Genesis and several Pauline texts in the New Testament. In 1 Corinthians 3:16–17, for example, Paul reminds Christian converts about the need to remain holy: "Do you not know that you are God's temple and that God's spirit dwells in you? If anyone destroys God's temple, God will destroy that person. For God's temple is holy, and you are that temple." Although Paul was likely not addressing issues of sexuality in this passage (he turns to sexual immorality in a later passage), the text was often used to admonish women. Chosen texts often included 1 Corinthians 7, in which Paul expressed a preference for virginity as a better path to holiness, explaining that unmarried (and thus virginal) men and women can be "anxious about the affairs of the Lord" rather than affairs of the world or their spouse.

He adds that this will "promote good order and unhindered devotion to the Lord" (1 Cor 7:35).

Early in the Christian movement it was generally accepted that original sin was passed on through the sexual act and that Jesus was born of a virgin, untainted by sexual intercourse. The teachings of the church fathers, and of Saint Augustine in particular, significantly influenced Christian views of sexuality.[49] Celibacy was the most desirable state for Augustine, who maintained that sexual activity was permitted only for the purpose of procreation; any kind of non-procreative sex, including masturbation, sexual engagement between homosexual persons, and the use of contraceptives, was sinful. Women were incomplete beings whose only purpose was to serve as vehicles of procreation. They were perceived as representing evil, sexual fleshy bodies in need of redemption: "the wily, wanton, seductress who destroys the innocence of man."[50]

From the very beginning Eve, the scapegoat for Adam, turned all women into sexual temptresses. In a letter to his wife, Tertullian, another church father, wrote:

> And do you not know that you are Eve? God's sentence hangs still over all your sex and his punishment weighs down upon you. *You* are the devil's gateway. *You* are the unsealer of that forbidden tree. *You* are the first deserter of the divine law. *You* are she who persuaded him whom the devil was not valiant enough to attack. *You* destroyed so easily God's image man. On account of *your* desert, that is death, even the Son of God had to die.[51]

These teachings about the sinful nature of sexuality shaped the way sexuality was perceived by Christians and strongly influenced Western attitudes toward sexuality. By the mid-seventh century, church dogma maintained that Mary, the mother of Jesus, was "forever virgin" and held her up as a model for all women.

Since Christian leaders have generally been expected to exemplify sexual control, women who were allowed to participate in some form of church leadership were expected to denounce their sexual bodies by remaining virgins or asexual.[52] This attitude toward women's sexuality has influenced teachings of the Roman Catholic Church around the world, including in Kenya. While Protestant churches in Kenya do not advocate vowed celibacy, they do emphasize sexual activity only for procreation.

In Kenya, Christian teachings are powerful sources for defining attitudes about sexuality as the majority of Kenyans are Christians. The myth regarding original sin, in which Eve is blamed for the fall of Adam, is often cited by both women and men to justify male dominance and female submission. Pauline teachings about women's submission to their husbands are interpreted to include sexual submission (e.g., Eph 5:22–26, Col 3:18). Similarly, most Kenyan Catholic women embrace the tradition of the virgin Mary as a model of the feminine.

The teachings of the Catholic Church about procreation, abortion, and contraception are strongly upheld by some women in Kenya, including non-Catholics. Indeed, debates within Kenya on issues of family planning and abortion often center on the perceived teachings of the Catholic Church. Similarly, the use of condoms for family planning and to prevent contracting infectious diseases such as HIV/AIDS has been and continues to be a significant source of conflict in Kenya, due in large part to Christian, and specifically Catholic, teachings on sexual abstinence, fidelity, and abortion. Christian teachings in general have significantly contributed to definitions of sexuality among women in Kenya.

The role the AICs play in defining Kenyan women's sexuality should not be overlooked. As mentioned earlier, some AICs incorporate both Indigenous and Christian teachings into their worship to define an African form of worship and promote African cultural values. Some of the AICs teach about the need to uphold virginity until marriage and to maintain fidelity in marriage, and they discourage the use of contraceptives and abortion as sinful. AIC leaders often quote from the Bible to justify the subordination of women, teaching that "if women keep to their traditions of subjugation, they will have a lot of blessings."[53]

It is important to note that Christian teachings about sexuality introduced new ideas of sexuality among Kenyans and also reinforced existing ones. Traditional patriarchal beliefs in male dominance and female subjugation were reinforced by Christian teachings. The control of women's sexuality was reinforced by the Christian ideas of virginity, fidelity, monogamy, and sex as a tool for procreation. The practice of female circumcision was justified by religious beliefs in the proper submissiveness of women, the need to control sexuality, and the need for purity and fidelity. Although the mainline churches reject indigenous practices such as polygamy, female circumcision, and widow inheritance, the AICs, which embrace indigenous attitudes on women's sexuality, allow them. For example, the African Independent Pentecostal Church and the Akorino churches of Kenya promote the sexual control of women by allowing polygamy and female circumcision.[54] A new sect in Kenya, the Thaai Fraternity Kenya (Mungiki), also promotes African values through female circumcision and polygamy.[55]

Islam and Women's Sexuality in Kenya

Islamic attitudes toward sexuality are not vastly different from those of Christianity. Islamic beliefs about social life are drawn mainly from the Qur'an, the *hadith* literature, and the *sharia*. For Muslims, the Qur'an, which was revealed to Muhammad between 610 and 632, has absolute authority as the literal and final word of God to Muhammad, the final prophet. Muhammad also elaborated on the meaning of the Qur'an and supplemented its rulings through his statements and actions. This body of information, known as the *sunna* (tradition) or hadith, also has a formative impact on Muslim ideas and attitudes about morality and proper behavior. Muslims seek to emulate actions of their prophet and may even interpret what Muhammad would have said in certain circumstances. This is true in the case of female circumcision. There is some controversy about the authenticity of the *sunna*. While the Qur'an was collected and recorded soon after Muhammad's death, it took almost two centuries to collect, verify, and record the *sunna*.[56] Because the *sunna* remained in oral form during a long period of exceptional turmoil in Muslim history, some *sunna* reports are still controversial.

The *sharia* is the vast body of jurisprudence in which individual jurists express their views on the meaning of the Qur'an and *sunna* and the legal implications of these views. It is used to govern every aspect of life for a devout Muslim. Although most Muslims believe the *sharia* to be a single logical entity, there is significant diversity of opinion among the various schools of thought and also among different jurists of a particular school. The principles of the *sharia*, which are formulated in terms of moral duties rather than legal obligations, rights, and specific temporal remedies, categorize all fields of human activity and behavior as either permissible or prohibited and recommended or reprehensible. As Abdullahi Ahmed An-Na'im, a Muslim scholar, observes, the *sharia* addresses the conscience of the individual rather than the institutions and corporate entities of society or state.[57]

Interpretation by individual jurists leads to a certain inconsistency, and this is evident in attitudes toward women and sexuality. For example, although the Qur'an affirms sexuality as an integral part of God's plan for humankind, most Muslims hold to dualistic notions that view sexuality as the opposite of spirituality. The Qur'an affirms heterosexual marriage as a natural human need for sexual satisfaction and intimacy. It can be said that marriage is perceived as a way to protect human beings, especially men, from immorality by providing them with a religious framework in which their sexuality and other energies can be constructively channeled. According to the Qur'an, God did not prescribe a monastic lifestyle similar to that which followers of Jesus imposed upon themselves. Renunciation of the world and celibacy are not required of Muslims who wish to dedicate their lives to the service of God or to spiritual pursuits.[58]

Unfortunately, this Qur'anic attitude toward sexuality is not reflected generally in Muslim attitudes toward women's sexuality. Muslim scholar Riffat Hassan points out that attitudes toward the sexuality of Muslim women are different from the message of the Qur'an because of divergences from Qur'anic teachings, individual hadith, and pre-Islamic attitude toward women and sexuality. In other words, the cumulative (Jewish, Christian, Hellenistic, Bedouin, and other) biases against women that existed in the Arab-Islamic culture of the early centuries of Islam infiltrated the Islamic tradition, largely through the hadith literature, and undermined the Qur'an's egalitarian message.[59] Because of such influences, Muslims generally consider that men are "above women" or have "a degree of advantage" over them.[60]

Like Jews and Christians, most Muslims believe that Adam was God's primary creation and that Eve was made from Adam's rib, a myth rooted in the Yahwist account of creation in Genesis 2:18–24. This myth has no basis in the Qur'anic account of human creation. As Hassan observes, there is no statement in the Qur'an saying that man was created prior to woman or that woman was created from man.[61] Muslims also believe that since the fall of man was caused by a woman, an allegation not even mentioned by the Qur'an, a woman is believed to be a tempter, deceiver, and the seducer of Adam. This has perpetuated the myth of feminine evil also in existence in Judeo-Christian beliefs. Women are agents of sexuality, which is regarded as the *shaitan's* (devil's) chief instrument for defeating God's plan.

The belief that woman was created for man is also grounded in the Hadith and in some Qur'anic passages. Surahs 4:34 and 2:288 are generally cited to support the belief that men have a degree of advantage over women:

> Men are the managers of the affairs of women because Allah has made the one superior to the other and because men spend all of their wealth on women. Virtuous women are, therefore, obedient; they guard their rights carefully in their absence under the care and watch of Allah. As for those women whose defiance you have cause to fear, admonish them and keep them apart from your bed and beat them. Then, if they submit to you, do not look for excuses to punish them: note it well that there is Allah above you, who is Supreme and Great. (Surah 4:34)[62]

This attitude toward women and their sexuality is reinforced by the Bedouin notion of honor and shame (*ird*), which is linked to beliefs in women's chastity and proper sexual behavior. *Ird* was considered sacred, and Bedouin Arabs were so fearful of having their *ird* compromised by a daughter's loss of chastity that they were willing to kill any who violated this ideal.[63] In pre-Islamic Arabia, Bedouin Arabs believed that women were bound to bring shame to their families due to their oversexed nature. The birth of a daughter, therefore, was received with reservations. Surah 16:58–61 makes reference to this practice:

> When one is told of the birth of a female child, his face is overcast with gloom and he is deeply agitated. He seeks to hide himself from the people because of the ominous [bad] news he has had. Shall he preserve it despite the disgrace involved or bury it in the ground?[64]

Although the term *ird* does not appear in the Qur'an, most Muslim men's concept of honor is shaped by this idea. A woman's sexuality is seen as a man's possession. Women are incapable of controlling their sexual desires; men possess greater reason and rationality (*aql*).[65]

As Janice Boddy observes, women are believed to differ from men in the amount of animal life force (*nafs*) they possess. This includes lusts, emotions, and desires as opposed to *aql* (reason, rationality), which includes the "ability to control one's emotions and to behave in socially appropriate ways." Although men are believed to develop considerable *aql* as they mature, "the amount that women are able to develop is less."[66] Therefore, women are said to be governed by their carnal natures and to be less intelligent than men and thus they are unable to exercise conscious restraint. Women must be protected from themselves and from men, or, in other words, men should be protected from women. According to Hassan, this idea continues to dominate Mediterranean societies to the extent that "honor killings still go on in many Muslim societies in which a woman is killed on the slightest suspicion of what is perceived as sexual misconduct."[67]

Because of this notion of honor, Muslim women's bodies are subjected to external social controls. The nature, purpose, and boundaries of women's sexuality in Islam are defined by dress and other restrictive measures such as virginity until marriage, female circumcision, denial of birth control, and the institution of *purdah* (segregation and veiling of women). These measures are intended to promote honor.[68] Virginity and chastity are social contracts into which a girl is initiated by other women. Fertility is valued, and birth control is discouraged as morally wrong because it interferes with God's purpose of procreation. Birth control is believed to promote promiscuity and unchaste behavior, which are contrary to the notions of honor and the teachings of Islam.[69]

The institution of *purdah* "protects" women from their supposedly uncontrollable sexual emotions. *Purdah* is part of the notion of *qawama*, meaning "guardianship and authority." According to Surah 4:34 of the Qur'an, "men have *qawama* over women because of the advantage they [men] have over them [women] and because they [men] spend their property in supporting them [women]."[70] The *sharia* interprets this verse to mean that men, as a group, are the guardians of and superior to women as a group, and the men of a particular family are the guardians of and superior to the women of that family.[71] *Purdah* ensures that married and unmarried women are kept in isolation from men and strangers. *Purdah* translates into elaborate rules restricting the free expression of emotion, physical touching, laughter, and requiring male-relative chaperonage for all women. In some communities wooden bars are installed on windows to ensure that the person inside is able to see out while no one outside can see in.[72] In traditional Muslim societies a woman is not allowed to go out except in the company of her husband or her mother-in-law.

Related to the institution of *purdah* is the institution of the veil, or *al hijab*. This means more than the requirement that women cover their bodies and faces in public. According to interpretations of Surahs

24:31, 33:33, 33:53, and 33:59 in the *sharia*, women are supposed to stay at home and not leave except when required to do so by urgent necessity. When they are permitted to go outside the home, they must do so with their bodies and faces covered. According to An-Na'im, "*al hijab* tends to reinforce women's inability to hold public office and restricts access to public life" because they "must not mix with men even in public places."[73] The use of the veil protects men from the lustful temptation that women allegedly embody.[74] Some veils cover women's bodies from head to toe to prevent others from seeing even their eyes. Most Muslim communities today believe that the Qur'an gives Muslim women the right to work, earn, and go about their daily business without fear of sexual harassment. To ensure this, however, they should be veiled (Surah 4:37).

Some Muslims reject the practice of *purdah* and *al hijab*. According to Hassan, the notion of *purdah* is not in the Qur'an. Surah 4:15 prescribes confinement to the home as a punishment for unchaste women. Further, the Qur'anic law of modesty addressed to men and women merely tells women not to dress or act as sex objects.[75] A renowned Muslim feminist scholar from Egypt, Nawal El Saadawi, sees *purdah* as a patriarchal perversion of the Qur'an. According to her, the authentic identity of a Muslim woman is not to be veiled and the veil is not even authentically part of Islamic dress. It is a practice reverted to by fundamentalist movements in order to return to a culture where women are dominated by men.[76]

Female circumcision as practiced in pre-Islamic Arabia and continued among some Muslims is a form of control of women's sexual desire and activity. It ensures the purity of these women while assuring the man that his wife's children are indeed his.[77] Circumcision, especially infibulation and re-infibulation, ensures the maintenance and renewal of this "virginity." It is believed that uncircumcised women are capable of bringing irreparable shame to their family through misbehavior. (The influence of religion on female circumcision is examined at length in the following chapter.)

Like Christianity, Islam has introduced and reinforced traditional notions of honor and women's sexuality in Kenya and traditional practices such as virginity, circumcision, widow inheritance, and polygamy. Muslim communities such as the Swahili, the Somali, the Rendile, the Boran, the Luyia, and other ethnic groups in the interior of Kenya continue to believe in the value of virginity, dowries, initiation rites, fidelity, and female circumcision. Today some of these beliefs are understood as Islamic. Among the Luyia, for example, male circumcision, which was traditionally practiced, is justified as a teaching of Islam.

Islamic beliefs in female subordination are commonly found among Kenyans. As Margaret Strobel observes, female obedience is a lesson learned both in female puberty rites and in didactic literature directed to young women. An example is the poem titled "The Advice of Mwana Kupona upon the Wifely Duty," which was composed in the 1850s on the northern Swahili coast and is still popular among those Muslim communities today. In this poem, which is translated by Strobel, Mwana Kupona, an aristocratic woman, advises, "She who obeys her husband, hers are honour and charm; wherever she shall go, her charm is published abroad. Be gay with him that he be amused; do not oppose his authority. If he brings you ill God will defend you."[78]

Most Kenyan Muslims also refer to the Genesis story of the creation and fall of humankind to justify their belief that a woman was responsible for the fall of man, due to her inability to control her sexual desire. Most Kenyan Muslim communities practice *purdah* as a way of protecting women from sexual perversion and as a way of elevating their status.[79] Circumcision is regarded by these Kenyan Muslims as a cardinal religious duty in Islam that is necessary to curb and socialize sexual desires. One of my Muslim informants described female circumcision as "an injunction of Islam required of every Muslim."

SUMMARY

It is most important to acknowledge how significant religion is in defining gender roles and women's sexuality for Kenyan women. It is evident that all religions in Kenya define women's sexuality in a way that potentially marginalizes and oppresses them. Commenting on religion and the status of women, El Saadawi asserts that all religions of the world, both East and West, have patriarchal principles that make women submissive to men.[80] These principles influence social attitudes toward women, including women's own attitudes toward sexuality. It is important to note that religion also justifies and internalizes cultural stereotypes emanating from Arab, Western, and indigenous cultures, stereotypes that have been internalized by members of communities within which these religions operate. In this way religion acts as a powerful instrument to legitimate and thus control women's sexuality.

Feminists have responded to the religious justification of women's oppression in different ways. Some reject all forms of religion as an oppressive and negative force, a trap that hinders women in the struggle for material change in their lives. Others believe that there is a spiritual as well as a material aspect to life, and they seek alternatives to male-defined religions through goddess worship and other forms of women-centered theology. Yet another group of feminists, while recognizing the patriarchal bias inferred by Christian, Muslim, or indigenous world views, believes that there are spiritual truths in these religions, truths that cannot be denied and should not be abandoned. These truths can be used to reform these religions rather than to break away from them. I belong to this group. In my opinion, because religion is one of the most powerful institutions for perpetuating sexism and patriarchal authority, it also has the potential to address the very problem of oppression. Religion can be a powerful instrument to deconstruct oppressive social stereotypes and to work to transform attitudes and social behavior.

5

Religion and Female Circumcision

Although female circumcision is associated primarily with cultural belief systems, its practitioners include followers of different religions, including Christianity, Islam, and Indigenous religions. Most Kenyans are very religious people, and in Kenya Christianity, Islam, and Indigenous religions all have large numbers of followers. The role religion plays in promoting female circumcision varies from one tradition to another and from one community to another. Its influence may be direct or indirect: direct by citing religious statements that justify female circumcision, or indirect by interpreting religious texts in ways that justify a culturally accepted practice. Because religion so strongly influences social practices in general, it is important to understand the significant role religion plays in constructing the practice of female circumcision.

THE RELIGIOUS ORIGINS OF FEMALE CIRCUMCISION

Although the origins of female circumcision remain vague, the practice seems to date back thousands of years. Early accounts of this practice can be found in an account of Herodotus in the fifth century B.C.E., which attributes female circumcision to the Phoenicians, Hittites, Ethiopians, and Egyptians.[1] The Greek geographer Strabo also mentions female circumcision in connection with Egyptians around 25 B.C.E. Two doctors, Soramus, who worked in Alexandria in the second century, and Aetius, who worked in Rome in the sixth century, are said to have left behind fairly precise descriptions of the operation and the instruments used to perform the ritual.[2]

According to historian Catherine Coquery-Vidrovitch, female circumcision probably originated in Egypt and then spread to other parts of the world. It was widely practiced in Rome. She attributes infibulation or "pharaonic circumcision" to ancient Egypt and claims that this practice may have been performed on girls of the aristocracy during the first millennium, an assumption unproved by the analysis of mummies, as she acknowledges.[3] The practice could be related to the notions of natural androgyneity, intrinsic bisexuality, and physical hermaphroditism that are part of the Egyptian pharaonic belief in the hermaphroditic nature of indigenous deities.

According to this belief, human beings, who are created as androgenous, must be circumcised in order to perfect their femininity or masculinity. It was believed that if they were not circumcised, the inherent bisexual natures would compete during sexual intercourse to disrupt coitus and the reproductive process. Further, it was believed that by circumcising both girls and boys, human beings could and should prevent this bisexual nature, a characteristic attributed only to the extraordinary nature of gods.[4] This story is still widely used in most circumcising communities in Africa to explain the religious origin of all forms of circumcision. In Rome, circumcision was widely practiced on slave boys and slave girls to keep them from engaging in sexual activity.[5] In some pastoral societies, according to Coquery-Vidrovitch, female circumcision was also practiced, including infibulation, to prevent the rape of shepherd girls during the long periods of time when young people tended animals in faraway fields.[6]

Although Kenyans cite varying reasons for performing female circumcision, religion is a prominent reason for the practice (see Table 4). It is important to note that in Kenya, and in other African communities, *tradition* describes the various elements that legitimate the social structure and that culture is rarely distinguished from religion. After interviewing fifty women about the practice of female circumcision in their community and after carefully considering their responses, I classified the reasons given for practicing female circumcision in four general categories: (1) sociological, (2) psychosexual, (3) hygienic and aesthetic, and (4) religious.[7]

Sociological Factors for Circumcision

Female circumcision is viewed by most circumcising communities as an initiation into womanhood.[8] It ensures female fertility, provides

Table 4. Reasons for the Practice of Female Circumcision in Kenya (Sample of Fifty Women)

Reason	N	%
Social status	45	90
Tradition, culture, religion (including Christianity, Islam, and Indigenous religion)	45	90
To curb sexual aggression	50	100
To attain a marriage partner	30	60

Source: Data collected by author in personal interviews. Clearly, most interviewees listed more than one reason.

a source of identity, and prescribes a social status; the lack of circumcision can lead to social exclusion and shunning. Circumcision is perceived as a test of courage in preparation for the pain of childbirth, a sign of maturity, a source of respect among peers, and an honor for the girl's family. In some communities it becomes a passport to marriage as it is performed on the wedding day or is required before marriage. The elaborate ceremonies such as songs, dances, chants, and teachings about wifely duties create immense social pressure to conform. Furthermore, the strong value attached to the production of children compels women to become circumcised, albeit often out of fear or ignorance. Other reasons include the need to maintain cultural values and the need for self-definition of one's femininity or personhood.

Psychosexual Factors

Most communities that perform female circumcision believe that the clitoris is an aggressive organ responsible for a woman's oversexed nature and therefore is threatening to the male organ.[9] Kenya's Rendile people, for example, believe that circumcision will reduce a wife's sexual desire and help her to control her sexual desire during the often long absences of a husband who may be away for months at a time caring for animals in the bush or working in a larger town.[10] This argument is based on an understanding that circumcision diminishes sexual desire and enjoyment for women while enhancing sexual fulfillment of men. The removal of the clitoris and the labia minora destroys sensitive parts of a woman's reproductive organ. Further, the narrowing of the vaginal opening can lead to painful intercourse, and the pain experienced during the procedure can lead to the association of sex with pain, resulting in frigidity and/or a minimal desire for sexual engagement.[11] Circumcision is, it is believed, necessary to preserve a woman's chastity and protect women from immorality. As noted before, a high value is placed on chastity, virginity, and fidelity among women in communities where female circumcision is practiced. All fifty informants cited the control of sexual aggression in women as one of the reasons for the practice of female circumcision.

Hygiene and Aesthetics

In some communities in Kenya, female circumcision is performed to purify or beautify a woman's "dirty" or "ugly" genitalia. Fifty-eight-year-old Kemunto said that she views an uncircumcised woman as a prostitute and that such a woman also "smells." There is also a belief in some communities that if the clitoris is not eliminated it can grow as big as a penis, or that the larger a clitoris, the dirtier and uglier it is, an assertion echoed by Gitobu, another informant.

This understanding of female circumcision is also illustrated by comments of some women in the film *The Day I Will Never Forget*. An exciser argues that circumcision makes girls "well behaved and clean, not dirty anymore. . . . It looks beautiful when it [clitoris] is not there. It is very clean; there is no nook and cranny where dirt can collect."[12] The concept of circumcision as a form of purification exists among Jews, Arabs, and Africans. According to Jewish Law, an uncircumcised man is not allowed to celebrate the Passover or to eat the sacrifice dedicated to this ceremony because of his uncleanliness (Ex 12:43–49). In Arabic, circumcision is called *tathir* (male) or *tohara* (female), meaning "purification" or "purity." The Kikuyu of Kenya undergo a cleansing process prior to circumcision. Watoro, a Kenyan woman, recalled her experience:

> On the morning of *irua* [circumcision], we who were candidates were taken to the river by women of our clan to wash. The reason we were washed was to wash away *mugiro*—the dirt the girl was coming to *irua* with. That state of being uncircumcised was termed "dirty" and had to be washed away.[13]

The cleansing rite prior to circumcision is also perceived as a help in maintaining good mental and physical health in a woman, her husband, and her children.

Many communities also consider female circumcision to be an aesthetic practice, a body alteration to beautify a woman's genitalia.[14] In communities where infibulation is practiced, smoothness and "being enclosed" are culturally valued and considered beautiful. A vulva without infibulation is deemed ugly and male like.[15]

Religious Factors

Despite the difficulty in distinguishing religious factors from social, psychological, and aesthetic ones, female circumcision is usually legitimated by some form of religious reasoning. In communities that practice it, Muslims, Christians, and believers in Indigenous religions generally perceive it to fulfill certain religious duties. It may be perceived as a cleansing ritual or a method of ensuring sharp differentiation between the sexes that will eradicate the "bisexual" state of the soul, thereby perfecting the woman's femininity. It is also believed to be a decree of the supernatural to be adhered to by all in order to attract blessings from the gods, ancestors, and parents, and to avoid misfortunes associated with the anger of supernatural beings, including infertility, still births, and the death of one's children or husband.

When I asked my informants why female circumcision is practiced in their community, Chebet, a twenty-six-year-old woman from Marakwet and a victim of early marriage, said, "I agreed to be circumcised because my mother told me that it would make me into a clean, attractive woman who can give her husband beautiful children. She told me to go through it in order to receive the blessing of my parents and ancestors."[16] Kemunto, a fifty-six-year-old Christian circumcised woman from the Kisii community, said that "uncircumcised women smell and their children may die from the curse of ancestors for disobeying tradition. . . . You know, *muacha mila ni mtumwa* [one who abandons her culture is a slave]."

According to Ndara, a forty-eight-year-old Samburu woman, "the experience is exciting in the small world of culture, but is it necessary?" She explained further: "It was exciting to belong to an adult group. . . . I was proud, rewarded by my parents. . . . But I think this practice is unnecessary. . . . Myths associated with this practice, like the immorality of uncircumcised women, death of children, and infertility, are not true." Maisha, a forty-nine-year-old Digo woman and a Muslim, explained that some Muslims believe in "female circumcision as an Islamic injunction." She added, "That is why religious leaders have the obligation to stop this practice." A forty-five-year-old Kikuyu woman described female circumcision as "a rite of passage from childhood into adulthood and meant also to attract ancestral blessings."

An elaborate relationship between religion and female circumcision was outlined by Gitobu, a Christian Meru woman.

Female circumcision connects one with ancestors, like Abraham and Jesus, who were also circumcised. . . . It is also believed that the clitoris of uncircumcised woman will grow too long and touch the ground and she will be dirty and her clitoris will obstruct sexual intercourse, therefore she will not have children and her husband will marry another wife. . . . Some new religious movements endorse the practice claiming that the Old Testament supports the practice. . . . I was not circumcised because I believe in Christ as the final sacrifice.[17]

The role of religion is illustrated further in a speech by Ngonya, the leader of Thaai Fraternity of Kenya. In the film *The Day I Will Never Forget*, he explains that female circumcision is believed to be instituted by God:

Our organization is called Thaai Fraternity of Kenya. Our aims and objectives are very simple. We are bent on salvaging our sinking boat or ship of our African traditional religion through reviving the lost values of our forefathers. I am not propagating anything but I am saying what our forefathers were instructed by the almighty, the creator, so in our society we do not have mutilation. What we have and we still advocate for it is female clitoridectomy. This is very simple biologically for those who know that a man and a woman have got both organs. A female has got a male organ and also she has a female organ. So, I, Ngonya, before I was circumcised I had both organs. I had two organs in me and time had to come when the two organs were supposed to be separated. For the woman, the female organ is that thing they keep fighting for—the clitoris. And for the man, what represents the woman in the man is the foreskin. So you see, because of the wisdom of the almighty the creator, the foreskin had to be taken off and that other thing hanging had to be taken off, so that now we can meet free people together.[18]

HOW RELIGION SANCTIONS FEMALE CIRCUMCISION

Religion has been a significant tool used to legitimate numerous forms of physical harm, including death, throughout history. In some cases religion has sanctioned harm to "atone for sins" or in response to the "will" of the spirits.[19] In some indigenous communities in Kenya, the birth of twins has led to the burning or killing of the infants and their mother, or to their abandonment, because of the belief that twins are a bad omen.[20] The sacrifice of virgins to the gods has been practiced among the Kikuyu, the Kalenjin, and the Maasai of Kenya.[21] Mutilations considered as sacrifices to the gods or to appease divine anger are believed to lead to blessings.

Religious narratives such as myths, taboos, curses, and ancestral decrees are used to instill fear in believers and thus legitimate physical harm. Violating purported religious decrees can be disastrous. Thus religion is an effective method of instilling fear and enforcing certain customs. As the collective beliefs of a given community, religious narratives make customs normative and, most important, they contain the sacred authority to maintain them.

Female circumcision is one of the sociocultural practices sanctioned by religion. In most circumcising communities it is performed to conform to stories or decrees of the gods or ancestors or to emulate revered religious leaders in order to draw some form of blessing or to prevent misfortune.[22] In Kenya the role of religion is more complex for a number of reasons. First, Kenya's three main belief systems—Indigenous religions, Islam, and Christianity—are all cited as justifying this practice. Second, because of the collective nature of African communities and the interrelation between religious beliefs and sociocultural practices, it is often difficult to distinguish religious reasons for female circumcision from social myths. Third, the encounter of Indigenous religions with Christianity and Islam and the ensuing introduction of foreign values, rituals, and sexist attitudes toward women and their sexuality complicate the issue; it is not possible to attribute female circumcision to a specific religion because all are used to reinforce its practice.

Finally, the association of Christianity with the colonialist and imperialist cultures of the West and the resulting politicization of female circumcision through the resistance movement make it difficult to delineate specifically religious concerns. It is essential to highlight each belief system's perspective regarding this practice to understand how the sociocultural fabric draws from and contributes to these religious systems and attitudes.

HOW INDIGENOUS BELIEFS DETERMINE FEMALE CIRCUMCISION

Indigenous beliefs are frequently cited to justify female circumcision. Most Kenyans—and my informants agreed—believe that female circumcision is a practice that conforms to tradition, a concept in Kenya that is virtually indistinguishable from culture and religion. In other words, female circumcision is believed to have been decreed by the ancestors or the gods. Every member in the community is expected to adhere to the tradition in order to receive blessings and to avoid any misfortunes associated with disobedience to the wishes of the gods and one's ancestors or parents.

The Myth of Bisexuality/Hermaphroditism

As noted briefly above, a common myth used to justify female circumcision in most African communities has to do with a belief in the bisexuality of the soul. Perhaps stemming from an early Egyptian understanding of the unique and extraordinary nature of the gods, this myth reflects a belief in the hermaphrodite nature of all human beings, maintaining that at birth they possess both male and female sexual organs.

According to this myth, which is narrated in different versions in various circumcising communities in Africa, the Supreme Being created the earth from clay. After creation, the earth lay down in the form of a female body facing upward. Its vulva was an ant hill and its clitoris a termite hill. The Supreme Being, feeling lonely, approached the earth to have intercourse. However, intercourse could not take place due to the obstruction of the union by the earth's clitoris. However, since the Supreme Being was omnipotent, he used his power to cut the clitoris of the earth in order for intercourse to take place without any further obstruction. According to this myth, the clitoris obstructed any sexual union because it "housed" the jealous male aspect of the female earth that resisted the Supreme Being's sexual advance.[23]

This myth is part of the oral tradition in many circumcising communities in Africa, including Kenya.[24] Every individual is born with aspects of both a male and a female soul. Everyone's soul is revealed in and through the reproductive organs. The female soul of a man is believed to be located in his prepuce or foreskin, while the male soul is believed to be located in a woman's clitoris. As they grow, boys are expected to shed their female soul by removing the prepuce, a necessary condition for admission into masculine society. Meanwhile, girls are expected to shed their male soul by removing part of or the entire clitoris and the labia in order to be admitted into feminine society. Prayer, which is offered after this ritual, stabilizes the initiates' souls by releasing the unwanted masculine or feminine spiritual force.[25] The circumcision of boys is believed to free them from any signs of femininity that they may possess in childhood, and the circumcision of girls frees them from any aspects of masculinity. Circumcision, therefore, is a process of perfecting the masculinity of a man and the femininity of a woman. It also ensures the removal of any "obstruction" to intercourse (the clitoris) in order for a perfect sexual union to take place between husband and wife. All forms of circumcision are considered a form of rebirth, from bisexuality into femininity or masculinity.

In Kenya, even in communities that do not have an elaborate form of this myth, notions of the bisexuality of individuals and the resulting need for circumcision remain a significant part of their narratives. Among the Maasai, for example, female circumcision is considered necessary because it entails the removal of the clitoris, which is believed to connote maleness; male circumcision is necessary to remove the prepuce of the penis, which connotes femaleness. Among the Somali and the Okiek of Kenya, female circumcision is said to remove the "hard male parts," making a woman "forever soft and feminine." Among the Kikuyu of Kenya, circumcision rids the individual of the masculine or feminine aspects believed to interfere with his or her social role as a man or a woman.[26] According to Ngonya, every person is born with two sexes that must be separated during circumcision.[27]

Unlike most Western gods, which generally have masculine attributes, most African gods are gender neutral. Mercy Oduyoye observes: "The African mind contains an image of a motherly Father or a fatherly Mother as the Source Being. . . . In the Source Being, there is no question of male preceding female."[28] The bisexual characteristics of these gods are often used to distinguish them from ordinary human beings. Circumcision, then, becomes a symbolic act to rid mortal human beings of the extraordinary nature belonging only to the gods.

The notion of bisexuality reflects a sense of balance between the sexes and in some communities even suggests equality by placing females on a par with males, since they both possess an extraordinary element that can be eliminated only through circumcision. It is on this basis that claims of the oppression of women and use of terminology such as *mutilation* are resisted. Although this explanation of the function of female circumcision makes sense to some, it does not explain or discount the social inequalities that exist in patriarchal communities that practice female circumcision.

Female Circumcision as a Decree of the Supernatural

The belief in ancestors is a very strong component in most Indigenous belief systems.[29] Whereas missionaries considered belief in the ancestors, witchcraft, misfortunes, and curses superstitious and ineffective, Africans continue to believe these are part of the reality of human life. Most African communities, even those that do not practice female circumcision, regard ancestral decrees with awe. Violators of these decrees draw upon themselves ancestral wrath in the form of misfortunes as well as social ridicule.

Female circumcision is believed to be a decree of one's ancestors or the gods. Rotich, a thirty-five-year-old Kalenjin woman, explains:

> Women are circumcised because it is our tradition. Our ancestors believed that everyone must be circumcised and we must respect that. An uncircumcised woman is believed to be dirty, you know. Men would not want such a woman for a wife. . . . There are other stories about infertility and the death of children. . . . Yes, that is why women get circumcised.[30]

Adherence to decrees of the ancestors or the gods is believed to bring blessings, including fertility and good health for siblings, the couple, and their relatives—in other words, for the individual and the community.[31] Disobedience could bring the opposite: infertility, stillbirths, the death of siblings or spouses, incurable illnesses, and insanity. It is also a common belief in some of these communities, such as the Nandi, that the mother's clitoris, if uncut, will kill the baby upon contact during childbirth and may also render their husbands impotent or infertile.[32] The Nandi also believe that, if left uncircumcised, the clitoris will "grow long and develop branches" and the children of the uninitiated woman will be "abnormal." Any misfortune befalling an uncircumcised woman is usually attributed to "the missing link in her ritual growth."[33]

As noted earlier, fertility and procreation are very important in Africa because they determine the social status of an African woman. The female sex organ is a symbol of life. Its cutting is believed to "unlock the issues of life," which, consequently, "unlock the flow of life." It is believed that the shedding of blood during circumcision symbolically binds the individual to the living community members as well as to the ancestors (the living dead) and to the Supreme Being. Female circumcision, therefore, symbolizes a process of dying, living in the spirit world, and being reborn with blessings from the spirit world. It is a form of rebirth that unites the individual with the family. It is a rebirth that emphasizes a new personality and responsibility in society and that assures fertility.[34]

Among the Akamba ethnic group an important part of the ritual is the "spitting of beer" over the initiates. The spitting of beer, especially on the reproductive organs, is considered a special blessing for each initiate as the circumcisers who perform this act are believed to possess some form of spiritual powers as physical representations of the ancestral wishes.[35] Seclusion of initiates from the community, a practice in most communities, symbolizes death. The initiates visit the community's sacred tree during this period as a reminder that this is a religious obligation to be observed by all. This visit is also a symbolic encounter with the living dead and the ancestral spirits that reside in the tree. The ancestors are believed to be present during the ceremony, acknowledging and blessing the initiate. Initiates' parents are expected to engage in ritual sexual intercourse at the end of the ceremony as a way of offering their blessings to the initiates and acknowledging their child is now fertile. This act grants the initiate authority to marry, procreate, and generate a new community. The end of seclusion symbolizes the rebirth of a new person, an adult with new responsibilities in the community.[36]

Among the Maasai the application of white clay during both male and female circumcision symbolizes death, and the washing away of the clay symbolizes rebirth into a new state of life, a new personality, and a new social status. Those initiated together bond mystically and ritually for the rest of their lives, becoming "one body" and "one people." Men symbolically become brothers and are allowed to share everything, including wives, as a sign of solidarity and oneness. Circumcision gives them the right to participate in a corporate existence.[37] Although the Maasai girls' circumcision mirrors that of men, their ritual leads to a prearranged marriage, separation from family and friends, and subjugation to a husband's authority. Unlike men, who look to circumcision with a sense of pride, women view their circumcision with apprehension because of the pain and social separation that comes with it. In spite of this, the ritual remains symbolic to them because it opens the door to marriage, childbearing, and the status of motherhood.

Belief in the double causality of illness continues to influence the perceptions of Africans. This belief draws from a general understanding that disease is both a physical and a mystical symptom. In other words, physical health can be affected by mystical entities like ancestral spirits or gods. Because of this, diagnosis of any illness must explore both physical and mystical explanations. For instance, a person ill with malaria may want to know if a particular ancestor caused the anopheles mosquito to bite out of displeasure with his or her actions. While it is common knowledge that mosquitoes cause malaria, there is always the need to know whether this particular occurrence is natural or mystical.[38] Such beliefs are dismissed in the West as superstitious or unscientific.[39] In Africa, however, diviners continue to be visited today.

The belief in double causality is manifested in the practice of female circumcision, especially when the ritual does not go as expected. Mistakes in the procedures are explained in a variety of ways; they can be attributed to evil spirits or to some form of misconduct by the initiate or a member of her family. If death or hemorrhage ensues, oracles are consulted to determine why.[40] In the end, such beliefs often exonerate careless practitioners of crimes. The circumciser may claim, for example, that a sacrifice to a fetish or a sacred place was not carried out or was poorly performed. In the case of death, the circumciser may disclaim responsibility by claiming that the victim's parents committed adultery or that her grandparents or someone else in the family violated a taboo.

A death resulting from circumcision is believed to be a form of sacrifice by the initiate's family to appease the demands of an angry god or ancestor. Thus, the circumciser is rarely sued because such an action would be interpreted as a revolt against the gods or ancestors. This, in turn, would create more problems for the community. Such beliefs obstruct any efforts to change attitudes toward the practice.[41] However, in the event that a circumciser causes numerous deaths, as in the case cited in Chapter 1, the community may intervene.

Although the advent of Christianity has had significant influence on Indigenous beliefs, such as the adoption of monogamy and the abandonment of sacrificing virgins to gods or the killing of twins as bad omens, the belief that the ancestors can trigger misfortune is still common among some communities, especially those in rural areas. Further, the association of female circumcision with fertility and healthy children explains the attitude of most African women who see infertility as a tragedy because their social status, potential for marriage, and self-respect are defined for the most part by the number of children they have. As Hosken notes, to be barren is to be a nobody, a person who is incomplete and considered a child.[42] In some communities a barren woman is referred to as a male, and men who marry such women are ridiculed for having married "fellow men." To avoid disgrace, such men end up marrying a second wife to beget children.

Female Circumcision and Taboo

In Africa, the practice of female circumcision is not the only one shrouded by secrecy and taboos. Rather, the entire concept of sexuality is a topic not for discussion except during circumcision rituals. This is why the health consequences of female circumcision and even the deaths that sometimes occur are rarely discussed. As noted by Obiora, it is thus impossible to determine the death statistics related to female circumcision. Similarly, very few records exist about the victims of the harmful effects of female circumcision and how these girls actually feel about the practice. In communities that perform this practice, the uncircumcised are considered violators of taboos, which offends the ancestral spirits of the community. The uncircumcised will draw upon themselves the misfortunes associated with ancestral wrath and are likely to be disowned, excommunicated, or even killed by members of the community for the disrespect they have exhibited. To avert misfortune after violating a taboo, a purification ceremony, including a ritual of "vomiting the evil deeds," must be performed.[43]

The corporate existence of African communities makes it even more difficult for a young girl to avoid circumcision; sooner or later she becomes the object of ridicule by her relatives and neighbors. If she happens to encounters misfortunes associated with ancestral wrath, ridicule can become ostracism, preventing any communal support at a time when it is most needed. The fear of separation from the community poses a serious dilemma, even for informed persons. And it is difficult to convince a woman who is not circumcised that the death of her child had nothing to do with her uncircumcised body when everyone around her insists that it is so.

Although some people are beginning to understand that myths about female circumcision are untrue, they continue the practice because of traditional social and religious beliefs associated with it. Although many female-circumcising communities, particularly in rural areas, are characterized by illiteracy and ignorance regarding biology and hygiene, it is a misconception that ignorance and illiteracy are the only reasons behind the practice. It is essential to demystify traditional beliefs associated with female circumcision in order to sensitize these communities to the harmful effects of this practice.

ISLAM AND FEMALE CIRCUMCISION

Although the term *female circumcision* is not mentioned in the Qur'an, Islam is widely cited as a source to justify the practice. According to Sami Awad Aldeeb Abu-Sahlieh, female circumcision is "completely unknown" in "the majority of Muslim countries."[44] However, when asked why they practice female circumcision, some Muslim informants responded that female circumcision is demanded by their religion. Most Muslims who practice female circumcision consider it *khitan al sunna* or *al-sunna*, which means "compliant to the Islamic tradition of Mahomet."[45] This assertion is confirmed by Kenyan

Muslims such as Maisha, who said that some Muslims believe in female circumcision as "the will of Allah expected of all Muslims." It is believed to be a "sign of purity," a claim that is confirmed by women in the film *The Day I Will Never Forget*.[46] Whereas those who perform female circumcision consider it a way of ensuring purity, other Muslims oppose it, denying its religious origin. These conflicting opinions indicate a significant controversy regarding the divine authorization of female circumcision.[47]

Muslim justification of female circumcision draws from various sources in the Islamic tradition, including the Hadith, inferences from narratives, pronouncements of religious leaders, and inculturation (the encounter of Islam with Indigenous religious beliefs and practices). These Islamic teachings and sources are interpreted to sanction the practice of female circumcision.

Female Circumcision in Pre-Islamic Communities

Prior to Islam, female circumcision existed in some Arab countries, including Egypt, Sudan, Somalia, Yemen, and even in Saudi Arabia, where Muhammad lived.[48] In Egypt, where it is said to have originated, it was referred to as pharaonic circumcision, implying that it originated during the reign of the pharaohs. It is speculated that Somalia and Sudan, as close neighbors of Egypt, adopted this practice through migration. In these communities infibulation was common because the chastity of its women was central to a family's honor. Honor was and continues to be determined by the size of the virginal opening. The smaller the infibulated opening, the higher the honor and bride price for the girl's family.[49]

In Saudi Arabia female circumcision is believed to have been practiced even at the time of Muhammad. This assumption is derived from the response of Aisha, Muhammad's wife, to the question of whether or not a man should clean himself after intercourse even if he does not ejaculate. She is said to have responded, "If the two circumcisions meet or touch each other, it is necessary to wash."[50] It is inferred from this response that women were circumcised during Muhammad's time, and, therefore, that Muslim women should be circumcised. Jews who lived in Saudi Arabia considered male circumcision an action of purity (see Jos 5:9 and Jer 9:23). Some speculate that the notion of female circumcision as a form of purification was influenced by Jewish practice.[51]

Female Circumcision according to the Hadith

Most Muslim advocates of female circumcision believe that the Prophet Muhammad established the practice. They generally base their argument on the three main narratives in the Hadith. The first narrative speaks of Abraham's (Ibrahim) circumcision, which, by implication, sanctions all forms of circumcision, including female circumcision, as a sign of faith in God. It is important, however, to note that the narrative of Abraham's circumcision is not drawn from the Genesis story but from narratives of Muhammad in the Hadith.[52]

Second, some Muslim advocates of female circumcision believe that Muhammad advised both men and women to be circumcised. According to Abu-Sahlieh, some Muslims argue that Muhammad believed in circumcision as *sunna* (obligatory) for men and *mankrumah* (a meritorious act, but not obligatory) for women, an assertion that has been challenged for implying that female circumcision is not valued to the same degree as male circumcision.[53] Despite this challenge, most supporters of female circumcision refer to this narrative.

Third, some Muslims refer to a narrative in which Muhammad is said to have held a discussion with a female circumciser of slaves, advising her on the proper procedure. There are two recorded versions of this narrative. According to the first, Muhammad is said to have conversed with a woman named Um-Atiyyah, who used to circumcise *jawari* (female slaves or girls). He is said to have advised her, saying, "Cut little and do not overdo it because it brings more radiance to the face and it is more pleasant for the husband." In the second and more elaborate version, Muhammad is said to have met a woman named Um-Habibah, who used to circumcise *jawari*. He asked her whether she intended to continue practicing her profession. Um-Habiba answered yes, "unless it is forbidden and you order me to stop doing it." Muhammad replied, "Yes, it is allowed. Come close so I can teach you: if you cut, do not overdo it, because it brings more radiance to the face and it is more pleasant for the husband."[54] Thus Muhammad is said to have legitimized female circumcision. Those who support female circumcision argue that if female circumcision were wrong, Muhammad would have disapproved of it in these conversations. Instead, his specific modification indicated approval. Opponents of female circumcision have responded that Muhammad was cautious about stopping a custom that was entrenched in the community's culture and that, in order to avoid conflict, he modified it as the first step toward changing attitudes about it.

Inferences from Other Religious Leaders

Some Muslims advocate or justify female circumcision based on utterances of other religious leaders, such as Ali, the fourth caliph (successor) of the Prophet Muhammad. It is reported that Ali also sanctioned female circumcision by saying that women's circumcision is a "meritorious act, but a man's circumcision is indispensable." Ali is said to have added, "What thing is better than a meritorious act?" leaving little choice for women but to get circumcised. However, as Abu-Sahlieh observes, there is nothing in this response that says Muslim women must be circumcised.[55]

Another narrative cited to support female circumcision tells of Hagar's circumcision. Hagar, who is considered as the foremother of Muslims, is a very important figure in Muslim history. According to Judaism, Christianity, and Islam, Hagar was an Egyptian slave girl of Abraham and Sarah. Realizing that she could not give her husband a child, Sarah offered Hagar to Abraham in order to give him an heir. Later Sarah became jealous and threatened Hagar. At this point the Muslim narrative departs from the reading in Genesis. According to the Muslim account, fearing that Sarah would cut off her nose and ears, Abraham ordered Sarah to pierce Hagar's ears and to circumcise her. Hagar gave birth to Ishmael, Abraham's son, through whom Muslims claim descent from Abraham. Since that time female circumcision is believed to have become a law *(sunna)* instituted by God for believers in memory of God's friend Abraham and in honor of Abraham's faith.[56] Muslims who cite this narrative argue that circumcision is practiced among Muslims in memory of Abraham and Hagar.

Fatwas

Fatwas (opinions of Muslim religious leaders) are a very important aspect of Islamic tradition and are respected within the Muslim community as Islamic injunctions.[57] Some *fatwas* have been used to justify the practice of female circumcision. While some *fatwas* are less rigid by actually sanctioning the abandonment of female circumcision because of the harm or immorality associated with the practice, others are very rigid on the need to uphold it. Popular *fatwas* have been issued by modern contemporary scholars, especially those who have served as sheikhs of Al-Azhar in Cairo, the most famous university in the Islamic world. One such *fatwa* was issued by Sheikh Mahmoud Shaltout:

> Islamic legislation provides a general principle, namely that should meticulous and careful examination of certain issues prove that it is definitely harmful or immoral, then it should legitimately be stopped to put an end to this damage or immorality. Therefore, since the harm of excision has been established, excision of the clitoris of females is not mandatory obligation [*sic*], nor is it a *sunna*.[58]

Another *fatwa*, issued in 1981 by another former sheikh of Al-Azhar in Cairo, said the Prophet Muhammad favored female circumcision and urged Muslims not to give it up. He argued that the lessons of the Prophet should not be abandoned in favor of the teachings of infallible beings such as doctors. He also maintained that parents have the responsibility to ensure that their daughters are circumcised and that those who avoid it are violating their duty.[59] Rigid *fatwas* with regard to the need to continue the practice of female circumcision are largely responsible for the persistence of female circumcision in a number of Muslim communities.

Female Circumcision as a Purification Rite

Like Jews and practitioners of Indigenous religions, most Muslims also believe in female circumcision as a form of purification. According to Zeinab, a Somali informant, "Female circumcision is understood as a purification rite that cleanses the dirt that would hide the devil. It is important because it prevents immorality among women." As indicated earlier, the concept of purification as incorporated in Islam draws from notions of chastity and honor of the pre-Islamic Bedouin Arabs and also from Jewish understandings of circumcision as a form of purification.[60]

As Abu-Sahlieh notes, organs cut during circumcision are believed to be "superfluous excrescence" whose removal rids a woman of the "dirty surpluses that if left would hide the demon."[61] To prepare a woman's body for womanhood and complete and purify a child's natural sexual identity, Boddy reports, the vestiges of maleness are removed, signaling a triumph of *aql* (reason) over *nafs* (emotion). The enclosure of the "vaginal meatus and her womb make it enclosed, impervious and virtually impenetrable and ostensibly fertile," a desirable state for a woman before marriage.[62]

Female Circumcision among Kenyan Muslims

Female circumcision in Kenya is also adopted or reinforced by Islam through proselytism. In other words, the expansion of Islam in Kenya contributed extensively not only to the spread of female circumcision, but also to the reinforcement of existing practices. As Hicks observes, the geographic area penetrated by Islam, such as Sudan, Ethiopia, and Somalia, coincides with the general distribution of infibulation. All populations that practice female circumcision, especially infibulation, are to some degree Muslim. Hicks further explains that the extension of female circumcision in Africa can be attributed to the expansion of Islam; those who practiced partial clitoral excision ended up performing infibulation after conversion to Islam.[63] In Uganda, infibulation is reported in areas that adopted Islam and traditionally did not circumcise women.[64]

In Kenya, Islam brought a number of rituals in addition to female circumcision. Its tolerant attitude toward indigenous cultures led to the melding of Islamic beliefs with local customs. So long as the basic precepts are followed, Kenyan Islam is very tolerant of other religious systems and practices. By introducing an ideology of gender that draws heavily upon notions of purity, honor, and the control of women's sexuality, Islam reinforced existing sexual asymmetry and male dominance, cultural attitudes of the Kenyan people.[65] The traditional circumcision of boys and girls practiced in Kenyan communities before Islam was integrated into Islamic rituals in which prayers were offered to the Prophet Muhammad seeking his intercession during the puberty rites. Among the Swahili of Kenya the circumcision of boys is justified as an emulation of the covenant of Abraham with God.[66] Female puberty rites were left to coexist alongside Islamic rituals, with Islamic prayers added. Today the preservation of virginity, *purdah*, *al hijab*, and female circumcision are common among Kenyan Muslims.

Among the Somali ethnic group of northern Kenya, who are mostly Muslim, infibulation ensures proof of virginity and chastity.

At marriage, the infibulated opening has to be reopened by a traditional circumciser or the husband of the bride. Anesthesia is not allowed because it is believed to shame the man. This is illustrated in the film *The Day I Will Never Forget*, where the viewer sees a groom vehemently resisting the use of anesthesia before the surgical deinfibulation of his bride for fear of shame.[67] The film also shows a Somali exciser vowing to continue her profession under all circumstances because she believes it is a responsibility for which she must answer to God on Judgment Day.

Despite justifications of the practice of female circumcision among some Muslims, opponents of the practice object to any link between the Islamic faith and female circumcision for a number of reasons. First, they maintain that God cannot command an action that is harmful, painful, and as physically and psychologically damaging as female circumcision.[68] Second, Muhammad did not sanction female circumcision because he did not circumcise his daughters. According to a Muslim scholar, Sheikh Abd-al-Rahman Al-Najjar, "Muhammad had four girls and there is no mention in his biography that he circumcised them."[69] Third, female circumcision cannot be an Islamic injunction because it is unknown in some Muslim communities. In an Egyptian text from 1943, later published as an article in the magazine *Al-Risalah*, Muslim scholar Dr. Usamah denies the link between Islam and female circumcision on this basis. He dismisses arguments about cleanliness, chastity, and aesthetics associated with the practice and considers female circumcision a "crime against a girl's body that no one has the right to commit."[70]

Opponents consider narratives that justify female circumcision misinterpretations and corruptions of Islamic traditions because they are not part of the Qur'an.[71] Based on the disadvantages of female circumcision, which they consider to outweigh any possible benefits, opponents of female circumcision refer to it as ungodly because it damages a healthy organ in an innocent woman. Opponents criticize Islamic institutions for neglecting to establish programs to educate women about the harmful effects of circumcision.

Conflicting opinions on the subject of female circumcision among Muslims explain why some Muslims hold to this practice, while others oppose it; female circumcision has an ambiguous link to religious duty that results from inferences and interpretations of ambiguous scriptural verses to support a popular practice. Without a firm stand by religious leaders, it is difficult to convince believers of communities that promote female circumcision to end it. This is why the role of Islam in promoting female circumcision cannot be underestimated, whether teaching is implicit or explicit. It is the moral responsibility of religious leaders to show concern for the welfare of the Muslim women and the community at large by clarifying the ambiguity that surrounds female circumcision.

CHRISTIANITY AND FEMALE CIRCUMCISION

Christianity has been the most vocal in opposing the practice of female circumcision, primarily because of associated health concerns. Nonetheless, female circumcision is not only practiced by some Christians, but Christian teachings are cited as the reason for the practice. Yet no mention at all is made of female circumcision in the Bible. The early church disapproved of cultural laws such as circumcision as a requirement for the faithful. In the New Testament, Paul states: "Was anyone at the time of his call uncircumcised? Let him not seek circumcision. Circumcision is nothing, and uncircumcision is nothing; but obeying the commandments of God is everything. Let each of you remain in the condition in which you were called" (1 Cor 7:18–20).[72]

Like Islam, Christianity has promoted female circumcision through inferences and the interpretation of ambiguous texts. Sources to justify the practice include Christian narratives, missionary attitudes toward African communities and their cultures, resistance to the alignment of missionaries with the colonial government's attempts to curb the practice, the rise of AICs, and attempts to contextualize and inculturate African values within the Christian church.

The Use of Christian Narratives

Religious narratives are powerful sources of influence, regardless of the reality they claim to represent. A common narrative to justify female circumcision is that of Abraham, as recorded in Genesis 17:1–14. This narrative featured prominently in women's responses when I asked, "Why perform female circumcision?" While the narrative spoke only of male circumcision, Christians who cited this narrative believe that any form of circumcision is a covenant between an individual and God, and that God therefore requires female circumcision as well.[73]

Referring to this narrative, Gitobu, one of my informants, argued, "Since Abraham was circumcised as a sign of his faith in God, we also should emulate him if we want to be righteous before God as he was."

A second Christian narrative cited to justify female circumcision is the story of Mary found in the Gospels of Matthew and Luke (Mt 1:23ff., Lk 1:27). The Virgin Mary, who is portrayed as the model of a faithful woman of God, has become a model to emulate for many African Christians, especially Catholics. As Abu-Sahlieh observes, some Christian Africans interpret the term *virgin* to mean "an unmarried woman who has been through initiation, and therefore has been circumcised." Mary is believed to have maintained her virginity only because she was circumcised. And if she was circumcised, it is necessary that "Christian women be circumcised." This interpretation derives from circumcising communities' belief that a girl's virginity can be ensured only through circumcision.[74]

Whereas inferences such as these may seem illogical to some, it should be noted that interpretations of texts are heavily influenced by a person's cultural background and world view. Thus, these two narratives can be said to make the point that female circumcision emulates scriptural models of faithfulness.

Missionary Attitudes toward African Communities and Culture

Missionaries to Kenya undoubtedly had good intentions in attempting to curb indigenous cultural practices such as female circumcision. However, their actions became suspect when they associated with the oppressive colonial governments and their agents, a move that seemed to contradict the Christian message. This interaction contributed significantly to the resistance, rebellion, and persistence of female circumcision among some Kenyans today.

Missionary attitudes stemmed from the perceived goals of the missionary church of the time, that is, to save, educate, and civilize the "heathen" and "uncivilized natives" and to eliminate cultural practices and values that were superstitious, "barbaric," and ineffective. Thus motivated, missionaries in Kenya took on the task of condemning social and religious practices such as the dowry, polygamy, witchcraft, belief in the ancestral spirits, traditional dances, widow inheritance, sacrificial offerings, and, of course, female circumcision. Many of these practices were condemned as non-Christian because they were associated with sexual excesses. Monogamy, required of converts, was a condition of baptism. Polygamous men had to give up all their wives except one to become Christian.[75]

Renunciation of practices such as female circumcision and polygamy—and particularly requiring such renunciations in order to declare one's Christian loyalty—triggered anger among Kenyan converts who still believed in these practices. The excommunication of circumcised girls and their parents deepened the resentment developing within the church and in the Kenyan community in general.[76] Kenyans were unhappy with missionaries' perceptions of both their world view and their cultural practices. Their resentment deepened when Africans educated in missionary schools realized that some of the practices condemned by missionaries as heathen and superstitious were actually affirmed in the Bible. They wondered why God disliked their polygamous nature and yet religious figures such as Solomon and David found favor in God's eyes. David, the second king of Israel, had many wives and concubines (2 Sm 5:12), and Solomon had hundreds of wives and concubines (1 Kgs 11:3ff.). Kenyatta explains the dilemma of Kenyans regarding this issue:

> Faced with this acute problem, the African whose social organization was based on polygamy . . . set about to look for evidence in the Bible. In the holy book, the African failed to find evidence to convince him about the sacredness of monogamy. On the contrary, he found that many of the respected characters in the Book of God, *Ibuku ria Ngai* (as the Bible is translated in Gikuyu), are those who have practiced polygamy. On this evidence the African asked for further enlightenment from his missionary teacher, but the missionary ignored all these queries, with the assumption that the African was only suited to receive what was chosen for his simple mind, and not ask questions.[77]

Kenyans deduced from the conflict between the teachings of the missionaries and those in the Bible that the missionaries were either hypocritical or misinterpreting the Bible for their own purposes. Monogamy was considered to be an imposition of the missionary lifestyle upon Kenyan people intended to "decrease their population" and "wipe out of existence the African species."[78] Condemnation of female circumcision was imperialistic and disrupted their social norms. As Kenyatta explains, female circumcision was compared to the Jewish rite of circumcision, which was a *conditio sine qua non* of the moral and religious teaching of the circumcising communities; therefore, any interference should be resisted.[79] This understanding, strongly supported by Kenyatta, the political figure who most symbolized nationalism and resistance to imperialism, strengthened Kenyan resistance to any attempt to curb the practice of female circumcision.

It is possible that such missionary teachings might have been tolerated, or even ignored, if it were not for the missionary alliance with the colonial governments and imperialistic control, which worsened the situation among converts. While the missionaries preached against oppression, they aligned themselves with oppressors, contradicting the message they preached. The missionaries became symbols of European oppression whose actions derived more from prejudice than from concern for the freedom and safety of females. When missionaries requested Kenya's colonial government to prosecute those who performed female circumcision, they were perceived as aligning themselves with injustice and the colonial evil of social control; they were seen as enemies of the African people. Even Kenyans such as Harry Thuku, a Kenyan nationalist who fought in the Mau Mau movement against colonialism and who had been committed to missionary work, began to suspect the missionaries' intentions and to accuse them of "being agents of the settlers."[80] Cynicism and bitterness increased as missionaries remained silent about the injustices of the colonial government.

According to Christian historian Jan Ham Boer, the most detested teaching was that "natives" should "not lay up treasures on earth," which enabled the colonists to grab their earthly treasures—the land.[81] As the Europeans seized the most fertile land, many Kenyans became squatters on their own land. Issues of land motivated national resistance to colonial rule. Kenyan converts increasingly aligned themselves with nationalistic movements to resist both colonial and missionary attempts to control them and to strip them of their culture and property. Kenyans began to demand that their schools be independent of missionary control. They also began to establish their own churches (AICs) in order to worship God without missionary restrictions on female circumcision or polygamy.[82]

The condemnation of female circumcision by missionaries and the excommunication of those who performed or experienced the practice led to a significant loss in converts. For example, the membership of the Methodist Church of Meru dropped from seventy to only six within weeks of instituting the excommunication rule.[83] Fearing such losses, the Methodist Church in Kenya resorted to a modified "Christian circumcision," while the Roman Catholic Church and the Salvation Army decided not to interfere with those practicing female circumcision.[84] "Christian circumcision" entailed the physical operation without the "heathen" ritual of feasting and ceremonies associated with traditional circumcision.[85] This resulted in mixed feelings among some Kenyan Christian converts who speculated about what the true Christian attitude toward female circumcision really was. These mixed messages, it seems, actually reinforced resistance to abandoning the practice. Jocelyn Murray observes, "It would seem that the institution of 'Christian circumcision' actually led to prolonging the custom."[86]

Something similar occurred in the seventh century when Roman Catholic missionaries in Ethiopia attempted to discourage female circumcision, leading to a great loss of converts. The missionaries then sought advice from Rome. Dorkenoo reports that the papacy "officially supported genital mutilation after a medical mission was sent from Rome to Ethiopia to confirm whether Ethiopian women suffer from hypertrophy of the clitoris."[87] The Roman Catholic Church decided not to interfere.

In the 1920s, while the Anglican and the Scottish Presbyterian Churches in Kenya attempted to stop female circumcision by excommunicating parents who circumcised their daughters, the Roman Catholic Church remained silent. A member of the Roman Catholic Church is reported to have said: "The Roman Catholic Church does not mind whether girls are circumcised or not, Christians who circumcise girls are not excommunicated."[88] It is important to note that although the missionaries' understanding of and pursuit of morality was paramount, there seemed little or no concern for the harmful effects of the practice on women.

The Rise of the African Initiated Churches

A primary reason behind the rise of the AICs was the dismissive and denigrating missionary attitudes toward African cultures. Missionary demands for the renunciation of practices such as polygamy and female circumcision caused resentment. It seemed that cultural change was being forced upon the people by an alliance between the missionaries and colonial interests. Advocates of resistance and rebellion demanded schools and churches independent of missionary control.[89]

In 1929 agitated Kenyans from the central province came up with a *mithirigu* dance song that mocked missionaries and colonialists opposed to female circumcision. They demanded their own churches and schools so that members could practice Christianity and educate their youth without worrying about who practiced or did not practice polygamy or female circumcision. The Kikuyu Independent Schools Association (KISA) was formed as Christians left the Anglican and other Protestant missions in Kikuyu, Embu, and Meru. In 1930 the colonial government banned the *mithirigu* dance.[90] However, AICs associated with KISA allowed members to practice both polygamy and female circumcision. These churches included the Arathi, also known as Watu wa Mungu (God's People), Anabii (Prophets), Iremba, and Akurinu churches.[91]

Because the goal of these new churches was to Christianize Africans without Europeanizing them, most AICs became more or less syncretistic. The Arathi Church, for example, incorporates both Christian and African customs such as female circumcision and polygamy and scorns Western adornment. Those who abandon the practice of female circumcision or polygamy are labeled Westernized and are believed to have the potential to destroy "tribal" symbols that perpetuate the spirit of collectivity and national solidarity.[92]

The rise of AICs became part of Kenya's two major nationalistic movements, the Kikuyu Central Association and the Mau Mau rebellion. Both sought independence from British colonial control and cultural imperialism. Female circumcision played a major role in the nationalist movements, particularly in efforts to mobilize support and to show patriotism and loyalty to the traditional ways of life. Those who vowed to fight the colonial government took an oath in the name of their ancestors to, among other things, uphold and preserve this practice, their country, and African values. By taking an oath to preserve female circumcision, they felt bound to their communities, including the demands of the ancestors and gods. As Strobel observes, at this point female circumcision became a symbol of "an early part of anti-colonial struggle."[93] Kenyatta's defense of female circumcision helped him to enlist broad support among men—a universal male brotherhood to control the sexuality of women—greatly strengthening his political power.

Kenyan resistance today to Western culture should be placed in this perspective. The rise of sects such as the Thaai Fraternity of Kenya, with its advocacy of female circumcision and its claim to be rooted in the Mau Mau movement, stems from the early identification of female circumcision with the nationalist movements. The Thaai Fraternity calls upon Kenyans, especially those in the central province, the heart of the Kikuyu community, to embrace their culture as a tribute to their ancestors and gods. Members of this sect are encouraged by their leader, Ngonya, to practice polygamy and female circumcision. Ngonya himself has five wives. He believes that female circumcision is a way of the ancestors established by God. Some members of this sect are extreme. There are reports that they have stripped women found wearing trousers and coerced them into female circumcision. Such actions have made this sect unpopular.

The AICs challenge the other Christian churches in Africa to contextualize and inculturate their theology, that is, to reflect on the Christian gospel in light of their own culture.[94] Whereas acknowledging the value of culture is commendable, contextualization or inculturation that does not distinguish between just and unjust social and cultural practices compromises the Christian message of justice for all. Allowing female circumcision without *informed* consent ignores the potentially harmful consequences of the practice. This is contrary to Christian teachings about promoting social justice. In an effort to contextualize Christianity, AICs and other mission churches should begin with a critical analysis of the culture in which the gospel of Christ is preached and promote only those cultural practices that ensure the welfare of all members of the community.

In order to modify a social practice, it is essential to interrogate how the social matrices shape a particular social practice, such as female circumcision, and to understand the social values associated with it. In Kenya, for example, the social web—of which female circumcision is one part—controls women's sexuality, but it also ensures family and community honor, appeases ancestral spirits, enhances the initiate's social status and respect, and promotes social harmony.

The centrality that religion—whether AICs, Islam, Christianity, or Indigenous—has had in justifying the practice of female circumcision must be of concern. In order to transform attitudes it is essential to explore and be aware of these religious dimensions. Most important is the need to acknowledge when and when not to exonerate religion for a given social ill. Accepting responsibility is the first and most significant step toward action. As Abu-Sahlieh has observed, religion is "an important factor for maintaining or abolishing both male and female circumcision." Religious leaders, by "engaging in the operation, justifying it, or by their silence about injustices, harmful effects and relevance for women in their congregations," are thus also responsible for its persistence.[95] By acknowledging the harmful effects and social injustice of female circumcision, they can play a powerful role in transforming attitudes and ending its practice.

6

Transforming Attitudes toward Female Circumcision

Numerous concerns about female circumcision have been raised both within and outside of Africa. There have also been many failed attempts to curb the practice. Not surprisingly, Muslims, Christians, and indigenous people have played and will continue to play a role in perpetuating this practice, either by sanctioning it or by creating resistance to religio-cultural change. Although religious beliefs have negatively affected attempts at transformation, religion *can* play a role in fostering positive social change without necessarily undermining cultural values or the welfare of women.

The complexity of values and issues involved in the practice of circumcision—social, cultural, and religious—poses a dilemma. It is unrealistic to expect easy change of a deeply rooted cultural practice perceived as the norm in a given society. The dilemma becomes clear in the controversial discussions of female circumcision and also by the strongly held positions of women in circumcising communities who are confused by the sudden shift of attitude regarding the practice of it. The story of Shuriye, an exciser who had much pride in her work, work she came to regret after realizing the harm it causes, illustrates this dilemma.[1] Shuriye is not alone in feeling this way. As Tables 5 and 6 show, changes in attitude regarding this practice, even by some elderly women, can be attributed to social changes that are taking place in these communities.

*Table 5. Positions on Female Circumcision by Age
(Interviews with Fifty Women)*

Age	Support Circumcision	Percent of Total	Oppose Circumcision	Percent of Total
< 20	–	0	–	0
21–30	2	4	13	26
31–40	6	12	14	28
41–49	5	10	5	10
50–59	3	6	2	4
>59	–	0	–	0
Total	**16**	**32**	**34**	**68**

*Table 6. Levels of Education and Attitudes toward Female Circumcision
(Interviews with Fifty Women)*

Level of Education	Percent That Supports Circumcision	Percent That Opposes Circumcision
College/Graduate	2	12
Secondary	10	30
Primary	20	26
Total	**32**	**68**

THE REALITY OF SOCIAL CHANGE IN KENYA

Change is a reality in Kenyan communities today. Over time, traditional values tend to be reevaluated and perhaps discarded, sometimes with little regard for the outcome. Differing notions of social good compete with one another. A crucial point to note, however, is that social and cultural systems, whether traditional or contemporary, may incorporate social injustices. What might appear acceptable to some might be repugnant to others, a reality behind social conflict in any society. It is important to seek strategies in social transformation that pursue values that do not compromise the welfare of some, for example, children and women in circumcising communities.

All cultures have values that promote the social good of all the members, and those values should be embraced to benefit the members of the community. Initiation rituals, for example, prepare young people for adulthood, which is an essential good for the community. It is important, however, to examine the practical applicability of traditional values in the contemporary world. Traditional values that endorse and maintain oppressive social structures, values, or practices in the name of cultural identity should not escape evaluation. In the past, for example, patriarchal systems and practices that discriminated against women were generally the rule; in contemporary societies such systems are subject to critique.

In Kenyan communities such as the Akamba, the Kikuyu, and the Kalenjin, the traditional belief in the sacrifice of a virgin girl as a religious ritual to "induce" rain has lost popularity.[2] Among the Maasai and the Kalenjin communities the norm that permitted the "stealing" of any cow found outside one's homestead is no longer acceptable. Based on the traditional belief that all cows belonged to certain ethnic groups, the norm was a source of ethnic raids in many communities in Kenya. Today community ownership of cattle is recognized. Other traditional practices that have lost value include the practices of widow inheritance and the killing of twin babies in the belief that they are a bad omen. These are a few examples of traditional values and practices that have been abandoned because of the potential harm they pose. In the same way, female circumcision, which served the cultural needs of some indigenous communities, can be slowly abandoned. The time seems right, given the social changes that are taking place in these communities, especially health hazards and increasing concerns for the human rights of women and children.

Christine J. Walley, a feminist anthropologist, observes that rituals involving female circumcision have changed over time. The agency of the individual is slowly becoming an accepted form of resistance to social norms, as women from circumcising communities are currently uncircumcised and yet happily married.[3] Similarly, Robyn Cerny-Smith observes that in some communities the female circumcision ritual has become more of a private ceremony, with virtually no ritual accompaniment, "leaving only the residue of the physical operation."[4] If rituals associated with female circumcision are no longer valued, why would we insist on an aspect of this ritual, especially when it is harmful to our children?

Kenyan Micere Githae Mugo explains how such changes can lead to social transformation:

> On the eve of the twenty-first century, I do not see physical initiation as a necessary rite of passage, even if it is in the form of "ritualized marking of female genitalia . . . where the clitoris is barely nicked or pricked to shed a few drops of blood." . . . There are other forms of self-assertion that are more relevant to current-day needs in which women can engage. . . . All society's resources in terms of time, energy, focus, and material support should be put into aiding women to acquire skills and experience that empower them with liberating choices so that they can become true agents of change.[5]

Effective Strategies for Transformation

Some attempts to curb the practice of female circumcision have not only encountered obstacles but have exacerbated the original situation. In some cases ineffective strategies have forced the practice underground, compounding the health risks associated with it. The failure of such strategies lies in a number of factors, including (1) disregard for the cultural context, values, and reality that inform the practice; (2) failure to distinguish among the forms of the practice; (3) imperialistic assumptions about the practice and the communities that perform it; (4) the tendency of these strategies to adopt an alien, coercive, or confrontational approach; and (5) failure to acknowledge the agency of women in circumcising communities and the need to empower them to critique and transform social behavior.

In very general terms the first step in an effective transformatory strategy is to acknowledge the reality of the social context and the potential for social change of a circumcising community. Have new values been adopted by members of these communities? Do some women and parents in circumcising communities want the practice abandoned? A second step is to construct educational materials to sensitize community members to issues that surround this practice, including health risks and social injustices such as gender discrimination.

What Is the Cultural Reality?

Most communities in Kenya have in place a patriarchal structure with ruling relations that shape the reality of women's experience. Since there is a significant association among poverty, illiteracy, the low status of women, and the practice of female circumcision, it is important, as Mugo observes, to understand the models of patriarchal hierarchies that exist in economics, politics, religion, and social practices, and especially how and why they resist social change.[6] Mugo's observation resonates with that of Mercy Oduyoye, who notes that "when dealing justly with African women, one ought to take seriously women's questions and concerns about their status, to listen to their voice and to respect their standpoint by acknowledging obstacles to their search for enhanced social status."[7] In other words, a strategy for curbing female circumcision should endeavor to challenge the oppressive realities that contribute to perpetuating its practice.

It is essential to address female circumcision not as an entity, per se, but in relation to its larger context. It should be perceived and addressed as one of the social practices that perpetuate the ruling relations in the community. This is to say, female circumcision must be viewed as one of the many social practices drawing from and promoting the values and world view of the community that embraces it. World views and values affect many aspects of a community's life, including its economic system, religious practices, family organization, and political forces. Interrogating such systems aids in identifying the practices harmful to women, understanding why they persist and are accepted by women, and recognizing sources of resistance that can help create change.[8]

It should never be taken for granted that women are "content with their situation just because visible resistance is absent."[9] Attempts to curb female circumcision should evaluate other efforts to end female circumcision, such as those discussed by Mugo.[10] Why were they ineffective? How can such programs be improved? The work of organizations such as MYWO in Kenya, RAINBO in New York and London, and AAWORD in Africa, as well as others, should be acknowledged. In addition, in order to solve specific problems, local forms of resistance must be identified and analyzed in order to evaluate where and why certain aspects of a strategy failed.

To be effective, a strategy should also seek solidarity among women and men in fighting social injustice. Kenyan Musimbi Kanyoro emphasizes the need for collective solidarity among women in Africa, who must resist both alien and cultural values that are oppressive.[11] Solidarity among women must be supplemented by the support of men, because female circumcision is a socially instituted practice that serves the interests of both men and women.

An effective strategy should also promote networking among advocacy groups and organizations. Networking enables communication among social institutions to help them become aware of the social injustices of a given behavior. Networking also can identify individuals in these institutions who are willing to participate in efforts toward social change. Joyce Umbima, a Kenyan feminist, observes that various organizations can network and work together through the use of "campaigns, brochures, stickers, and posters to educate the public on issues and concerns of justice."[12]

It is also important that strategies for social justice ensure support for the victims of injustice. This entails moral, psychological, medical, and material support to assure victims that they will be protected and that their needs will be met regardless of their position. This support can take many forms, including providing shelter, counseling services, workshops, medical services, legal resources, and economic support.

Any strategy seeking to be effective must be accompanied by speaking out about oppression. As Robyn Cerny-Smith observes, women's voices on this issue must be heard and a theory of justice must be created in order to recognize the power relations involved in social practices such as female circumcision.[13] Curbing female circumcision in Kenya requires enabling Kenyan women to break the silence about their situation by motivating and enhancing their agency. They need to be enabled to question the structure of institutions that promote oppressive practices. The film *The Day I Will Never Forget* illustrates how women can be given a voice in this matter.[14] And youth should not be forgotten. Incorporating and involving girls in efforts to curb female circumcision can lead to changes in attitude and set the groundwork for a system of peer support.

Finally, and most important, strategies employed in attempts to curb the practice of female circumcision must be grounded in the religious systems of these communities. Female circumcision is a practice that involves religious justification. A strategy that does not incorporate the religious perspective of the community is bound to fail.

It is important to integrate religion into a strategy for transformation for three primary reasons. First, if a practice is considered sacred within a community, such religious convictions can be most effectively challenged by alternative religious traditions. Second, religious systems embody attributes such as holiness or virtue that can transform social behavior and motivate social action. Third, when a community is strongly influenced by religious faith, as is true in Kenya, a religious appraisal of the issues affecting it is vital. In interviews with fifty Kenyan women, twenty-two indicated that they were not circumcised. Fifteen of those women cite religion, specifically Christianity, as an influence on their decision not to be circumcised (see Table 7). (Some interviewees declined to indicate their status, a position that the interviewer respected.) Forty-three of the fifty women interviewed felt religion should be part of any educational process aimed at curbing female circumcision (see Table 8). Incorporating religion into strategies for curbing female circumcision can serve to demystify the myths used to legitimize this practice.

As shown in Tables 7 and 8, many informants responded affirmatively to the question, "Do you think religion can change attitudes toward female circumcision?" Others described the potential of religion to transform attitudes and elaborated on how religion can be used. Gitobu, a Christian Meru woman, noted that "religion motivates change of behavior. Religion tends toward unification." A Kisii woman, Kemunto, stated that religion will "impart some enlightenment on the subject of female circumcision." Another Kisii woman, Nyachae, said that religious teachers should teach women "not to look at circumcision as the ultimate end in itself."

Table 7. The Influence of Religion on Decisions Not to Be Circumcised

Reasons	Total (N=22)	Percent
Christianity	15	68
Islam	0	0
Indigenous religion	0	0
Education (other)	7	32

Table 8. Views on Possible Strategies to Curb Female Circumcision

Views	Total (N=50)	Percent
Use law or prosecute those encouraging female circumcision	10	20
Educate and sensitize communities on risks	49	98
Seek alternative rite of passage *(ntaanira na mugambo)*	14	28
Reward girls who say no to female circumcision	13	26
Use religion to teach about attitudes toward female circumcision	43	86

Other respondents had more specific suggestions. According to a Kalenjin woman, Chebet, religion can transform attitudes toward female circumcision by "condemning the practice and educating its members on the various side effects." Ndara, an agricultural extension officer, said that "since Muslims have justified circumcision, claiming that it is a religious injunction . . . they should be sensitized and trained on consequences of circumcision. . . . Involve them in awareness creation [and] train peer educators from within the group of religious leaders. . . .These then will be the ones to help discourage the practice." Lang'at, also from the Kalenjin group, commented that "Christianity can change attitudes regarding female circumcision by teaching values against this practice, values which are appreciated in these communities." Hadija, a leader in the RAINBO organization, argues that religion can contribute to the transformation process "by involving religious leaders in efforts to educate circumcising communities on the consequences of the practice."[15]

The success of religious systems in addressing the issue of female circumcision is also demonstrated by the work of some churches, especially one in which leaders not only have sheltered girls who have resisted the practice but also have established programs to address the issue. Through its development program the Norwegian Lutheran mission in the Pokot area in Kenya has worked hard to curb the practice of female circumcision through education. Ingrid Naess describes the success of the mission in an *Afrol News* article: "For years we have been teaching about the complications that follow such an intervention. Now we can see that it is of use and we want to carry on with our information services."[16] Similarly, Loice Chepkieny, a trained teacher who coordinates the Norwegian Lutheran program, has found "Pokot women hungering for education and information and being receptive to information about health complications following female genital mutilation (FGM)."[17] More and more mothers in this community are sparing their daughters from being circumcised. Although the article does not specifically discuss if or how religion forms part of this educational program provided by the Norwegian Lutheran church, it is a religious institution, and that is probably why it is having a significant impact on the Pokot community.

The film *The Day I Will Never Forget* includes scenes of churches sheltering victims of early marriage and circumcision and describes numerous incidences when churches have sheltered girls who have run away from home to evade circumcision.

RELIGION AS LIBERATIVE

The notion of liberation arises in the debate on female circumcision because of the social injustice associated with the practice. Throughout history, social and emancipation movements have mobilized collective action against injustice and have resisted social change that is contrary to justice or that in some way harms human welfare.[18] While there are always individuals hungry for power who seek to oppress others, most human beings have a tendency to be motivated by reason, the needs of the community, and religious values and therefore to reject oppression. Religious or spiritual values teach them to conquer moral evil by analyzing and critiquing the social institutions that promote it.

Religious institutions also have a history of organizing movements based on religious or spiritual values to sensitize communities and to motivate action that will enhance social transformation.[19] The twentieth century saw the rise of a number of social movements based on the need to respect the human worth of every individual. Liberal, Marxist, humanist, and religious organizations have sought to embrace the moral principles based on the UN's Universal Declaration of Human Rights. These principles are predicated on the need to dismantle structures in society that oppress human beings. In general, such liberation movements call for the dismantling of institutional evils that promote oppression and injustice, such as poverty, dehumanization, and forms of political bondage that cause physical or psychological harm.

As an agent of social construction, religion can be a potent force because it grounds reality in the extraordinary—the sacred.[20] As an ideology, religious systems are about ideals, about how the world should be. Religious systems thus critique the current inadequate social manifestation of their visions or ideals. Religious beliefs act as legitimating agents that can inhibit or promote social change because they are thought to transcend human frailties and wrongs. In constructing social behavior, religion sanctions social practices that either promote what is deemed good or assure social stability.[21] However, and history makes this all too obvious, what is deemed good by one group may conflict with the views or needs of other groups in the society.

The notion of religious systems as potentially liberative draws from a deep historical relationship between emancipation movements and religious faiths and the realization that liberation can be absent or present in a society's social structures. Christian liberation theology, for example, perceives human society as a social construction that can be transformed for the good of all rather than as a fixed creation of God. Human relations are presented, therefore, as capable of reconstruction in "ways that promise greater justice and participation." Christian liberation theologians perceive salvation as intimately linked to liberation in this world even as it also transcends this world. Thus Christians are called into the world to cooperate with God and with each other for their own individual transformation as well as for the transformation of their communities and of the world.[22] This argument is also found among some Muslims. Islamic scholar Muhammad Mashuq Ibn Ally explains that Islamic theology grapples with the task of rediscovering the relevance of Islam for present-day problems.[23]

Religious systems that embody and legitimate the values of morality, justice, human responsibility, and the general good of society ought to be a source of condemnation for those causing social evil and human suffering. As pointed out in Table 4 (p. 101) the practice of female circumcision has been and continue to be influenced significantly by religion. It is noteworthy that 68 percent of twenty-two Kenyan women interviewees cited religion as the reason they decided not to be circumcised (see Table 7, p. 133). Of the fifty women interviewed, 98 percent expressed the need to educate communities on the health consequences of female circumcision (Table 8, p. 134), and 68 percent believe that integrating religious beliefs in this process will yield significant results (Table 6, p. 128). The ability of religious systems to act as tools of liberation and social transformation lies in a number of factors, including religion's transcendent motivation, its moral imperatives, the organizational resources of religious institutions, the shared and unifying identity of members in a given religion, and the modes of resistance and interpretation a religious system can provide.

Transcendent Motivation

According to Smith, religious systems are powerful tools of legitimation because they have a "transcendent motivation."[24] By aligning a social cause with the sacredness associated with divine commands, eternal truths, and the absolute moral structure of the universe, religion gives power to a social cause that is otherwise unchallengeable. While "God's will" or its equivalent is usually not negotiable, people can often negotiate and compromise on issues that are not rooted in religion. By rooting social activism in the sacred, religion often reflects "uncompromising and tenacious certainty and commitment that sustains activism in the face of great adversity."[25] Religion has the power to grant a divine imperative to a social cause that infuses a struggle against injustice with nonnegotiability.

Thus, a social practice such as female circumcision can be rendered illegitimate as long as such a position is clearly articulated in religious terms. For example, Christianity or Islam can legitimate the need to curb this practice without negotiation or compromise by critiquing it in terms of the religious values of social justice for all and the need to ameliorate human suffering. Aligning campaigns against female circumcision with the sacred, eternal truths or with the absolute moral structure of the universe can also legitimate transforming the gender stereotypes associated with it.

Moral Imperatives

Religious systems also have moral imperatives or principles that can place a situation in an "injustice frame."[26] Christian liberation theology uses Jesus as a model for its teachings on the need for social justice and for the equality of human beings before God. It is then the responsibility of Christian leaders to condemn any practice that jeopardizes these values. Female circumcision can be condemned on the grounds of jeopardizing women's health and degrading their worth as Christians who are equal before God, according to texts such as Genesis 126–27 and Galatians 3:28.[27] Islam also teaches the values of justice and respect for human worth, values that Islamic leaders can draw upon to condemn attempts to justify female circumcision using religion. For instance, Surah 4:75 teaches protection of the weak and oppressed.

Drawing on such principles, religion provides a source of moral standards with which to criticize an oppressive situation and a measure of what should be—how people should live and how the world ought to operate. Religion has great potential to conscientize believers and to empower communities to pursue the common good.

Organizational Resources Activism

Social liberation movements need a variety of organizational resources to use to mobilize and channel energy for transformation.[28] Christian and Islamic institutions alike have the potential to offer trained and experienced leaders and leadership resources, financial resources, and grassroots activist networks. They can provide effective administration by coordinating communication channels and overseeing various aspects of a program. Trained leaders can inspire commitment within a congregation and the community at large because they speak with authority. The institutions they serve can also train them in strategies and tactics that will, if effectively coordinated, calm any form of insurgence, resolve internal conflicts, and articulate grievances of both "insiders" and "outsiders." As Abu-Sahlieh observes, religious authorities become responsible for female circumcision by doing the operation, by trying to justify it, or by remaining silent.[29] In order to transform attitudes about practices such as female circumcision, religious leaders must refuse to be silent and join the struggle.

But religious leaders can transform attitudes only if they themselves are conscientized and given the tools to face the challenge of opposing female circumcision. It is a serious challenge because it involves transforming long-held views and principles. Critical analysis is required to determine the actual teachings of a particular religion. Religious leaders need to be trained to integrate their religious beliefs and convictions with their new knowledge of the social dynamics of the communities in which they live. Awakening their consciences to the fact that social change is always taking place is a significant first step in asserting that outdated values and practices have to be discarded as new values that speak to the essence of humanity are embraced. Religious leaders can help community members understand female circumcision as a practice that is outdated in the contemporary world.[30]

Once religious leaders are equipped with the critical skills to assess the social context of female circumcision, they should begin to demystify the practice and any other social practices that compromise the welfare of members of their congregations or the society at large. Deconstructing the myths surrounding the practice helps clear the veil of religious illusion that can blind members of circumcising communities to the resulting injustices and health consequences. This is not an easy task, as even religious systems that promote injustice have power within a culture to enforce social practices; this power should not be denied. In any case, demystification is an important tool to disentangle more transcendent religious beliefs from particular cultural practices.

Second, religious leaders have a responsibility to establish programs in their institutions to educate their congregations on the injustice of and health risks associated with female circumcision. In defining the content to be communicated to the communities, these leaders must ensure that the content is appropriate to that particular community.

Religions also have the potential to generate financial resources to support social causes. Their institutions can generate funds through donations from governments, NGOs and private individuals, at home and abroad. A morally convincing cause is likely to secure both moral and financial support.

Similarly, religions have the ability to network and coordinate their efforts with other channels through newsletters and bulletins, weekly announcements, mass media programs, and their own synods and councils. Some of these channels are not only educative but authoritative as well. Worship bulletins can include notices about social action programs or requests for donations and volunteers; however, if a religious leader such as an *imam*, sheikh, or minister announces details of a planned protest or action at the end of prayers, such an announcement bears authority. To curb a practice that is as deeply entrenched in people's attitudes as female circumcision, authoritative strategies that go beyond networking and coordination with other channels seem essential.

A practice such as female circumcision that is strongly entrenched in rural communities also needs grassroots activists to get the word out. As institutions that are found to a lesser or greater degree in every community, religious systems have great potential to coordinate grassroots activism and to become sanctuaries of counseling and education.

Religious systems also have the potential to support those who are willing to stand against female circumcision and its victims. As a sanctuary of the oppressed, religious institutions can offer shelter to those who face rejection by their families or communities for opposing an entrenched cultural practice. There are churches in Kenya that support and shelter girls who have run away from their homes for fear of being circumcised. One Kenyan woman, Lang'at, reported that the teachings she received in a Christian church influenced her decision not to be circumcised and that her pastor sheltered her:

My family, even my mother, talked to me about the importance of getting circumcised. They told me how I would never get a man to marry me and how my children will die in childbirth because of a curse from my ancestors for refusing to be circumcised. Yet as a Christian, I did not believe in these things any more. My attempts to convince my mother not to have me circumcised led to rebukes on how I was going to shame them. When I realized that no one in my family would support me, I packed a few of my belongings while everyone was asleep and escaped at 3 a.m. a few days before the circumcision ceremony. . . . I could not go to any of my relatives because they would bring me back home for the ritual. My only refuge was my pastor's house. When I told his wife that I was there because I did not want to be circumcised, she was kind and allowed me to stay with them until the ceremony was over. When I went back home everybody was furious with me, but I did not care. I only felt sorry for my mother, who had been beaten for supposedly "teaching me bad manners" just because she was not able to convince me to be circumcised. . . . Luckily, I met a Christian man who was not interested in a circumcised woman. . . . Sure! There are men out there who do not support female circumcision, especially Christians. I am now happily married and have three children. . . . Yes, it is unfortunate. Many girls have to go through this crude practice for fear of offending their parents. . . . Not all pastors are as good as mine. Some believe in this practice, which makes it difficult for some girls who might want to seek their help.[31]

Whereas sheltering victims is a commendable gesture, it is not enough in itself. Religious institutions should offer counseling and education to those willing to denounce this practice by empowering them and affirming their choice not to be circumcised. Religious leaders also have a responsibility to work to reconcile these individuals with their communities.

Supporting the basic needs of victims is another crucial area. Women have shied away from challenging the practice for fear of being abandoned by their families. They fear for their very survival if they lose the support of their parents. A few who have managed to escape circumcision speak of the hardships they faced. The story of a Togolese woman, Fauziya Kassindja, is not unique. She encountered numerous difficulties, including imprisonment, before finally getting asylum in the United States.[32] It is important, therefore, that religious institutions use their capability to ameliorate the situation of circumcision resisters.

Shared Identity and Social Resistance

Religious systems can offer a shared and unifying identity that leads to solidarity, an essential component of effective resistance to an unjust practice.[33] Religious systems provide solidarity in that their moral codes require adherents to uphold certain values and to operate in a certain way. In this sense religions offer a "yardstick" of acceptable behavior. Social activists in religious institutions have an opportunity to explain what principles they stand for, what kind of society they hope to create, and how this is supported by the values of their religion.

Most religions have concepts of human worth, human rights, and social justice ingrained in their teachings. Even though these beliefs may propound different perceptions of human rights, the centrality of human worth found in all religions can be a common ground for articulating social justice. For a practice such as female circumcision, activists within a religious institution have an opportunity to explain to the public how it denigrates the values of justice, human worth, and the treatment of each person with dignity. As most religions provide a sense of fellowship and community for their members, such connections among members can become a base on which to build solidarity for social transformation. If all Christians or Muslims were to denounce female circumcision because of the social injustices associated with it, Christian and Muslim solidarity could become an emblem of justice to be embodied by all.

Interpretation of Religious Systems in the Light of Social Reality

Another potent tool of religion is the power to interpret sacred texts. This tool has been effectively used in liberation theology to relate the social reality of the poor to the texts and teachings of Christianity. Liberation readings that engage scripture from the perspective of the oppressed have taken the form of explicit advocacy and have inspired social movements for change. The effectiveness of this tool in bringing about social transformation makes it key in efforts to curb female circumcision.

Liberation theologian Juan Luis Segundo maintains that theology is explicitly or implicitly intertwined with existing social situations and that the interpretation of scripture must begin with an experience or analysis of a given social reality. Segundo refers to his model of scriptural interpretation as a hermeneutic circle, an approach that provides continuing interaction between a scriptural text and its interpretation in various periods or contexts.[34] The hermeneutic circle is a method of reflection that acknowledges the need for continuous change in the way scripture is interpreted because of continuing changes in present-day reality, both at individual and social levels.

Segundo enumerates four steps that the hermeneutic circle takes as it relates theology to social reality.[35] He maintains that it is essential to "force theology to come back down to reality and ask itself new and decisive questions."[36] The first step begins with an analysis of social reality in order to evaluate a given social expedience. The second step involves the application of "ideological suspicion" that arises from such an evaluation to theology and all other "ideological superstructures" that exist in the experience. During the third step "theological reality" is experienced differently as a result of the social experience that is interposed with religious and other social ideals. This experience leads to suspicion that "the prevailing interpretation of the Bible has not taken important pieces of data into account."[37] At the fourth and final level a new hermeneutic is developed, a new way to interpret a scriptural text based on new reality.[38] Segundo emphasizes that before a given reality can change, someone must to some extent be dissatisfied with it and raise questions about it, "questions rich enough, general enough, and basic enough to force us to change our customary conceptions of life, death, knowledge, society, politics and the world in general."[39] Questions and new convictions will require a new look at scripture, which can in the end bring about social transformation.

The great potential of the hermeneutic circle lies in its focused reflection on the problem at hand and in its commitment to find a solution for correcting social injustice. This method of analyzing social reality and interpreting scripture perceives faith as an educational process in which people should be involved throughout history. In other words, Christianity should be understood as continuous divine revelation in which new insights are sought and applied to new realities in contemporary situations. For Segundo, the meaning of scripture is to be found through the process of learning how to reconstruct the scripture in relation to contemporary situations. Use of the hermeneutic circle allows the religious values of a community, including a practice such as female circumcision, to be interrogated in relation to their social reality.

As Elisabeth Schüssler Fiorenza notes, Segundo's method of interpreting scripture affirms the need to perceive scripture as "a significant tool in the struggle for liberation and an acknowledgement that 'the God of the Bible is a God of the oppressed.'"[40] She and other feminist theologians criticize this position. They claim that it is a revisionist model of interpretation. According to Schüssler Fiorenza, such a revisionist interpretation of scripture does not allow for critical evaluation of biblical ideologies that are sometimes false and an evaluation of the process of interpretation of the scripture as well. It does not take into account women's struggles for liberation from the sexist oppression and violence that are perpetuated by Christian scriptures and thus undermines the struggle of women for liberation. Schüssler Fiorenza explains further that this model exemplifies the reluctance of theologians like Segundo to acknowledge the fact that women are exploited and oppressed. That is, Segundo's model lacks a critical element that evaluates religion as an ideology with a "false consciousness" that can inhibit the struggle of the oppressed for liberation. It is important, therefore, that critical evaluation be applied to "biblical texts and upon the process of interpretation within Scripture and tradition."[41]

Drawing from Elizabeth Cady Stanton's model of scriptural interpretation, which presents scripture as having been used as a political weapon against women's struggle for suffrage, Schüssler Fiorenza argues that scriptural theology is "inherently sexist and, therefore, destructive to women's consciousness." It is thus erroneous to assume that scriptures are "neutral," as does Segundo. Apart from being used as political weapons against women's rights and the struggle for liberation throughout history, religious scriptures have also been used to keep women in subjection. Yet, as Schüssler Fiorenza observes, scriptures have a "numinous authority" over women, given the fact that women are the most faithful of believers.[42]

Schüssler Fiorenza also argues that it is impossible to bring about social change in one area of society if social change is not advanced in all other areas. In her view, "one cannot reform law and other cultural institutions without also reforming religion. She recommends the need for a critical feminist interpretation to deconstruct religious teaching from the androcentric and sexist cultures that have shaped religions such as Judaism, Islam, and Christianity. Use of this model, which she refers to as a "feminist hermeneutic of suspicion," will enable women to comprehend how scriptures have and do function as tools of oppression and to distinguish between valid and invalid teachings, especially with regard to those that affect the welfare of women. The approach also reveals scriptural traditions that transcend "their oppressive cultural contexts even though they are embedded in patriarchal cultures." An example cited is Galatians 3:28, which teaches about equality between men and women, slaves and free, and has been used by feminists as a Magna Carta for the liberation of women.[43]

Use of these feminist methods of interpretation can (1) reveal forgotten roles of women in the social communities in which God's message was revealed, (2) reclaim the scriptural history as women's history, and (3) challenge androcentric constructions in sacred texts. A feminist critical hermeneutics or a hermeneutics of suspicion is, therefore, the base for an advocacy position demanding that oppressive and destructive scriptural traditions and cultures should not be granted any claim to truth or authority today.

AFRICAN FEMINIST HERMENEUTICS

African theologians such as Mercy Amba Oduyoye and Musimbi Kanyoro argue that any critical evaluation of the scriptures should be derived from a particular experience in order to formulate specific goals and strategies for the liberation struggle. This means that Kenyan women must seek to employ a tool that is particular to their situation. This would be true of any reflection on the practice of female circumcision.

Kenyan feminist theologian Musimbi Kanyoro is critical of any feminist analysis that does not interrogate a specific social context. In Africa, for example, while African women acknowledge men's role in oppression, they do not "throw stones," reasoning that this could pose a major threat to women's security and solidarity. As an example, according to Kanyoro, African women have had difficulty reaching consensus on matters such as rituals and initiation practices because of their cultural loyalty, and this may be misconceived as a "sign of lack of courage or inability to confront issues." Kanyoro argues, though, that this is usually a sign of "counting the cost and of taking stock of the gains and losses." She explains: "Some African women reason that they want a future in which men are friends. Building that future does not begin by attacking men, but by finding methods of bringing change together with them. This is a tall order, but it is the reality of the lived experience of African women."[44]

Employing a critical hermeneutics can also reveal that women are not only victims but also perpetrators of oppression against themselves. In most Kenyan communities women are the circumcisers, the instigators of divorce and polygamy, and the enforcers of rituals such as widow inheritance and female circumcision—all practices that compromise the welfare of women. As Kanyoro observes, these are areas of "women's violence against women," because women are socialized to accept such forms of violence as normative.[45] Socialization and the institutionalization of violence blinds them to the health risks and injustices associated with practices such as female circumcision, especially when those practices are cultural "givens" that are also sources of social identity and status.

The lens of an African feminist hermeneutics of suspicion can enable Kenyan women to reflect upon their own social situation in a more objective way. As Kanyoro explains, women will realize the need to "break the vicious circle of women violating other women in the name of culture."[46] In the same way, they will stop bemoaning socialization or colonization and learn to be accountable for the realities they live and to acknowledge their own part in their situation. As African women begin to confront the issues they face each day, they will judiciously condemn what is oppressive and raise up what is valuable.

Analysis that targets social dynamics that inform a given practice highlight and confront the complexities inherent in social situations. When used by women, it can be used to examine all questions regarding their welfare within the framework of culture. As Kanyoro observes, one should be able to sift the usable culture from what is unusable, acknowledging that not all cultures are free of negative practices nor immune to external change.[47]

RELIGIOUS SOURCES FOR TRANSFORMATION: A BRIEF ILLUSTRATION

Drawing upon the insights of African feminist hermeneutics, it is possible to suggest how this method of interpreting sacred texts might be useful in transforming the practice of female circumcision. It is important to begin by highlighting the liberative aspects of each set of religious beliefs.

Christian Sources

The theme of social transformation and liberation in Christianity is based on history, social values, teachings, and the actions of religious leaders. As Asghar Ali Engineer observes, Christianity originated as a protest movement against prevailing social injustices. Its main concern at the moment was "the Palestinian serfs under the political domination of the Byzantine Empire."[48] The Exodus event is often referred to as the watershed of liberation in Christianity because the Israelites, who were enslaved in Egypt, gained their freedom through a historical action of God. The proclamations of the Old Testament prophets also underscore the theme of liberation in expressing concern for those who suffer from economic, social, and political distress. Amos, for example, denounced the exploitation of the poor (Am 8:5–6). The salvific mission of Jesus Christ is also characterized as liberative; at the start of his public ministry Jesus echoed the Exodus theme of liberation when he read the following message from the prophet Isaiah:

"The spirit of the Lord is upon me,
    because he has anointed me to bring good news to
        the poor.
He has sent me to proclaim release to the captives
    and recovery of sight to the blind,
        to let the oppressed go free,
to proclaim the year of the Lord's favor." (Lk 4:18–19)

Jesus' teachings have been an inspiration for the poor and the downtrodden. Known as the redeemer of the poor and the oppressed, he critiqued the unjust status quo of his time. Even today Jesus' Sermon on the Mount provides hope for the dominated. Wholeheartedly accepting Jesus' message of liberation demands a radical conversion from the old ways of perceiving reality and renouncing all the sinful and oppressive parts of one's life. This was true as well in the early church. The often-cited Pauline text of Galatians 3:28 called for equal treatment of all, since in Christ "there is no longer Jew or Greek, there is no longer slave or free, there is no longer male or female; for all of you are one in Christ Jesus." Christ's liberating message of equality freed converts to the early church from the bonds of Jewish Law, including traditional practices such as male circumcision.

Today, because most Kenyans are Christians, the scriptural stories of liberation and the salvific message of Jesus can serve as significant resources for reflecting on female circumcision. In an earlier study I sought to determine if Kenyan women were aware of the redemptive mission of Jesus and the Christian faith.[49] That project attempted to determine the degree of influence that Christ and the Christian message have on the views and attitudes of Nandi women concerning female circumcision. Many of their responses demonstrated the strong influence of Christian teachings. For example, Chepkwony, a Kalenjin, reported viewing Christ as a personal savior who frees her from "fear of any evil force and tradition"; for this reason she no longer believes in female circumcision. Koech said that Christ is a "source of courage" who enables her to face the challenges of life. He is a friend who has "never let me down." When forsaken by others, even close relatives, "Christ is always there for me" when she needs him. Because of this, she refused circumcision. Rotich said that Christ is "everything" to her. In Christ, she explains, "I am able to attain anything in this world. . . . I fear nothing." Rotich does not object to circumcision because, in her view, it is "my culture and I do not condemn those who practice it as long as it is their own choice."[50]

I also interviewed women from other ethnic communities in Kenya. According to Kemunto of the Kisii ethnic group, Christ is the conqueror of every evil and all suffering. She believes that, although she may experience suffering here on earth, her suffering means nothing to her as long as she believes in Christ. When the time comes, she believes she will have peace in heaven. Circumcision is an earthly thing and thus insignificant to her faith in God. Circumcision does not make a difference in what God requires of humanity. Kemunto equated Paul's denunciation of the Jewish tradition of circumcision among Christian converts as a denunciation of circumcision among African Christians. She believes that Christian faith does not depend on following the Old Testament Law because Christ's blood "washed away earthly forms of sacrifices" so that Christians could abandon all form of sacrifice.

For Wanjiku, Christ is her "comforter in times of trouble and a friend that never lets one down." She dislikes female circumcision because she has never understood "why women are made to go through such a painful experience." However, she believes that "each individual should make her own choice on whether she wants to embrace the practice or not." As a Christian, however, Wanjiku strongly opposes female circumcision, arguing that "it is outdated for Christians, who belong to a different world view."

The responses of these Kenyan women reveal their awareness of the mission of Christ as redeemer, and they see this mission being fulfilled in their lives. They see Christ as a savior, a friend, and a source of consolation and of courage to resist the pressure to be circumcised.

These attitudes resonate with what Kenyan feminist theologians Anne Nasimiyu-Wasike and Teresia M. Hinga outline in their study of women from different communities in Kenya.[51] According to Hinga, Kenyan women perceive Christ as a personal savior and friend. He accepts them "as they are" and meets "their needs at a very personal level." The image of Christ is that of one who helps them "to bear their griefs, loneliness, and suffering." Christ is also an "embodiment of the Spirit, the power of God, and the dispenser of the same to those who follow him." He is "the voice of the voiceless, the power of the powerless, . . . the iconoclastic prophet" who conquers and criticizes the status quo that "engenders social injustices." As Hinga asserts, Christ champions "the cause of the voiceless . . . by giving them power and a voice to speak for themselves."[52]

Because Kenyan women perceive Jesus Christ as liberator and see his mission and teachings as liberative, it is not difficult to apply the Christian message to Kenyan communities that practice female circumcision. However, because there are Christians who believe that Christian teachings actually sanction practices such as female circumcision and because segments of a community may not be Christian, it is important to employ a variety of strategies in designing educational programs. Education about female circumcision should critique Christian beliefs that sanction social injustice against women while emphasizing those that promote social justice. To be effective, a program should also acknowledge the traditional functions of female initiation rites and simultaneously raise awareness of the social injustice and related health risks of female circumcision. It is to be hoped that the Christian message of justice and liberation, following the example of Jesus, can change attitudes favoring the practice. Jesus' message should be presented to Christians in Kenya as a message of liberation from *all* practices that harm and dehumanize people. Christ seeks to empower those who are unaware of their oppressive cultural practices.[53]

The Christian message of liberation for women is an affirmation of their human worth before God. In the Christian scriptures Jesus recognizes the fact that women should also lead healthy and fulfilling lives (see, for example, the story of the hemorrhaging woman in Luke 8:43–48). Just as the Jewish tradition of male circumcision, along with other customs, lost validity with belief in Jesus Christ, so should female circumcision lose its validity among Christians. As a practice laden with serious and long-lasting health risks, it represents an injustice for women.

It should be noted—and this has been pointed out by feminist critiques of scripture, including those of Elisabeth Schüssler Fiorenza—that the Christian tradition is not devoid of repressive teachings. Christian texts such as "in all the churches of the saints, women should be silent in the churches. For they are not permitted to speak, but should be subordinate, as the law also says" (1 Cor 14:34–35) and "let a woman learn in silence with full submission. I permit no woman to teach or to have authority over a man; she is to keep silent" (1 Tm 2:12) have been used to oppress women in both society and church.[54] It is important to deconstruct and demystify such "culturally conditioned" texts in order to distinguish them from universal truths that promote social justice. Because religion is a significant source of authority, it is important to draw on the resources of the Christian tradition to empower and liberate all people, including Kenyan women.

It is also extremely important to emphasize that embracing Christian values does not necessarily mean abandoning all cultural practices. A distinctly African hermeneutics exists that can be used in critiquing cultural practices, such as female circumcision, that result in social injustices or violate moral principles. Such a model of interpretation can introduce Kenyans to ways of understanding their responsibility to reflect on social practices that have lost their meaning in the contemporary landscape.

Islamic Sources

I have dwelt at length on Christianity because such a large number of Kenyans are Christian. However, Islam also has the potential to liberate and to bring about social transformation. According to Muhammad Mashuq Ibn Ally, Muslims, like Christians, are grappling with the task of rediscovering the relevance of Islam for present-day problems and formulating answers to the challenges of modern society. Islamic liberation represents "a rebellion against imposed heterogeneous, political, economic, and cultural models" and reflects the Muslim people's search for a "new order which ensures justice for all human beings in seeking the ideological fulfillment of the *ummah* (community)." Mashuq Ibn Ally outlines the four pillars of a contemporary Islamic program: (1) it seeks "the renewal of Islamic thought, to meet the modern ideational challenge"; (2) it reaches out "to the persons who are disposed to righteousness" and draws them together "into an organized body—*jama'hi*" (a moral entity that goes beyond biological, political, geographical, linguistic, and cultural links); (3) it strives to promote societal change through individual conversion and collective education in order to promote social development; and (4) it seeks to develop "a new cadre of leaders at the intellectual, social, and cultural levels."[55] Like Christianity, Islam is concerned with interpreting and reinterpreting its doctrine to make it relevant for the contemporary world and to promote social justice.

To understand the role of Islam in the transformation of social practices such as female circumcision, it is important to remember that Islam began as a movement for social justice, equality, and brotherhood. The Prophet Muhammad's message chastised the rich and the corrupt while drawing closer to the poor and the oppressed of Mecca, including slaves.[56] In Islam, messages of liberation can be drawn from the Qur'an and from Muhammad's teachings. It is significant that the Qur'an defines piety in terms of justice. According to Surah 5:8, Muslims are instructed to "be just; this is closest to piety."[57] The Qur'an also enjoins Muslims to fight for the liberation of the weak and the oppressed:

> And what reason have you not to fight in the ways of Allah, and of the weak among the men and the women and the children, who say, "Our lord, take us out of this town, whose people are oppressors, and grant us from thee a friend and grant us from thee a helper." (Surah 4:75)

The Qur'an categorically denounces oppression (*zulm*). Moses is presented as the leader of the oppressed because he launched a struggle to liberate the oppressed Israelites from Egypt. The Egyptian pharaoh is denounced in the Qur'an as the oppressor (*zalim*) for enslaving the Israelites.

The Qur'an also has a liberative message for women and elevates their status. African Muslim feminist theologian Rabiatu Ammah points out that the Qur'an sees a woman as an individual who, in the sight of God, "is completely free and in respect of her moral and spiritual status. . . . She is equal to man for when God instructs humankind in the Qur'an to worship God, both men and women are addressed."[58] A woman in the Islamic tradition is given an identity with a soul, an identity she did not have in the pre-Islamic era. She is made accountable to God, rewarded or punished according to her deeds, and given property, a right that she did not have in the pre-Islamic era.[59]

The teachings and actions of the Prophet Muhammad can be a source of liberation for Muslim women. The Prophet's prohibition on infanticide against female children, a practice that was prevalent in the pre-Islamic communities of Arabia, is one indicator of his struggle for justice for women.[60] Another is his reported discouragement of extreme forms of female circumcision, which were prevalent in Arabia before Islam.[61] Muhammad also attempted to control reckless polygamous marriages among Muslims by advocating monogamy except for those men able to ensure equal provision and love for their wives. In fact, Muhammad limited the number of wives per man to only four, contrary to pre-Islamic times when men were permitted to have an unlimited number of wives.[62] Regarding polygamy, the Qur'an instructs men:

> If you fear you cannot be equitable to orphan girls (in your charge, or misuse their persons), then marry women who are lawful for you, two, three, or four; but if you fear you cannot treat so many with equity, marry only one, or a maid or captive. This is better than being iniquitous. (Surah 4:3)

It is also important to note that polygamy as instituted in Islam should be understood in its context; it was one way of providing for a widow (and children) after her husband's death in the ethnic wars that were prevalent at the time, including the holy wars fought by Muhammad and his followers. As Ammah observes:

> The trend in the Koran is toward monogamy, a situation which was not possible at the time due to the prevailing social conditions. The widely accepted practice of polygamy and the existence of the many widows and orphans left by war and therefore in need of protection through marriage militated against outlawing it properly.[63]

Muhammad married some of these widows himself to protect and provide for them. But, as Engineer observes, this is just "a contextual justification, not a normative one, and hence its applicability must be seen as dated, not for all times to come."[64]

According to Muslim feminists such as Leila Ahmed, the egalitarian and liberative passages of the Qur'an and Muhammad's teachings were later misread or misinterpreted, intentionally or unintentionally, by some Muslims in androcentric and patriarchal societies in order to reinforce the culture of male superiority over women.[65] This misinterpretation reinforced some of the hadith teachings, which, as already noted, are somewhat controversial with regard to their religious authority. Because of the inevitable association of Islam with the cultural values of pre-Islamic Arabia, Islam has been used to sanction some cultural practices that oppress women, and many Muslim women are socialized to believe in their subordinate state. Believing this to be the norm, these women unconsciously participate in their subordination by claiming the inferior status and roles assigned to them. The pronouncements of Muslim leaders are normally sacrosanct for believers and rarely challenged.

Methods similar to those of Christian feminists can be employed to distinguish the liberative messages in Islamic teachings from those repressive of women. Leila Ahmed uses critical hermeneutics as articulated by Schüssler Fiorenza to explain how a close examination of the history of Muslim teachings on women can trace the limitations that were gradually placed on women and how their rights were progressively curtailed. Eventually this resulted in practices that were detrimental to women and a decline in their social status.[66] The process of rereading and reconstructing Islamic scriptures and Muhammad's original message can bring to the surface the androcentric cultural corruption that penetrated and shaped Muslim practices over time and can reveal the egalitarian message intended by God and Muhammad for all Muslims, and particularly for women.

Ahmed points out that a critical evaluation of the practices sanctioned by Muhammad within the first Muslim society can reveal far more positive attitudes toward women. This is because the social context within which the "Islamic textual edifice was created was far more negative for women," a situation that led to the suffocation of the egalitarian voice of Islam, a reality that Muslim leaders must acknowledge.[67]

Using feminist critical interpretation allows readers to discern within Islam a variety of role models for women that can be sources of inspiration for women's agency and social transformation. The story of Hagar (Gn 16:1–16), which describes her struggle to overcome the obstacles and injustices she encountered as a slave and as a woman, can be a great source of inspiration and courage for Muslim women. Hagar did not give up hope after being sent away by her mistress Sarah; rather, she confronted with courage the odds against her. Her faith in God enabled her to overcome the difficulties she faced in a culture that despised slave women.

Other role models for women include Khadija and Aisha, Muhammad's wives; his daughter, Fatima; and Zubayd, the queen of Harun al Rashid. These women are also sources of inspiration for Muslim women who struggle with social injustice. Their courage in cultural contexts that oppressed women can inspire contemporary women to struggle for social justice in their own societies. Khadija's immense contribution to the development of Islam and her constant support for Muhammad, even when he was in doubt about his revelations, displayed great courage. Zubayd is remembered by Muslims for showing that "piety could flourish in the midst of palatial surroundings."[68]

As with other religious texts, it is important critically to evaluate Islamic scriptural interpretation to separate androcentric and sexist beliefs used to oppress women from universal truths of social justice. Similarly, other Islamic sources of social behavior such as the Hadith and *fatwas* should be critically evaluated in order to identify ideologies that compromise the welfare of women.

Ten of the Kenyan women interviewed as part of this study were Muslim; all view the Qur'an as absolute truth. Whereas some of these women believe that the Qur'an has an egalitarian message for women, others think that cultural practices associated with Islam, such as female circumcision, are mandated because they are Islamic. Maisha, a Muslim woman, stated, "I am a Muslim, and since female circumcision is an Islamic injunction, I have to be circumcised. It is my religion. . . . I do not want to be judged by God because I did not get circumcised." Similar sentiments are expressed in the film *The Day I Will Never Forget*. Some of the Muslim women interviewed, especially those aware of feminist attacks against Islam for promoting oppressive practices, were defensive about their religion. In one of my classes on Islam and women, a Muslim student said, "People think Muslim women are oppressed by Islam. They are wrong. Muslim women have been saved from *jahiliya* [a state of ignorance that predated Islam]."

The faith of Kenyan Muslim women must be respected. Consequently, any attempt to change their attitudes or behavior demands patience and care. There is certainly a need for basic conscientization. It is possible to deconstruct passages from Islamic texts to identify the liberative message within. This task must become a priority for Muslim feminist scholars and activists concerned with ending female circumcision.

Indigenous Religion Sources

Although little has been done to analyze Indigenous religions in order to outline sources of liberation for the oppressed, it should be possible to use an African feminist critical hermeneutics, such as the model developed by Musimbi R. A. Kanyoro, to reflect upon examples of social injustice and liberation in these religions. A first step can be to examine themes of justice and liberation in social struggles, such as the struggle for independence from colonialism and the efforts of ethnic groups to overcome different forms of social injustice.

A number of African women stand out as role models, including the voices of women in matriarchal societies. In Kenya, significant stories of empowerment include the stories of nationalists such as Mary Muthoni Nyanjiri, who led the Mau Mau warriors during the political movement in Kenya. Muthoni Nyanjiri was one of the two hundred women who participated in a procession that gathered outside the Nairobi prison on March 16, 1922, to demand the release of Harry Thuku. Me Katilili is another Kenyan woman role model; she led her people against the colonialists in the Giriama community of Kenya.[69] Their courageous acts of participating in liberation struggles against colonial masters not only countered stereotyped roles for women but their courage was rewarded by the political independence they helped gain for their country. In addition, countless unnamed courageous women who carried food into the forests to sustain the warriors and hid firearms and messages in their skirts as they traveled to detention camps serve as great role models for women at the grassroots level in the struggle against social injustice. While their contributions were seen as ordinary and not significant, the struggle could not have been won without them.[70]

Women role models can also be drawn from other communities in Africa. In the Akan community of Ghana, for example, the story of Oheema (the queen mother, a female ruler) and her sister rulers is a great source of inspiration not only for Ghanaian women but also for women in other African countries. In Ghanaian traditional politics, women played a significant role in policymaking. The Oheema was a female ruler in this traditional system and "the king maker in the traditional political system of the Asante." The leadership position held by the Oheema represented authority and the power behind the throne. It demonstrates a dynamic in social power, a power that equals that of men and therefore should be acknowledged. This can empower agency.[71] After naming female circumcision a cultural practice that promotes injustice, opponents of female circumcision can draw on these models for inspiration and courage to be firm and strong as they confront this injustice.

Since the fear of ancestral spirits and misfortunes associated with female circumcision is a great motivation for performing this practice, offering a religious explanation would contribute significantly to the process of demystifying the religious myths that promote this practice. An effective explanation could draw from African beliefs in spirit possession. Spirit possession is a cultural phenomenon consisting of various symbols and associations. Mediums or those skilled in the interpretation of the message of a possessed individual can construct an event to render it meaningful and evaluate it along culturally standardized lines.[72] Commenting on spirit possession as a strategy for resistance, anthropologist Vincent Crapanzano argues that "once the experience is articulated, once it is rendered an event, it is cast within the world of meaning and may provide a basis for action."[73]

Africans who believe in this form of resistance see it as an intervention in the spirit world for answers to counter social situations. In some cases those possessed by spirits are able to challenge unjust social situations. Boddy explains how spirit possession, as perceived in some African communities, resonates with a similar idea of spirit possession in most Kenyan communities. She describes spirit possession as a form of "relieving illness or personal distress," usually fraught with tension and surprise. Although this state of being "is considered as affliction and expressed as illness," the motive of spirit possession is considered to surpass the misery that the possessed goes through because the messages delivered by the possessed may "influence people's perceptions and behavior in the cause of daily life."[74]

Since Kenyan circumcising communities embrace all these religious systems, how this form of social resistance can function or has functioned for women in relation to practices such as female circumcision could be one area of exploration. Spirit possession is a very powerful mode of social resistance among communities that strongly believe in the potency of ancestral spirits and exorcism.

The Christian and Islam traditions also include forms of spirit possession and exorcism. In Kenya, spirit possession has been incorporated into some Christian churches and is interpreted as a case of possession by the Holy Spirit. In many AICs in Kenya, such as the Roho and the Akurinu churches, women are continually being possessed by the Holy Spirit and exercising charismatic roles. An example of this phenomenon is found in leaders such as Mary Akatsa, a leader of the Jerusalem Church of Christ in Nairobi; Veronica Kanunkuchia, a prophetess and healer in the Mugwe Church (Organization for Christian Acts of Mercy); and Gaudencia Aoko, founder of the Legion of Mary Church. These women started their churches through the message of spirit possession. Their ministries include "revelations and healings, exorcisms, preaching, counseling, and witch-finding" and people flock to them with issues of conflict to be resolved through consultation with the "mysterious world" that people believe they can access.[75]

As Hannah Kinoti observes, Akatsa's gift of spirit possession is "coated" with Pentecostalism. Acquired during her upbringing, it is interpreted as the work of the Holy Spirit. Among her activities are revelations, healings, exorcisms, preaching, counseling, and witch finding, and people travel long distances to seek out her services. She is believed to possess mystical power and claims to be Christ's tool or vessel. Akatsa uses the Bible as a "fetish with which to hit her patients" in her therapeutic sessions rather than as a source of texts.[76] Many other women in Kenya possess similar charisms and have influence that can be tapped and used as tools for social transformation.

It is important to emphasize that all religious systems in Kenya must first liberate themselves from social injustices, including patriarchal and oppressive interpretations of sacred texts, before they can play a major role in liberating Kenyan women from unjust practices such as female circumcision. In the words of Kenyan feminist Nyambura J. Njoroge, Christianity in Africa "must first liberate itself from centuries of misuse, abuse and misinterpretation and from patriarchal, colonial, and racist foundations it has embraced since the days of slave trade" if it is to succeed in its mission to liberate Kenyans.[77]

In Kenya the first crucial step in transforming attitudes toward female circumcision is conscientizing Kenyan communities to the injustice of the practice. Religious systems must be part of this process and employ their resources of sacred texts and liberating hermeneutics to confront all obstacles to social justice. Religious leaders need to assist Kenyan women in the process of examining and reflecting on the social practices and religious beliefs and values of their communities. Religions also need to reexamine their mission in the world and redefine the special roles they can play in establishing a more humane and just society. The authority of religion in Kenya and other African countries makes it a powerful agent of transformation.

Conclusions
and Recommendations

Do you recall the story I began with in Chapter 1? During a visit with my friend Jane, I heard about the death of Leah Yatich, a primary-school girl. She died from excessive bleeding after being circumcised by a traditional exciser. And later that day the exciser also died, killed by angry villagers. This all happened "to uphold tradition." My hope is that on my next visit to Kapsabet town in the Rift Valley Province to see my friend, I will hear instead about a young girl who has successfully completed primary school and is now a promising student in secondary school, perhaps thinking one day of becoming a doctor.

But much must change for this to happen. Leah's death was a consequence of a family adhering to tradition. Tradition carries with it great social pressure to conform; in Kenya to ignore tradition is to risk being ostracized. The traditions enveloping female circumcision also spell out the serious misfortunes that might result from refusing the practice: Leah may be made barren, she may not find a husband, death might come to her family, or her clitoris might grow so long that it would offend her community and the gods. These myths are part and parcel of tradition, and they continue to hold hostage many families in Kenya and other parts of Africa. It is time to challenge, demystify, and abandon these myths.

The beginning of this new millennium seems the right time. Young people are increasingly embracing values that promote individual agency and social justice. As a result, many young people are choosing to dissociate themselves from indigenous practices that are harmful, such as female circumcision. As education and communication become more accessible, there are more frequent cries for change, cries that Kenyan communities must address. Girls are risking their lives to flee their homes at night, staying in the bush or with strangers, until the time for circumcision has passed. There are also recurrent conflicts between parents and their daughters over circumcision, some of which have been resolved by the courts.

While the reality of social change cannot be ignored, it is important to recognize the importance of cultural identity. Considering the influence and power of culture on a community and on individuals, it must be acknowledged that a deeply rooted practice such as female circumcision cannot be easily changed. However, this does not mean that it cannot be eliminated if appropriate strategies are adopted. Claims of cultural identity are important, but structural injustice perpetuated against children and women in our societies in the name of culture and religion must be condemned. It is time that female circumcision is perceived within this framework. It is time that our communities protect the weak from social cultural practices that endanger their lives.

It is also important to note that women cannot do this on their own, without the help of men. Social values are a network of structural values that everyone is socialized to accept as normative. A practice such as female circumcision is part of the social structures and values of the community. One of my colleagues, a university professor, came to my office one day for coffee and happily announced to a group of other faculty, "My wife is planning to circumcise our daughters this weekend." Most of us were bewildered by this announcement from a man we considered educated. When questioned about stopping the ritual, he responded, amused, that he could not interfere because "that is the women's department." Although he was well educated, he was ignorant of the serious health risks and the violations of basic human rights to which his daughters would be exposed. It is, therefore, essential that both men and women be made aware of the reality of cultural and also religious practices that jeopardize the wellbeing of the community or bring injustice to parts of it.

Female circumcision should also be addressed in the context of patriarchal societies. This means raising the larger issues of sexism and the unfair treatment of women as subordinate to men. This would include addressing social practices such as widow inheritance; the prohibition on women owning property or holding leadership positions such as political office; wife battering; forced marriages, including the marriage of young girls; the violation of women's integrity by checking their genitals at marriage to ensure virginity or by breaking the hymen and showing the blood-stained towel to the public as proof of virginity; and the general treatment of girls as inferior to boys. Given the challenges HIV/AIDS poses to women in our communities, it is time for the welfare of women to become a central concern. Attempts should be made to acknowledge the worth of women, to educate girls in the same way as boys, and to treat all people with dignity.

All institutions that educate—schools, religious bodies, and the mass media—should be part of the social network that communicates gender-related messages of equality with the goal of transforming social attitudes, values, and practices. Challenging a social and cultural practice such as female circumcision is not an easy task, and change will not happen overnight. Strategies that are alien to or disrespectful of a community's social context or a people's world view have little chance of succeeding. Alienating members or parts of the community fuels resentment and resistance, as has happened in Kenya in the past. An effective strategy must acknowledge the weaknesses and strengths of a given people. It must appreciate their values even as it critiques areas of concern. Romanticizing tradition tends to cloak social injustice in the veil of culture. In other words, efforts to transform attitudes toward female circumcision must be pursued not because it is illegitimate (or barbaric, some might say), but because it poses serious health risks and human rights concerns.

A strategy to transform female circumcision through education must inform the entire community of both the physical consequences and the human rights issues that the practice involves. While education is a significant factor in the process of social transformation, *effective* education must be tailored not only to educate people about the physical consequences and human rights issues associated with female circumcision, but also to empower agency. Recall the account of the university professor who labeled female circumcision "the women's department." Education to empower agency must first raise awareness and then create the conviction that gives voice. Voices raised can lead to action. An effective strategy cannot gloss over these issues in the name of culture or tradition. It must call upon community members to act in defense of the weak, who, in this case, are primarily children.

Since age is a significant variable and since most elderly members of a community are in favor of female circumcision as a traditional practice, an effective strategy must consider the elderly, who are being asked to abandon something that was considered the norm in their societies. Education must provide sufficient opportunity for questions and responses to each of their concerns before any attempt can be made to dismantle these long-held attitudes. The attitudes of youth will change more quickly, as they are in the midst of formulating their life principles. Younger age groups are less likely to support female circumcision.

Religion, a significant source of attitudes and values, is another important variable in social behavior. Table 4 (p. 101) shows that 90 percent of fifty women interviewed cited religion as a factor motivating the practice of female circumcision. Yet 68 percent of the uncircumcised women cited religion as a factor in their decision *not* to be circumcised (see Table 7, p. 133). Because religion has been used to sanction female circumcision, religious beliefs should also be included in all efforts to transform attitudes. Because religion integrates divine authority in its interpretation of scripture or in the messages of religious leaders, it invokes sacred power, which has significant appeal to and influence on the community. As an agent of liberation, religion should seek to demystify any social myths that damage the social welfare of the vulnerable.

Yet, in any mission of liberation the oppressed must be willing to embrace their liberation. For this reason religious education should never seek to stifle agency. The goal should be to empower victims— in this case, women—to voice their concerns about female circumcision and other practices they endure in the name of culture. They must be empowered to realize that they have voices and that they can play a significant role in determining the shape of their lives. Apathy is the greatest enemy of social justice. While apathy leads to inaction, speaking out is a significant and active step. If Kenyan women cannot speak for themselves, someone else will speak for them, a situation that heightens the possibility of misrepresentation, as has happened in the controversy over female circumcision.

In order to stimulate agency through religion, a critical evaluation of scriptural texts is necessary to discern a message of emancipation for women. Agency can also be promoted by the many strong women who have defied tradition and circumcision. Such women leaders include the first African Nobel Peace Prize winner, Professor Wangari Maathai, and politicians Charity Ngilu, Martha Karua, Sally Kosgei, Winifred Nyiva Mwendwa, Dr. Julia Ojiambo, and Jael Mbogo, to mention just a few. Women in religious congregations who have successfully overcome challenges to harmful cultural practices should also be held up as models. Men who have defended their daughters and wives against this practice should also testify and be lifted up. Emphasis should be given to numerous women of courage in the Qur'an and the Bible, such as Khadija and Aisha in Islam, and Esther, Deborah, Mary, and Martha in Christianity. Contemporary writers of African fiction, curriculum materials, and popular theater, whether practitioners of Islam, Christianity, or Indigenous religion, can also be involved in this task.

And finally, it should be noted that because of changing values and the abandonment of some traditional practices, fewer people are trained in indigenous procedures such as excision, a factor responsible for even greater health risks. A program with the goal of transforming attitudes and, finally, ending the practice of female circumcision must acknowledge the realities in circumcising communities. It must go beyond a study of religious and social values to include a community's power dynamics, the economic well-being of all its members, and weaknesses in its infrastructure, such as transportation and access to medical care. The story of Leah, the young girl, and Nifa, the exciser, clearly illustrates how such social matrices integrate.

My dream is to bring together scholars from different disciplines, health practitioners, sociologists, educators, lawyers, economists, political leaders, and leaders from Kenya's different religious groups to share information as well as their concerns, successes, and failures in transforming attitudes toward female circumcision and other social practices that endanger the welfare of women. Such a conference on religion and social change could promote dialogue on how to address the issue of female circumcision in the larger social context. Such a conference could also explore ways religion could be integrated in educational programs to address the social issues of sexism, with particular reference to practices such as female circumcision. A white paper produced by the conference could be disseminated to Kenya's educational agencies, including its religious institutions, to serve as a basic reference on methods to curb the practice of female circumcision. Each community would share basic information but be free to design a program to suit local needs.

Significant change in ending the social oppression of women can take place only through a critical analysis of social structures and cultural and religious beliefs. Because of the significant role religion plays in determining social values and social behavior, religious leaders are key to this process. The fate of Kenya's children, wives, and mothers lies in the decisions of those who have the ability to voice their concerns and act as leaders. The authority of leaders ought to serve the good of our communities. Women must be empowered with voice and agency in order to challenge harmful practices such as circumcision. The goal is that Kenyan women—Leah, Nifa, Maisha, Amina, Lang'at and millions of others, including those outside Kenya—will live lives of abundance as human beings with equal rights and as women at home in their own cultures.

Notes

1 THE CONTROVERSY

1. Nation Correspondent, "Teenager Dies in Hospital after Secret 'Cut' at Home," *Daily Nation on the Web*, December 9, 2003. Available online.

2. Nation Correspondent, "Girls Get Ill after Being Circumcised," *Daily Nation Online*, October 1, 2004. Available online.

3. Editorial, "Charge Them with Murder," *Daily Nation Online*, December 7, 2004. Available online.

4. Female circumcision is also known as female genital mutilation (FGM), female genital cutting, clitoridectomy, excision, and infibulation. The controversy surrounding the terminology to be used in reference to this practice arises out of the perceived connotation of some of the terms and the inadequacy of other terms to describe the operation. For instance, the term FGM is resented among some African scholars and circumcising communities because it connotes intentional harm not intended by parents who circumcise their daughters. The debate on terminology is discussed at length in Chapter 4. In this book I use the term *female circumcision* not only to avoid offensive overtones associated with the term *FGM* but more especially to acknowledge and respect social values that bring about the use of this term in communities where this practice is found. This is not to overlook my reservations about the practice.

5. Anika Rahman and Nahid Toubia, *Female Genital Mutilation: A Practical Guide to Laws and Policies Worldwide* (New York: Zed Books, 2001), 7–8.

6. Female circumcision has also been reported in Australia, Asia, Latin America, the United States of America, and Europe. See Rahman and Toubia, *Female Genital Mutilation*, 6–7; and Robin Morgan and Gloria Steinem, "The International Crime of Genital Mutilation," in *Outrageous Acts and Everyday Rebellions*, ed. Gloria Steinem (New York: Henry Holt and Co., 1983), 331–32.

7. The exact number of women affected by this practice is unknown. Statistics are not released and even more difficult to obtain since the practice is related to sexuality, a subject that is considered a taboo in many communities.

8. Maendeleo Ya Wanawake Organization (MYWO), *Harmful Traditional Practices That Affect the Health of the Women and Their Children* (Nairobi: MYWO, 1993), 2.

9. L. Amede Obiora, "Bridges and Barricades: Rethinking Polemics and Intransigence in the Campaign against Female Circumcision," *Case Western Reserve Law Review* 47, no. 2 (1997): 275–378.

10. Fuambai Ahmadu, "Rites and Wrongs: An Insider/Outsider Reflects on Power and Excision," in *Female "Circumcision" in Africa: Culture, Controversy, and Change*, ed. Bettina Shell-Duncan and Ylva Herlund (Boulder, CO: Lynne Rienner Publishers, 2000), 283–312.

11. Sylvia Wynter, "'Genital Mutilation' or 'Symbolic Birth'? Female Circumcision, Lost Origins and the Aculturalism of Feminism/Western Thought," *Case Western Reserve Law Review* 47, no. 2 (1997): 503; see also Obiora, "Bridges and Barricades," 277; and Ahmadu, "Rites and Wrongs," 284.

12. Ahmadu, "Rites and Wrongs," 284.

13. Micere Githae Mugo, "Elitist Anti-Circumcision Discourse as Mutilating and Anti-Feminist," *Case Western Reserve Law Review* 47, no. 2 (1997): 464.

14. Lynn Thomas, "*Ngaitana* (I Will Circumcise Myself): Lessons from Colonial Campaigns to Ban Excision in Meru, Kenya," in Shell-Duncan and Herlund, *Female "Circumcision" in Africa*, 129. The Njuri was an officially sanctioned local council of male leaders who served the community on behalf of the colonial government.

15. Ibid., 137.

16. Christine J. Walley, "Searching for 'Voices': Feminism, Anthropology, and the Global Debate over Female Genital Operations," in *Genital Cutting and Transnational Sisterhood: Disputing US Polemics*, ed. Stanlie M. James and Claire C. Robertson (Urbana: Univ. of Illinois Press, 2002), 31–32.

17. Claire C. Robertson, "Grass Roots in Kenya—Women Genital Mutilation and 'Collective Action,'" in *Unspoken Rules: Sexual Orientation and Women's Human Rights*, ed. Rachel Rosenbloom (London: Cassell, 1996), 624; and Walley, "Searching for 'Voices,'" 31.

18. Mugo, "Elitist Anti-Circumcision Discourse as Mutilating and Anti-Feminist," 464.

19. Uma Narayan, *Dislocating Cultures: Identities, Traditions, and Third-World Feminism* (New York: Routledge, 1997), 29.

20. Ibid., 3.

21. Ibid., 31.

22. Ibid.

23. Mark Lacey, "Genital Cutting Shows Signs of Losing Favor in Africa," *The New York Times*, June 8, 2004.

24. Kim Longinotto, *The Day I Will Never Forget* (London: Women Make Movies), 2002.

25. The term *religion* is used here to refer to the belief systems of any given community.

26. Efua Dorkenoo, *Cutting the Rose: Female Genital Mutilation: The Practice, and Its Prevention* (London: Minority Rights Publication, 1994), 36–39, 95–96.

27. Obiora, "Bridges and Barricades," 295–98.

28. John S. Mbiti, *African Religions and Philosophy* (London: Heinemann Educational Books, 1990), 118–29.

29. Sami Awad Aldeeb Abu-Sahlieh, *Male and Female Circumcision among Jews, Christians and Muslims: Religious, Medical, Social, and Legal Debate* (Warren Center, PA: Shangri-La Publications, 2001), 16–130.

30. Jomo Kenyatta, *Facing Mount Kenya: The Tribal Life of the Gikuyu* (New York: Vintage Books, 1962 [1938]), 129–48.

31. All forms of discrimination and mistreatment, which can be assumed to apply to female circumcision, are restricted under the Universal Declaration of Human Rights (Article 2); the United Nations Charter (Articles 1 and 55); the International Covenant of Civil and Political Rights (Article 2 (1)); the Convention on the Elimination of All Forms of Discrimination against Women (CEDAW) (also knows as the Women's Convention) (Article 1); the Economic, Social and Cultural Rights Covenant (Article 22); the African Charter on Human and Peoples' Rights (the Banjul Charter) (Article 18 (3)); the Convention on the Rights of the Child (Article 19); and the Declaration on the Elimination of Violence against Women. For further details, see Rahman and Toubia, *Female Genital Mutilation*, 18–39. Several individual nation-states have also banned female circumcision, including the United States, Britain, and Sweden, which punishes violators with a five-year prison sentence. In Kenya, numerous attempts have been made by the government to ban this practice, with the latest attempt made in the year 2001. The Kenyan government passed the "children's bill," which defines a child as a person below eighteen years of age. According to this bill, a child should not be subjected to circumcision and any other rite that is defined as harmful to the development of a child.

32. Angela Wasunna, "Towards Redirecting the Female Circumcision Debate: Legal, Ethical, and Cultural Considerations," *McGill Journal of Medicine* 5 (2002): 105–7.

2 RELIGION AND THE SOCIAL BEHAVIOR OF KENYANS

1. Clifford Geertz, *The Interpretation of Cultures* (New York: Basic Books, 1973), 127.

2. Ibid.

3. John S. Mbiti, *African Religions and Philosophy* (London: Heinemann Educational Books, 1990), 102–4.

4. Harold D. Nelson, ed., *Kenya: A Country Study* (Washington, DC: The American University, 1984), 105.

5. Mbiti, *African Religions and Philosophy*, 104.

6. Susan Moller Okin, *Women in Western Political Thought* (Princeton, NJ: Princeton Univ. Press, 1997), 3.

7. Lance F. Morrow, "Women in Sub-Saharan Africa," in *The Cross-Cultural Study of Women: A Comprehensive Guide*, ed. Margot I. Duley and Mary I. Edwards (New York: The Feminist Press, 1986), 291.

8. L. Amede Obiora, "Bridges and Barricades: Rethinking Polemics and Intransigence in the Campaign against Female Circumcision," *Case Western Reserve Law Review* 47, no. 2 (1997): 302.

9. Bettina Shell-Duncan, Walter Obungu Obiero, and Leunita Auko Muruli, "Women without Choices: The Debate over Medicalization of Female Genital Cutting and Its Impact on a Northern Kenyan Community," in *Female "Circumcision" in Africa: Culture Controversy and Change*, ed. Bettina Shell-Duncan and Ylva Hernlund (Boulder, CO: Lynne Rienner Publishers, 2000), 119.

10. Wanjiku Mukabi Kabira, "Images of Women in African Oral Literature: An Overview of Images of Women in Gikuyu Oral Narratives," in *Understanding Oral Literature*, ed. Austin Bukenya, Wanjiku Mukabi Kabira, and Okoth Okombo (Nairobi: Nairobi Univ. Press, 1994), 77.

11. Ellen Gruenbaum, *The Female Circumcision Controversy: An Anthropological Perspective* (Philadelphia: Univ. of Pennsylvania Press, 2001), 42.

12. Kabira, "Images of Women in African Oral Literature," 77–78.

13. Gruenbaum, *The Female Circumcision Controversy*, 41.

14. Regina Smith Oboler, *Women, Power, and Economic Change* (Stanford, CA: Stanford Univ. Press, 1985), 58–60.

15. Kabira, "Images of Women in African Oral Literature," 77; and Catherine Coquery-Vidrovitch, *African Women: A Modern History* (Boulder, CO: Westview Press, 1997), 46.

16. Kabira, "Images of Women in African Oral Literature," 80; and Jomo Kenyatta, *Facing Mount Kenya: The Tribal Life of the Gikuyu* (New York: Vintage Books, 1962 [1938]), 12.

17. Kabira, "Images of Women in African Oral Literature," 81.

18. Mary Omosa, "Persistent Cultural Practices: A Review of the Status of Women in Kenya," in *From Strategies to Action: A Research Perspective*, ed. AAWORD (Nairobi: AAWORD, 1995), 64–65.

19. Jean Davison, *Voices from Mutira: Change in the Lives of Rural Gikuyu Women, 1910–1995*, 2nd ed. (Boulder, CO: Lynne Rienner Publishers, 1996), 119.

20. Such texts include Colossians 3:18 and Ephesians 5:22.

21. Central Intelligence Agency, *The World Factbook, 2006*. Available online.

22. The Norwegian Church Aid, "Women Rights as Human Rights: A Contradiction between Policy and Practice in Kenya," Occasional Paper Series No. 01/2004.

23. See S. W. Nasong'o, "Women and Economic Liberalization in Kenya: The Impact and Challenges of Globalization," in *Women in African Development: The Challenge of Globalization and Liberalization in the 21st Century*, ed. Sylvain Boko et al. (Trenton, NJ: Africa World Press, 2005).

24. For figures on poverty and gender disparity, see ibid.

25. Omosa, "Persistent Cultural Practices," 69.

26. Ibid., 61.

27. Rosalind I. J. Hackett, "Women and New Religious Movements in Africa," in *Gender and Religion*, ed. Ursula King (Oxford: Blackwell, 1994), 77.

28. Central Intelligence Agency, *The World Factbook, 2003*.

29. Maendeleo Ya Wanawake Organization (MYWO), *Harmful Traditional Practices That Affect the Health of the Women and Their Children* (Nairobi: MYWO, 1993), 2, 16–19.

30. Ibid., 2.

31. Ibid., 18.

32. Fran P. Hosken, *The Hosken Report: Genital and Sexual Mutilation of Females*, 4th ed. (Lexington, MA: Women's International Network News, 1993), 157; and Lynn Thomas, "*Ngaitana* (I Will Circumcise Myself): Lessons From Colonial Campaigns to Ban Excision in Meru, Kenya," in Shell-Duncan and Hernlund, *Female "Circumcision" in Africa*, 132–45.

33. Sami Awad Aldeeb Abu-Sahlieh, *Male and Female Circumcision among Jews, Christians and Muslims: Religious, Medical, Social, and Legal Debate* (Warren Center, PA: Shangri-La Publications, 2001), 266; Thomas, "*Ngaitana* (I Will Circumcise Myself)," 132–33; and Teresia M. Hinga, "Jesus Christ and the Liberation of Women in Africa," in *The Will to Arise: Women, Tradition, and the Church in Africa*, ed. Mercy Oduyoye and Musimbi R. A. Kanyoro (Maryknoll, NY: Orbis Books, 1992), 188.

34. Hosken, *The Hosken Report*, 162–64; and Jocelyn M. Murray, "The Kikuyu Female Circumcision Controversy, with Special Reference to the Church Missionary Society's 'Sphere of Influence,'" Ph.D. dissertation (Los Angeles: UCLA, 1974; Ann Arbor, MI: UMI Library West: DT433.575.M7x), 169–70.

35. Emmanuel Babatunde, *Women's Rights Versus Women's Rites: A Study of Circumcision among the Ketu Yoruba of South Western Nigeria* (Trenton, NJ: Africa World Press, 1998), 8; and Kenyatta, *Facing Mount Kenya*, 132.

36. Hosken, *The Hosken Report*, 165–66.

37. Babatunde, *Women's Rights Versus Women's Rites*, 7–8.

38. Thomas, "*Ngaitana* (I Will Circumcise Myself)," 137–41.

39. Henry J. Steiner and Philip Alston, *International Human Rights in Context: Law, Politics, Morals* (Oxford: Clarendon Press, 1996), 246; and Anika Rahman and Nahid Toubia, *Female Genital Mutilation: A Practical Guide to Laws and Policies Worldwide* (New York: Zed Books, 2001), 76.

40. Tervil Okoko, "Kenya's No-Win War against Female Genital Mutilation," *Panafrican News Agency*, October 12, 2000. Available online.

41. Ibid.

42. Malik Stan Reaves, "Alternative Rite to Female Circumcision Spreading in Kenya," *Africa News Service* (November 1997). Available online. For details on this program, see Chapter 3 herein.

43. Micere Githae Mugo, "Elitist Anti-Circumcision Discourse as Mutilating and Anti-Feminist," *Case Western Reserve Law Review* 47, no. 2 (1997): 463–76; Fuambai Ahmadu, "Rites and Wrongs: An Insider/Outsider Reflects on Power and Excision," in Shell-Duncan and Herlund, *Female "Cicumcision" in Africa*, 284–85; and Martha C. Nussbaum, *Sex and Social Justice* (New York: Oxford Univ. Press, 1999), 126.

44. Mugo, "Elitist Anti-Circumcision Discourse as Mutilating and Anti-Feminist," 477.

45. Jane Flanagan, "Kenyan Sisters Win Judgment on Circumcision," *News Telegraph*, December 17, 2000. Available online.

46. Kim Longinotto, *The Day I Will Never Forget* (London: Women Make Movies, 2002).

47. "Meru Elders Reject Female Cut," *The Nation* (Nairobi), March 30, 1999. Available online.

48. Peter Berger, *The Sacred Canopy: Elements of a Sociological Theory of Religion* (New York: Anchor Books, 1990), 32–33.

49. Details on how religion shapes gender and sexuality are discussed in Chapter 4 herein.

50. Dorothy Smith, *Writing the Social Critique: Theory and Investigations* (London: Univ. of Toronto Press, 1999), 49–50, 76–78.

51. Mbiti, *African Religions and Philosophy*, 2.

52. Ibid., 2. Note that Mbiti's claim that Africans cannot distinguish religion from daily lifestyles propagates an assumption that makes it difficult for social change to be promoted in African communities, especially when patterns of lifestyle are always interpreted in terms of the divine. In my opinion, religion is not really intertwined with culture, as Mbiti claims. It is and should be possible to distinguish the two.

53. Ibid., 106.

54. Ibid.

55. Ibid.

56. Bénézet Bujo, *Foundations of an African Ethic: Beyond the Universal Claims of Western Morality* (New York: Crossroad, 2001), 3–5.

57. Kenyatta, *Facing Mount Kenya*, 115.

58. Ibid., 87.

59. Bujo, *Foundations of an African Ethic*, 3.

60. Mbiti, *African Religions and Philosophy*, 165–66.

61. Ibid., 165–67; see also John S. Mbiti, *Concepts of God in Africa* (London: SPCK, 1970), 81–83.

62. Mugo, "Elitist Anti-Circumcision Discourse as Mutilating and Anti-Feminist," 477.

63. Nelson, *Kenya*, 114; see also David B. Barrett, George T. Kurian, and Todd M. Johnson, eds., *World Christian Encyclopedia: A Comparative Survey of Churches and Religions in the Modern World* (Oxford: Oxford Univ. Press, 2001), 245; and Central Intelligence Agency, *The World Factbook, 2006*.

64. Ibid.

65. Jan Knappert, *East Africa: Kenya, Tanzania and Uganda* (New Delhi: Vikas Publishing House, 1987), 101–33; and Mbiti, *African Religions and Philosophy*, 30–43.

66. Knappert, *East Africa*, 119–37.

67. Ibid., 104, 124; and Mbiti, *Concepts of God in Africa*, 80–87.

68. Mbiti, *Concepts of God in Africa*, 43–44, 81.

69. Ibid., 81–84.

70. Mbiti, *African Religions and Philosophy*, 81–83.

71. Mbiti, *Concepts of God in Africa*, 124.

72. Mbiti, *African Religions and Philosophy*, 80.

73. Knappert, *East Africa*, 104.

74. Ibid., 112–13.

75. Mbiti, *Concepts of God in Africa*, 211–12.

76. Ibid.

77. Mbiti, *African Religions and Philosophy*, 167–69.

78. Ibid., 165.

79. Carl G. Rosberg, and John Nottingham, *The Myth of "Mau Mau" Nationalism in Kenya* (London: Pall Mall Press, 1966), 112; and F. B. Welbourn, *East African Rebels: A Study of Some Independent Churches* (London: SCM Press, 1961), 127.

80. Ram Desai, "Christianity in Danger," in *Christianity in Africa: As Seen by the Africans*, ed. Ram Desai (Denver: Alan Swallow, 1962), 20.

81. David B. Barrett, "The Expansion of Christianity in Kenya AD 1900–2000," in *Kenya Churches Handbook: The Development of Kenyan Christianity 1498–1973*, ed. David B. Barrett, George K. Mambo, Janice McLaughlin, and Malcolm J. McVeigh (Kisumu, Kenya: Evangel Publishing House, 1973), 183–89, 229–51; and Thomas Spear, "Toward the History of African Christianity," in *East African Expressions of Christianity*, ed. Thomas Spear and Isaria N. Kimambo (Nairobi: East African Educational Publishers, 1999), 14–17.

82. Exorcism is a traditional ritual in which evil spirits are driven out of an individual—an expressive and emotional phenomenon that counters fears of witchcraft and misfortune among Africans.

83. Central Intelligence Agency, *The World Factbook, 2003*, 285.

84. Nelson, *Kenya: A Country Study*, 117; and James D. Holway, "Islam in Kenya and Relations with the Churches," in Barrett et al., *Kenya Churches Handbook*, 295–96.

85. Holway, "Islam in Kenya and Relations with the Churches," 296.

86. Isa S. Wali, "Islam and Africa," unpublished, as quoted in Desai, "Christianity in Danger," 34.

3 THE DEBATE OVER FEMALE CIRCUMCISION

1. I am deeply indebted to works by Fran P. Hosken, *The Hosken Report: Genital and Sexual Mutilation of Females*, 4th ed. (Lexington, MA: Women's International Network News, 1993); Alice Walker, *Possessing the Secret of Joy* (New York: Harcourt Brace Jovanovich, 1992); Alice Walker and Pratibha Parmar, *Warrior Marks: Female Genital Mutilation and the Sexual Blinding of Women* (San Diego: Harcourt Brace and Co., 1993); L. Amede Obiora, "Bridges and Barricades: Rethinking Polemics and Intransigence in the Campaign against Female Circumcision," *Case Western Reserve Law Review* 47, no. 2 (1997): 275–378; Fuambai Ahmadu, "Rites and Wrongs: An Insider/Outsider Reflects on Power and Excision," in *Female "Circumcision" in Africa: Culture, Controversy and Change*, ed. Bettina Shell-Duncan and Ylva Herlund (Boulder, CO: Lynne Rienner Publishers, 2000); Ellen Gruenbaum, *The Female Circumcision Controversy: An Anthropological Perspective* (Philadelphia: Univ. of Pennsylvania Press, 2001); Efua Dorkenoo, *Cutting the Rose: Female Genital Mutilation: The Practice, and Its Prevention* (London: Minority Rights Publication, 1994); and Sami Awad Aldeeb Abu-Sahlieh, *Male and Female Circumcision among Jews, Christians and Muslims: Religious, Medical, Social, and Legal Debate* (Warren Center, PA: Shangri-La Publications, 2001), to name but a few.

2. Anika Rahman and Nahid Toubia, eds., *Female Genital Mutilation: A Practical Guide to Laws and Policies Worldwide* (New York: Zed Books, 2001), 4; and Gruenbaum, *The Female Circumcision Controversy*, 3–4.

3. Rahman and Toubia, *Female Genital Mutilation*, 4.

4. Eugenie Anne Gifford, "The Courage to Blaspheme: Confronting Barriers to Resisting Female Genital Mutilation," *UCLA Women's Law Journal* 4 (1994): 329; and Ahmadu, "Rites and Wrongs," 284–85.

5. Dorkenoo, *Cutting the Rose*, 4; and Gifford, "The Courage to Blaspheme," 329.

6. Gruenbaum, *The Female Circumcision Controversy*, 3–4; Bettina Shell-Duncan and Ylva Hernlund, "Female 'Circumcision' in Africa: Dimensions of the Practice and Debates," in Shell-Duncan and Hernlund, *Female "Circumcision" in Africa*, 6; and Rahman and Toubia, *Female Genital Mutilation*, 4.

7. Micere Githae Mugo, "Elitist Anti-Circumcision Discourse as Mutilating and Anti-Feminist," *Case Western Reserve Law Review* 47, no. 2 (1997): 461.

8. Obiora, "Bridges and Barricades," 290.

9. Martha C. Nussbaum, *Sex and Social Justice* (New York: Oxford Univ. Press, 1999), 121.

10. Gifford, "The Courage to Blaspheme," 333; and Shell-Duncan and Hernlund, "Female 'Circumcision' in Africa," 1.

11. Leila Ahmed, *Women and Gender in Islam* (New Haven, CT: Yale Univ. Press, 1992), 247.

12. Nancy Bonvillain, *Women and Men: Cultural Constructs of Gender*, 3rd ed. (Upper Saddle River, NJ: Prentice-Hall, 2000), 278.

13. Walker and Parmar, *Warrior Marks*, 15–19.

14. Mary Daly, *Gyn/Ecology: The Metaethics of Radical Feminism* (Boston: Beacon Press, 1978), 156–59.

15. Bonvillain, *Women and Men*, 278.

16. Shere Hite, *The Hite Report: A Nationwide Study of Female Sexuality* (New York: Macmillan, 1976), 99.

17. Dr. M. Mahran, as quoted in Dorkenoo, *Cutting the Rose*, 21.

18. Dorkenoo, *Cutting the Rose*, 20.

19. Obiora, "Bridges and Barricades," 295–98.

20. Ahmadu, "Rites and Wrongs," 284.

21. Obiora, "Bridges and Barricades," 302; and bell hooks, *Feminist Theory: From Margin to Center* (Boston: South End Press, 2000), 9, 11.

22. Obiora, "Bridges and Barricades," 302–5; and Janice Boddy, *Wombs and Alien Spirits: Women, Men and the Zar Cult in Northern Sudan* (Madison: Univ. of Wisconsin Press, 1989), 53–58.

23. Mugo, "Elitist Anti-Circumcision Discourse as Mutilating and Anti-Feminist," 477.

24. Ahmadu, "Rites and Wrongs," 284; and Obiora, "Bridges and Barricades," 285.

25. Mugo, "Elitist Anti-Circumcision Discourse as Mutilating and Anti-Feminist," 468–69.

26. Ibid., 474; Gruenbaum, *The Female Circumcision Controversy*, 39–40; and Obiora, "Bridges and Barricades," 310.

27. Maendeleo Ya Wanawake Organization (MYWO), *Harmful Traditional Practices That Affect the Health of the Women and Their Children* (Nairobi: MYWO, 1993), 2.

28. Dorothy Smith, *Writing the Social Critique: Theory and Investigations* (London: Univ. of Toronto Press, 1999), 76–79, 91–95.

29. Bonvillain, *Women and Men*, 278.

30. Nussbaum, *Sex and Social Justice*, 126.

31. Mary R. Jackman, "Gender, Violence and Harassment," in *Handbook of the Sociology of Gender*, ed. Janet Saltzman Chafetz (New York: Kluwer Academic Plenum Publishers, 1999), 290.

32. Kim Longinotto, *The Day I Will Never Forget* (London: Women Make Movies, 2002).

33. Shell-Duncan and Hernlund, "Female 'Circumcision' in Africa," 14.

34. Dorkenoo, *Cutting the Rose*, 13–27.

35. Shell-Duncan and Hernlund, "Female 'Circumcision' in Africa," 14.

36. Dorkenoo, *Cutting the Rose*, 13–27; and Shell-Duncan and Hernlund, "Female 'Circumcision' in Africa," 14–18.

37. Shell-Duncan and Hernlund, "Female 'Circumcision' in Africa," 14.

38. Dorkenoo, *Cutting the Rose*, 14.

39. Ibid., 15–24; and Shell-Duncan and Hernlund, "Female 'Circumcision' in Africa," 14.

40. Catherine Coquery-Vidrovitch, *African Women: A Modern History* (Boulder, CO: Westview Press, 1997), 208.

41. MYWO, *Harmful Traditional Practices That Affect the Health of the Women and Their Children*, 24.

42. Wanyama, personal interview, July 2003.

43. Dr. Mark Besley, ABC News, 1993, as quoted in Dorkenoo, *Cutting the Rose*, 13.

44. Dr. Rosemary Mburu, as quoted in Judy Mann, "Torturing Girls Is Not a Cultural Right," *The Washington Post*, February 23, 1994; also cited in Dorkenoo, *Cutting the Rose*, 15.

45. Miriam Kahiga, "One Rite, Too Many Wrongs," *Daily Nation*, April 1994, 3–5.

46. Muliro Telewa, "Female Genital Mutilation Hospitalizes 21 Girls in Kenya," The British Broadcasting Company, October 31, 2001.

47. Chepkorir, personal interview, August 2002.

48. Gruenbaum, *The Female Circumcision Controversy*, 205; see also Alison Slack, "Female Circumcision: A Critical Appraisal," *Human Rights Quarterly* 10 (1988): 437–86.

49. Henry Steiner and Philip Alston, *International Human Rights in Context: Law, Politics, Morals* (Oxford: Clarendon Press, 1996), 244; and Dorkenoo, *Cutting the Rose*, 10.

50. Obiora, "Bridges and Barricades," 307–10; and Gruenbaum, *The Female Circumcision Controversy*, 141–43.

51. Obiora, "Bridges and Barricades," 291–92.

52. Ibid., and Ahmadu, "Rites and Wrongs," 284–85.

53. December Green, *Gender Violence in Africa: African Women's Response* (New York: St. Martin's Press, 1999), 51, 241; Stephen Makabila, "Over 100 Girls Flee FGM, Hide in Churches," *East African Standard*, February 7, 2003; and Kipchumba Kemei, "38 Girls Evade Circumcision," *East African Standard*, May 5, 2003. Abu-Sahlieh makes the same point about male circumcision (*Male and Female Circumcision among Jews, Christians, and Muslims*, 317–19).

54. Obiora, "Bridges and Barricades," 277; see also Steiner and Alston, *International Human Rights in Context*, 244–45; and Shell-Duncan and Hernlund, "Female 'Circumcision' in Africa," 27.

55. Shell-Duncan and Hernlund, "Female 'Circumcision' in Africa," 28; and Steiner and Alston, *International Human Rights in Context*, 244–45.

56. See Efua Dorkenoo and Scilla Elworthy, *Female Genital Mutilation: Proposals for Change*, Minority Rights Group International, Report 92/3 (1992), 11.

57. Scilla McLean, ed., "Female Circumcision, Excision, and Infibulation: The Facts and Proposal for Change," Minority Rights Group International, Report 47/3 (1985), 11.

58. Shell-Duncan and Hernlund, "Female 'Circumcision' in Africa," 30.

59. The International Human Rights movement began during the Second World War as a struggle against political absolutism. The failures of rulers to respect the principles of freedom and equality central to natural law philosophy were responsible for this development. See further details in Steiner and Alston, *International Human Rights in Context*, 168ff.

60. Ibid., 1156.

61. Ibid., 1148.

62. The UN Charter prescribes several powers and methods to create enforcement mechanisms throughout the international community to ensure that the human rights goals of the Charter are met. See Article 13 concerning the General Assembly; Article 60 on the implementation of international cooperation in economic, social, and human rights; Article 62 on defining the functions of the economic and social council; and Articles 76 and 87 on the trusteeship system. In addition, the Charter created and empowered specialized groups to address international concerns involving human rights. These groups include the Commission on Human Rights, the Commission on the Status of Women, and the Sub-commission on Prevention of Discrimination and Protection of Minorities.

63. Steiner and Alston, *International Human Rights in Context*, 192.

64. Obiora, "Bridges and Barricades," 284.

65. Ibid., 277.

66. Ibid., 278.

67. Sylvia Wynter, "'Genital Mutilation' or 'Symbolic Birth?' Female Circumcision, Lost Origins, and the Aculturalism of Feminism/Western Thought," *Case Western Reserve Law Review* 47, no. 2 (1997): 503–4.

68. Obiora, "Bridges and Barricades," 286; and Wynter, "'Genital Mutilation' or 'Symbolic Birth?,'" 506.

69. Wynter, "'Genital Mutilation' or 'Symbolic Birth?,'" 544.

70. Ibid.

71. Merrilee H. Salmon, "Ethical Considerations in Anthropology and Archeology or Relativism and Justice for All?," *Journal of Anthropological Research* 53 (Spring, 1997).

72. Wynter, "'Genital Mutilation' or 'Symbolic Birth?,'" 517.

73. Steiner and Alston, *International Human Rights in Context*, 221.

74. Ibid.

75. Kwasi Wiredu, *Cultural Universals and Particulars: An African Perspective* (Bloomington: Indiana Univ. Press, 1996), 32.

76. Ibid., 41.

77. Ibid.

78. Francis Beckwith and Gregory Koukl, *Relativism: Feet Firmly Planted in Mid-Air* (Grand Rapids, MI: Baker Books, 1998), 69.

79. Mugo, "Elitist Anti-Circumcision Discourse as Mutilating and Anti-Feminist," 465.

80. Linda Bell, *Rethinking Ethics in the Midst of Violence: A Feminist Approach to Freedom* (Lanham, MD: Rowman and Littlefield, 1993), 43–48, 234.

81. Julian Steward, "Comments on the Statement on Human Rights," *American Anthropology* 50, no. 2 (1948): 352.

82. Wiredu, *Cultural Universals and Particulars*, 77, italics added.

83. Ibid., 77.

84. Marion Iris Young, "Five Faces of Oppression," in *Rethinking Power*, SUNY Series in Radical Social and Political Theory, ed. Thomas E. Wartenberg (Albany: State Univ. of New York Press, 1992), 39, 163.

85. Abdullahi Ahmed An-Na'im, "Human Rights in the Muslim World," in Steiner and Alston, *International Human Rights in Context*, 211.

86. Ibid.

87. Ibid., 210.

88. Ahmadu, "Rites and Wrongs," 283.

89. For details, see Mugo, "Elitist Anti-Circumcision Discourse as Mutilating and Anti-Feminist," 466.

90. Ibid., 468; see Walker, *Possessing the Secret of Joy*, 324.

91. Jean Davison, *Voices from Mutira: Changes in the Lives of Rural Gikuyu Women, 1910–1995*, 2nd ed. (Boulder, CO: Lynne Rienner Publishers, 1996); and Boddy, *Wombs and Alien Spirits*.

92. Mugo, "Elitist Anti-Circumcision Discourse as Mutilating and Anti-Feminist," 468–75; see Walker, *Possessing the Secret of Joy*, 5–7.

93. Lynn Thomas, "*Ngaitana* (I Will Circumcise Myself): Lessons from Colonial Campaigns to Ban Excision in Meru, Kenya," in Shell-Duncan and Hernlund, *Female "Circumcision" in Africa: Culture, Controversy, and Change*, 137, 146.

94. Teresia M. Hinga, "Jesus Christ and the Liberation of Women in Africa," in *The Will to Arise: Women, Tradition and the Church in Africa*, ed. Mercy Amba Oduyoye and Musimbi R. A. Kanyoro (Maryknoll, NY: Orbis Books, 1992), 188.

95. Ibid..

96. Stanlie M. James, "Listening to Other(ed) Voices: Reflections around Female Genital Cutting," in *Genital Cutting and Transnational Sisterhood: Disputing US Polemics*, ed. Stanlie M. James and Claire C. Robertson (Urbana: Univ. of Illinois Press, 2002), 104–5; and Shell-Duncan and Hernlund, "Female 'Circumcision' in Africa," 37.

97. Shell-Duncan and Hernlund, "Female 'Circumcision' in Africa," 37.

98. Ylva Hernlund, "Cutting without Ritual and Ritual without Cutting: Female 'Circumcision' and the Re-ritualization of Initiation in the Gambia," in Shell-Duncan and Hernlund, *Female "Circumcision" in Africa*, 250.

99. Obiora, "Bridges and Barricades," 365–367; and Ahmadu, "Rites and Wrongs," 309.

100. Obiora, "Bridges and Barricades," 365.

101. Nahid Toubia, *Female Genital Mutilation: A Call for Global Action* (New York, RAINBO, 1995), 16.

102. Obiora, "Bridges and Barricades," 366.

103. Ifi Amadiume, *Daughters of the Goddess, Daughters of Imperialism: African Women Struggle for Culture, Power, and Democracy* (London: Zed Books, 2000), 152.

104. Obiora, "Bridges and Barricades," 361.

105. Mugo, "Elitist Anti-Circumcision Discourse as Mutilating and Anti-Feminist," 467.

106. Paulo Freire, "Conscientization as a Way of Liberating," in *Liberation Theology: A Documentary History*, ed. Alfred T. Hennely, SJ (Maryknoll, NY: Orbis Books, 1970), 9.

107. Ibid., 13.

108. Amadiume, *Daughters of the Goddess, Daughters of Imperialism*, 156.

4   SEXUALITY, GENDER, AND RELIGION IN KENYA

1. Sherry B. Ortner, "Introduction: Accounting for Sexual Meanings," in *Sexual Meanings: The Cultural Construction of Gender and Sexuality*, ed. Sherry B. Ortner and Harriet Whitehead (Oxford: Cambridge Univ. Press, 1981), 6–7.

2. John H. Gagnon, "The Interaction of Gender Roles and Sexual Conduct," in *Human Sexuality: A Comparative and Developmental Perspective*, ed. Herant A. Katchadourian (Berkeley and Los Angeles: Univ. of California Press, 1979), 243.

3. Ibid., 226–27.

4. Ibid., 223.

5. Pepper Schwartz and Virginia Rutter, *The Gender of Sexuality* (London: Pine Forge Press, 1998), 21–22.

6. Patricia Madoo Lingermann and Jill Niebrugge-Brantley, "Contemporary Feminist Theory," in *Sociological Theory*, 5th ed., ed. George Ritzer (New York: McGraw Hill, 2000), 454.

7. Catharine A. MacKinnon, "A Feminist/Political Approach: Pleasure under Patriarchy," in *Theories of Human Sexuality*, ed. James H. Geer and William T. O'Donohue (New York: Plenum Press, 1987), 69.

8. Ibid.

9. Ibid.

10. Schwartz and Rutter, *The Gender of Sexuality*, 72.

11. John DeLamater, "A Sociological Approach," in Geer and O'Donohue, *Theories of Human Sexuality*, 238.

12. Schwartz and Rutter, *The Gender of Sexuality*, 74.

13. Ibid., 72–73.

14. Judith Shapiro, "Cross-Cultural Perspectives on Sexual Differentiation," in Katchadourian, *Human Sexuality*, 269; and Rosemary Radford

Ruether, *Sexism and God-Talk: Toward a Feminist Theology* (Boston: Beacon Press, 1993), 72.

15. Sherry Ortner, "Is Female to Male as Nature Is to Culture?" in *Woman, Culture and Society*, ed. M. Z. Rosaldo and L. Lamphere (Stanford, CA: Stanford Univ. Press, 1974), 67–87.

16. Ruether, *Sexism and God-Talk*, 72.

17. Ibid., 75.

18. Amy-Jill Levine, "Sexuality," in *Encyclopedia of Women and World Religion*, vol. 2, ed. Serenity Young (New York: Macmillan Reference, 1999), 889.

19. Ruether, *Sexism and God-Talk*, 260.

20. Ibid., 80.

21. Shapiro, "Cross-Cultural Perspectives on Sexual Differentiation," 291.

22. Ibid., 290–91.

23. Catharine A. MacKinnon, "Sexuality," in *Feminist Theory: A Reader*, ed. Wendy K. Kolmar and Frances Bartkowski (Toronto: Mayfield Publishing Company, 2000), 438.

24. Celia Kitzinger, "Problematizing Pleasure: Radical Feminist Deconstructions of Sexuality and Power," in *Power/Gender Social Relations in Theory and Practice*, ed. H. Lorraine Radtke and Hendrikusj Stam (London: Sage Publications, 1994), 194.

25. Shere Hite, *The Hite Report: A Nationwide Study of Female Sexuality* (New York: Macmillan, 1976), and Nancy Friday, *My Secret Garden* (New York: Pocket Books, 1973).

26. Kitzinger, "Problematizing Pleasure," 202; and Schwartz and Rutter, *The Gender of Sexuality*, 80–84.

27. Elizabeth Amoah, "Violence and Women's Bodies in African Perspective," in *Women Resisting Violence: Spirituality for Life*, ed. Mary J. Mananzan et al. (Maryknoll, NY: Orbis Books, 1996), 84.

28. John S. Mbiti, *African Religions and Philosophy* (London: Heinemann Educational Books, 1990), 109–12.

29. Jean Davison, *Voices from Mutira: Change in the Lives if Rural Gikuyu Women, 1910–1995*, 2nd ed. (Boulder, CO: Lynne Rienner Publishers, 1996), 11; and Jomo Kenyatta, *Facing Mount Kenya: The Tribal Life of the Gikuyu* (New York: Vintage Books, 1962 [1938]), 152–56.

30. Davison, *Voices from Mutira*, 11.

31. Given the scourge of HIV/AIDS in Africa, it is a tragedy that men violate this taboo, assuming such a young girl is a virgin, in the erroneous belief that sleeping with a virgin cures HIV/AIDS.

32. Elizabeth Amoah, "Femaleness: Akan Concepts and Practices," in *Women, Religion and Sexuality: Studies on the Impact of Religious Teachings on Women*, ed. Jeanne Beecher (Philadelphia: Trinity Press International, 1991), 140.

33. Musimbi Kanyoro, *Introducing Feminist Cultural Hermeneutics: An African Perspective* (Cleveland: Pilgrim Press, 2002), 15–16.

34. Bénézet Bujo, *Foundations of an African Ethic: Beyond the Universal Claims of Western Morality* (New York: Crossroad, 2001), 36; and Mbiti, *African Religions and Philosophy*, 25–26.

35. Mbiti, *African Religions and Philosophy*, 107.

36. Bujo, *Foundations of an African Ethic*, 35–36.

37. Amoah, "Violence and Women's Bodies in African Perspective," 91.

38. Wanjiku Mukabi Kabira, "Images of Women in African Oral Literature: An Overview of Images of Women in Gikuyu Oral Narratives," in *Understanding Oral Literature*, ed. Austin Bukenya, Wanjiku Mukabi Kabira, and Okoth Okombo (Nairobi: Nairobi Univ. Press, 1994), 81.

39. Mbiti, *African Religions and Philosophy*, 143.

40. Henrietta L. Moore, *Space, Text, and Gender: An Anthropological Study of the Marakwet of Kenya* (London: Cambridge Univ. Press, 1986), 175.

41. Muturi, personal interview, August 2003.

42. Kabira, "Images of Women in African Oral Literature," 80.

43. Ibid.

44. Ibid., 81.

45. Ciarunji Chesaina, "Images of Women in African Oral Literature: A Case Study of the Kalenjin and the Maasai Oral Narrative," in Bukenya, Kabira, and Okombo, *Understanding Oral Literature*, 88; see also Margaret Carey, *Myths and Legends of Africa* (New York: Hamlyn Publishing Group, 1970), 92–97.

46. Carey, *Myths and Legends of Africa*, 92–97; and Chesaina, "Images of Women in African Oral Literature," 87–88.

47. Vern L. Bullough, "A Historical Perspective," in Geer and O'Donohue, *Theories of Human Sexuality*, 50; and Ruether, *Sexism and God-Talk*, 78–79.

48. Penelope Washbourn, "Process Thought and a Theology of Sexuality," in *God, Sex, and the Social Project*, ed. James H. Grace (New York: Edwin Mellen Press, 1978), 94.

49. Ibid., 52.

50. Saint Augustine, *The City of God*, trans. Marcus Dods (New York: Modern Library, 1950), 464–72; and Washbourn, "Process Thought and a Theology of Sexuality," 101.

51. Tertullian, *De Cultu Feminarum*, 1.1; see also as quoted in Ruether, *Sexism and God-Talk*, 167.

52. Celibacy was also advocated for male clergy in both Eastern and Western churches at various times and has been required of clergy in the Roman Catholic Church since the Second Lateran Council in 1139.

53. Cited in Kabira, "Images of Women in African Oral Literature," 78.

54. John Murray, "Varieties of Kikuyu Independent Churches," in *Kenya Churches Handbook: The Development of Kenyan Christianity 1498–1973*, ed. David Barrett et al. (Kisumu, Kenya: Evangel Publishing House, 1973), 129.

55. Kim Longinotto, *The Day I Will Never Forget* (London: Women Make Movies, 2002).

56. Abdullahi Ahmed An-Na'im, "Human Rights in the Muslim World," in *International Human Rights in Context: Law, Politics, Morals*, ed. Henry J. Steiner and Philip Alston (Oxford: Clarendon Press, 1996), 211.

57. Ibid., 212.

58. Riffat Hassan, "An Islamic Perspective," in *Women, Religion, and Sexuality: Studies on the Impact of Religious Teachings on Women*, ed. Jeanne Beecher (Philadelphia: Trinity Press International, 1991), 99.

59. Ibid., 116.

60. Ibid., 110.

61. Ibid., 102.

62. Surah 4:34, trans. A. A. Maududi, as quoted in ibid., 110.

63. Hassan, "An Islamic Perspective," 117.

64. *The Qur'an: The Revelation Vouchsafed to Muhammad the Seal of the Prophets* (in Arabic and English), trans. Muhammad Zafrulla Khan (London: Curzon Press, 1971; reprint 1985). See also Leila Ahmed, *Women and Gender in Islam* (New Haven, CT: Yale Univ. Press, 1992), 42.

65. Esther K. Hicks, *Infibulation: Female Mutilation in Islamic Northeastern Africa* (London: Transactions Publishers, 1996), 79; and Shapiro, "Cross-Cultural Perspectives on Sexual Differentiation," 291.

66. This can be compared to the Greek and Christian notion of dualism, whereby femininity is considered inferior. See also Janice Boddy, *Wombs and Alien Spirits: Women, Men, and the Zar Cult in Northern Sudan* (Madison: Univ. of Wisconsin Press, 1989), 53.

67. Hassan, "An Islamic Perspective," 117.

68. Ibid., 116–18.

69. Ibid., 119.

70. Surah 4:34, in An-Na'im, "Human Rights in the Muslim World," 214.

71. An-Na'im, "Human Rights in the Muslim World," 214.

72. Schwartz and Rutter, *The Gender of Sexuality*, 73–74.

73. An-Na'im, "Human Rights in the Muslim World," 215.

74. Shapiro, "Cross-Cultural Perspectives on Sexual Differentiation," 22. Today veiling is seen by some as a fashion among upper-class women. Among other Muslims it is an emblem of political, economic, and cultural emancipation and is perceived as a means to assert their multifaceted identities (Nawal El Saadawi, *The Nawal El Saadawi Reader* [London: Zed Books, 1997], 95).

75. Hassan, "An Islamic Perspective," 119.

76. El Saadawi, *The Nawal El Saadawi Reader*, 95.

77. Fran P. Hosken, *The Hosken Report: Genital and Sexual Mutilation of Females*, 4th ed. (Lexington, MA: Women's International Network News, 1993), 40; and Hassan, "An Islamic Perspective," 118.

78. Margaret Strobel, "Women in Religion and in Secular Ideology," in *African Women South of the Sahara*, ed. Margaret Jean Hay and Sharon Sticher (London: Longman Group, 1984), 98.

79. Strobel, "Women in Religion and in Secular Ideology," 94, 98. It is important to note that in Kenya, veiling is considered a sign of respect among some Muslim women.

80. El Saadawi, *The Nawal El Saadawi Reader*, 73, 86.

5 RELIGION AND FEMALE CIRCUMCISION

1. See Catherine Coquery-Vidrovitch, *African Women: A Modern History* (Boulder, CO: Westview Press, 1997), 207; and Angela Wasunna, "Towards Redirecting the Female Circumcision Debate: Legal, Ethical, and Cultural Considerations," *McGill Journal of Medicine* 5 (2002): 104.

2. Coquery-Vidrovitch, *African Women*, 207.

3. Ibid.

4. Sami Awad Aldeeb Abu-Sahlieh, *Male and Female Circumcision among Jews, Christians, and Muslims: Religious, Medical, Social, and Legal Debate* (Warren Center, PA: Shangri-La Publications, 2001), 223–24; see also Fuambai Ahmadu, "Rites and Wrongs: An Insider/Outsider Reflects on Power and Excision," in *Female "Circumcision" in Africa: Culture, Controversy and Change*, ed. Bettina Shell-Duncan and Ylva Herlund (Boulder, CO: Lynne Rienner Publishers, 2000), 295–96.

5. Coquery-Vidrovitch, *African Women*, 207; and Wasunna, "Towards Redirecting the Female Circumcision Debate,"104.

6. Coquery-Vidrovitch, *African Women*, 207.

7. These categories are also outlined in Wassuna, "Towards Redirecting the Female Circumcision Debate," 105–7; and Efua Dorkenoo, *Cutting the Rose: Female Genital Mutilation: The Practice, and Its Prevention* (London: Minority Rights Publication, 1994), 34–41.

8. John S. Mbiti, *African Religions and Philosophy* (London: Heinemann Educational Books, 1990), 121–29; see also L. Amede Obiora, "Bridges and Barricades: Rethinking Polemics and Intransigence in the Campaign against Female Circumcision," *Case Western Reserve Law Review* 47, no. 2 (1997): 296.

9. Wasunna, "Towards Redirecting the Female Circumcision Debate," 105.

10. Bettina Shell-Duncan, Walter Obungu Obiero, and Leunita Auko Muruli, "Women without Choices: The Debate over Medicalization of Female Genital Cutting and Its Impact on a Northern Kenyan Community," in Shell-Duncan and Hernlund, *Female "Circumcision" in Africa*, 118.

11. Dorkenoo, *Cutting the Rose*, 23.

12. Kim Longinotto, *The Day I Will Never Forget* (London: Women Make Movies, 2002).

13. Jean Davison, *Voices from Mutira: Change in the Lives of Rural Gikuyu Women, 1910–1995*, 2nd ed. (Boulder, CO: Lynne Rienner Publishers, 1996), 118.

14. Obiora, "Bridges and Barricades," 297.

15. Janice Boddy, *Wombs and Alien Spirits: Women, Men, and the Zar Cult in Northern Sudan* (Madison: Univ. of Wisconsin Press, 1989), 74; and Ellen Gruenbaum, *The Female Circumcision Controversy: An Anthropological Perspective* (Philadelphia: Univ. of Pennsylvania Press, 2001), 73.

16. Chebet, personal interview. All interviews in this section were carried out by the author between August 2002 and August 2004.

17. Gitobu, personal interview, August 10, 2003.

18. Ngonya, quoted in Kim Longinotto, *The Day I Will Never Forget.*

19. Abu-Sahlieh, *Male and Female Circumcision among Jews, Christians, and Muslims*, 206.

20. Mbiti, *African Religions and Philosophy*, 114.

21. Ciarunji Chesaina, "Images of Women in African Oral Literature: A Case Study of the Kalenjin and the Maasai Oral Narrative," in *Understanding Oral Literature*, ed. Austin Bukenya, Wanjiku Mukabi Kabira, and Okoth Okombo (Nairobi: Nairobi Univ. Press, 1994), 88; and Margaret Carey, *Myths and Legends of Africa* (New York: Hamlyn Publishing Group, 1970), 92–97.

22. Abu-Sahlieh, *Male and Female Circumcision among Jews, Christians, and Muslims*, 130; and Mbiti, *African Religions and Philosophy*, 118–19.

23. Geoffrey Parrinder, *Sex in the World Religions* (New York: Oxford Univ. Press, 1980), 130; Ahmadu, "Rites and Wrongs," 295–96, 187–89; and Abu-Sahlieh, *Male and Female Circumcision among Jews, Christians, and Muslims*, 223–24.

24. The concept of bisexuality also has its Western proponents; see details in Abu-Sahlieh, *Male and Female Circumcision among Jews, Christians, and Muslims*, 224.

25. Parrinder, *Sex in the World Religions*, 130; and Abu-Sahlieh, *Male and Female Circumcision among Jews, Christians, and Muslims*, 224.

26. See this narrative in Longinotto, *The Day I Will Never Forget.*

27. Ngonya's words are quoted in ibid.

28. Mercy Amba Oduyoye, *Daughters of Anowa: African Women and Patriarchy* (Maryknoll, NY: Orbis Books, 1999), 179.

29. Malcolm J. McVeigh, "Theological Issues Related to Kenyan Religious Independency," in *Kenya Churches Handbook: The Development of Kenyan Christianity 1498–1973*, ed. David B. Barrett et al. (Kisumu, Kenya: Evangel Publishing House, 1973), 140–43; and F. B. Welbourn and B. A Ogot, *A Place to Feel at Home: A Study of Two Independent Churches in Western Kenya* (Nairobi: Oxford Univ. Press, 1966), 166.

30. Rotich, personal interview, July 2003.

31. Mbiti, *African Religions and Philosophy*, 122; and Obiora, "Bridges and Barricades," 295–98.

32. Hosken, Fran P., *The Hosken Report: Genital and Sexual Mutilation of Females*, 4th ed. (Lexington, MA: Women's International Network News, 1993), 40, 51; and Abu-Sahlieh, *Male and Female Circumcision among Jews, Christians, and Muslims*, 216–17.

33. Mbiti, *African Religions and Philosophy*, 127; and Mary Nyangweso, "Christ's Salvific Message and the Nandi Ritual of Female Circumcision," *Theological Studies* 63 (2002): 584.

34. Hosken, *The Hosken Report*, 39, 40–51; and Maendeleo Ya Wanawake Organization (MYWO), *Harmful Traditional Practices That Affect the Health of the Women and Their Children* (Nairobi: MYWO, 1993), 20.

35. Mbiti, *African Religions and Philosophy*, 121–22.

36. Ibid., 122.

37. Men are given a spear after circumcision as a symbol of their adulthood. The initiate is expected to use the spear to confront and kill a lion to show his courage. The spear is also used to indicate to potential admirers of the woman to whom he is married or whom he has visited for the night that the house is already occupied. He does this by sticking the spear outside the entrance of the house.

38. Mbiti, *African Religions and Philosphy*, 165–166; and idem, *Concepts of God in Africa* (London: SPCK, 1970), 81.

39. Abu-Sahlieh, *Male and Female Circumcision among Jews, Christians, and Muslims*, 151; and Mbiti, *African Religions and Philosophy*, 165–66.

40. Hosken, *The Hosken Report*, 326–27.

41. Ibid., 171; and Abu-Sahlieh, *Male and Female Circumcision among Jews, Christians, and Muslims*, 151.

42. Hosken, *The Hosken Report*, 163; and Mbiti, *African Religions and Philosophy*, 107–8.

43. Jomo Kenyatta, *Facing Mount Kenya: The Tribal Life of the Gikuyu* (New York: Vintage Books, 1962 [1938]), 127, 175–76.

44. Abu-Sahlieh, *Male and Female Circumcision among Jews, Christians, and Muslims*, 122.

45. Ibid., 11.

46. Dorkenoo, *Cutting the Rose*, 36; Ladislav Holy, *Religion and Custom in a Muslim Society: The Berti of Sudan* (New York: Cambridge Univ. Press, 1991), 164; Abu-Sahlieh, *Male and Female Circumcision among Jews, Christians, and Muslims*, 110–27; and Longinotto, *The Day I Will Never Forget*.

47. Abu-Sahlieh, *Male and Female Circumcision among Jews, Christians, and Muslims*, 104–5, 122.

48. Leila Ahmed, *Women and Gender in Islam* (New Haven, CT: Yale Univ. Press, 1992), 175–76; and Riffat Hassan, "An Islamic Perspective," in *Women, Religion, and Sexuality: Studies on the Impact of Religious Teachings on Women*, ed. Jeanne Beecher, 93–128 (Philadelphia: Trinity Press International, 1991), 118.

49. Hosken, *The Hosken Report*, 40.

50. Abu-Sahlieh, *Male and Female Circumcision among Jews, Christians, and Muslims*, 112.

51. Ibid., 99.

52. Ibid., 100–101.

53. Ibid., 111.

54. Ibid., 112.

55. Ibid., 111–12.

56. Ibid., 114, 120; and Barbara Freyer Stowasser, *Women in the Qur'an: Traditions and Interpretation* (New York: Oxford Univ. Press, 1994), 147.

57. Dorkenoo, *Cutting the Rose*, 37–38; and Abu-Sahlieh, *Male and Female Circumcision among Jews, Christians, and Muslims*, 122.

58. Sheikh Mahmoud Shaltout, quoted in Dorkenoo, *Cutting the Rose*, 37. Although the exact date is not indicated, this *fatwa* was definitely issued before 1981.

59. Dorkenoo, *Cutting the Rose*, 37–38.

60. Abu-Sahlieh, *Male and Female Circumcision among Jews, Christians, and Muslims*, 143, 172–73; and Boddy, *Wombs and Alien Spirits*, 55–59.

61. Abu-Sahlieh, *Male and Female Circumcision among Jews, Christians, and Muslims*, 143.

62. Boddy, *Wombs and Alien Spirits*, 58, 74.

63. Hicks, *Infibulation*, 27–28; see also Abu-Sahlieh, *Male and Female Circumcision among Jews, Christians, and Muslims*, 215.

64. Mbiti, *African Religions and Philosophy*, 245.

65. Margaret Strobel, "Women in Religion and in Secular Ideology," in *African Women South of the Sahara*, ed. Margaret Jean Hay and Sharon Sticher (London: Longman Group, 1984), 91–92.

66. Ibid., 91–92.

67. Longinotto, *The Day I Will Never Forget*.

68. Abu-Sahlieh, *Male and Female Circumcision among Jews, Christians, and Muslims*, 150.

69. Sheik Abd-al-Rahman Al-Najjar, quoted in ibid., 109.

70. Dr. Usamah, quoted in ibid., 262.

71. Abu-Sahlieh, *Male and Female Circumcision among Jews, Christians, and Muslims*, 112–13; and Hassan, "An Islamic Perspective," 118.

72. See also Rom 2:28–29, Acts 11:3; Acts 10:28; 1 Cor 7:18–20; Gal 2:12; Gal 5:1–2, 4; and Abu-Sahlieh, *Male and Female Circumcision among Jews, Christians, and Muslims*, 73–74, 91.

73. Jomo Kenyatta, "Christianity and Clitoridectomy," in *Christianity in Africa: As Seen by Africans*, ed. Ram Desai (Denver, CO: Alan Swallow, 1962), 86; and Abu-Sahlieh, *Male and Female Circumcision among Jews, Christians, and Muslims*, 217–18.

74. Abu-Sahlieh, *Male and Female Circumcision among Jews, Christians, and Muslims*, 219.

75. Kenyatta, "Christianity and Clitoridectomy," 101; and Kenyatta, *Facing Mount Kenya*, 261.

76. Kenyatta, *Facing Mount Kenya*, 4; and Teresia M. Hinga, "Jesus Christ and the Liberation of Women in Africa," in *The Will to Arise: Women, Tradition,*

and the Church in Africa, ed. Mercy Amba Oduyoye and Musimbi R. A. Kanyoro (Maryknoll, NY: Orbis Books, 1992), 188.

77. Kenyatta, *Facing Mount Kenya*, 261.

78. Ibid., 266.

79. Kenyatta, "Christianity and Clitoridectomy," 86.

80. A. J. Temu, *British Protestant Missions* (London: Longman Group, 1972), 132; and Hosken, *The Hosken Report*, 169.

81. Jan Ham Boer, *Missionary Messages of Liberation in a Colonial Context: A Case Study of Sudan United Mission* (Amsterdam: Rodop, 1979), 237.

82. John Murray, "Varieties of Kikuyu Independent Churches," in Barrett et al., *Kenya Churches Handbook*, 129; and Kenyatta, *Facing Mount Kenya*, 261.

83. Lynn Thomas, "*Ngaitana* (I Will Circumcise Myself): Lessons from Colonial Campaigns to Ban Excision in Meru, Kenya," in Shell-Duncan and Hernlund, *Female "Circumcision" in Africa*, 132.

84. Jocelyn M. Murray, "The Kikuyu Female Circumcision Controversy, with Special Reference to the Church Missionary Society's 'Sphere of Influence.'" Ph.D. dissertation (Los Angeles: UCLA, 1974; Ann Arbor, MI: UMI Library West: DT 433.575.M7x), 339; and Hosken, *The Hosken Report*, 170.

85. Murray, "The Kikuyu Female Circumcision Controversy," 228; and Hosken, *The Hosken Report*, 169.

86. Murray, "The Kikuyu Female Circumcision Controversy," 228.

87. Dorkenoo, *Cutting the Rose*, 38.

88. In Dorkenoo, *Cutting the Rose*, 39.

89. Hinga, "Jesus Christ and the Liberation of Women in Africa," 188; Murray, "Varieties of Kikuyu Independent Churches," 129; and Strobel, "Women in Religion and in Secular Ideology," 96.

90. Thomas, "*Ngaitana* (I Will Circumcise Myself)," 132–33.

91. Murray, "Varieties of Kikuyu Independent Churches," 129.

92. Kenyatta, "Christianity and Clitoridectomy," 88.

93. Strobel, "Women in Religion and in Secular Ideology," 96.

94. Robert J. Schreiter, *Constructing Local Theologies* (Maryknoll, NY: Orbis Books, 1997), 1, 5–6.

95. Abu-Sahlieh, *Male and Female Circumcision among Jews, Christians, and Muslims*, 284.

6 TRANSFORMING ATTITUDES TOWARD FEMALE CIRCUMCISION

1. Mark Lacey, "Genital Cutting Shows Signs of Losing Favor in Africa," *New York Times*, June 8, 2004.

2. Margaret Carey, *Myths and Legends of Africa* (New York: Hamlyn Publishing Group, 1970), 92–97; John S. Mbiti, *African Religions and Philosophy* (London: Heinemann Educational Books, 1990), 59.

3. Christine J. Walley, "Searching for 'Voices': Feminism, Anthropology, and the Global Debate over Female Genital Operations," in *Genital Cutting and Transnational Sisterhood: Disputing US Polemics*, ed. Stanlie M. James and Claire C. Robertson (Urbana: Univ. of Illinois Press, 2002), 31.

4. Robyn S. Cerny-Smith, "Female Circumcision: Bringing Women's Perspectives into the International Debate," *Southern California Law Review* 65, no. 5 (1992): 2460.

5. Micere Githae Mugo, "Elitist Anti-Circumcision Discourse as Mutilating and Anti-Feminist," *Case Western Reserve Law Review* 47, no. 2 (1997): 464.

6. Ibid.

7. Mercy Amba Oduyoye, *Daughters of Anowa: African Women and Patriarchy* (Maryknoll, NY: Orbis Books, 1999), 171.

8. Traci West, *Wounds of the Spirit: Black Women, Violence, and Resistance Ethics* (New York: New York Univ. Press, 1999), 155.

9. Oduyoye, *Daughters of Anowa*, 160.

10. Mugo, "Elitist Anti-Circumcision Discourse as Mutilating and Anti-Feminist," 477.

11. Musimbi R. A. Kanyoro, "Cultural Hermeneutics: An African Contribution," in *Other Ways of Reading African Women and the Bible*, ed. Musa W. Dube (Geneva: WCC Publications, 2001), 106.

12. Joyce K. Umbima, "Kenya: Mothers in Action," in *Women, Violence and Non-Violent Change*, ed. Aruna Gnanadason, Musimbi R. A. Kanyoro and Lucia Ann McSpadden (Geneva: WCC Publications, 1996), 100.

13. Cerny-Smith, "Female Circumcision," 2502.

14. Kim Longinotto, *The Day I Will Never Forget* (London: Women Make Movies, 2002).

15. Hadija, personal interview, July 2003; the interviews were held 2002–3.

16. Ingrid Naess, quoted in "Missionaries Successful in Curbing Female Mutilation in Kenya," *Afrol News*, December 11, 2000. Available online.

17. Ibid.

18. Christian Smith, "Correcting a Curious Neglect or Bringing Religion Back In," in *Disruptive Religion: The Force of Faith in Social Movement Activism*, ed. Christian Smith, 1–25 (New York: Routledge, 1996), 1–3.

19. Ibid.

20. Peter Berger, *The Sacred Canopy: Elements of a Sociological Theory of Religion* (New York: Anchor Books, 1990), 27–32; Clifford Geertz, *The Interpretation of Cultures* (New York: Basic Books, 1973), 131.

21. Emile Durkheim, *The Elementary Forms of Religious Life*, trans. Karen E. Fields (New York: Free Press, 1995), 227.

22. Alfred T. Hennelly, ed., *Liberation Theology: A Documentary History* (Maryknoll, NY: Orbis Books, 1990), xx–xxi.

23. Muhammad Mashuq Ibn Ally, "Theology of Islamic Liberation," in *World Religions and Human Liberation*, ed. Daniel C. Cohn-Sherbok (Maryknoll, NY: Orbis Books, 1992), 46–60.

24. Smith, "Correcting a Curious Neglect or Bringing Religion Back In," 9.

25. Ibid.

26. William Gamson, W. Bruce Fireman, and Steven Rytina, *Encounters with Unjust Authority* (Chicago: Dorsey Press, 1982); Smith, "Correcting a Curious Neglect or Bringing Religion Back In," 10.

27. Galatians 3:28 reads, "There is no longer Jew nor Greek, there is no longer slave or free, there is no longer male or female; for all of you are one in Christ Jesus." Interestingly, the following verse, "And if you belong to Christ, then you are Abraham's offspring, heirs according to the promise," has been used to support female circumcision.

28. Smith, "Correcting a Curious Neglect or Bringing Religion Back In," 13.

29. Sami Awad Aldeeb Abu-Sahlieh, *Male and Female Circumcision among Jews, Christians, and Muslims: Religious, Medical, Social, and Legal Debate* (Warren Center, PA: Shangri-La Publications, 2001), 284.

30. Ibid., 285.

31. Lang'at, personal interview, August 2003.

32. Fauziya Kassindja was granted asylum in the United States after careful consideration of her case and after a Harvard University legal team substantiated her claim to refugee status (see Fauziya Kassindja, *Do They Hear You When You Cry?* [New York: Delacorte Press, 1998]).

33. Smith, "Correcting a Curious Neglect or Bringing Religion Back In," 17.

34. Juan Luis Segundo, *The Liberation of Theology* (Maryknoll, NY: Orbis Books, 1976), 8.

35. This is also discussed in Elisabeth Schüssler Fiorenza, *Bread Not Stone: The Challenge of Feminist Biblical Interpretation* (Boston: Beacon Press, 1984), 49–52.

36. Segundo, *The Liberation of Theology*, 9.

37. Ibid.; see Schüssler Fiorenza, *Bread Not Stone*, 50.

38. Segundo, *The Liberation of Theology*, 9.

39. Ibid., 8.

40. Schüssler Fiorenza, *Bread Not Stone*, 52.

41. Ibid.

42. Ibid., 55.

43. Ibid., 55, 61.

44. Kanyoro, "Cultural Hermeneutics," 106–7.

45. Ibid., 107.

46. Ibid.

47. Ibid., 66–67.

48. Asghar Ali Engineer, "Religion and Liberation," in *Religion and Liberation*, ed. Asghar Ali Engineer (Jawahar Nagar Delhi: Ajanta Publications, 1989), 3.

49. Mary Nyangweso, "Christ's Salvific Message and the Nandi Ritual of Female Circumcision," *Theological Studies* 63 (2002): 579–600.

50. Ibid., 595–96.

51. Anne Nasimiyu-Wasike, "Christology and an African Woman's Experience," in *Faces of Jesus in Africa*, ed. Robert J. Schreiter (Maryknoll, NY: Orbis Books, 1991), 72–73; and Teresia M. Hinga, "Jesus Christ and the Liberation of Women in Africa," in *The Will to Arise: Women, Tradition, and the Church in Africa*, ed. Mercy Amba Oduyoye and Musimbi R. A. Kanyoro (Maryknoll, NY: Orbis Books, 1992), 190–91.

52. Hinga, "Jesus Christ and the Liberation of Women in Africa," 191–92.

53. See Kofi Appiah-Kubi, "Christology," in *A Reader on African Christian Theology*, ed. John Parratt (London: SPCK, 1987), 74–75; and Nyangweso, "Christ's Salvific Message and the Nandi Ritual of Female Circumcision," 596–98.

54. For a detailed discussion of these texts, see Rebecca Merrill Groothuis, *Good News for Women: A Biblical Picture of Gender Equality* (Grand Rapids, MI: Baker Books, 1997), 209–29.

55. Muhammad Mashuq Ibn Ally, "Theology of Islamic Liberation," 45–46, 59–60.

56. Asghar Ali Engineer, "Religion, Ideology, and Liberation Theology," in *Religion and Liberation*, ed. Asghar Ali Engineer (Jawahar Nagar Delhi: Ajanta Publications, 1989), 143–44.

57. Surah citations in this chapter are taken from *Al-Qur'an: A Contemporary Translation*, rev. ed., trans. Ahmen Ali (Princeton, NJ: Princeton Univ. Press, 1988).

58. Rabiatu Ammah, "Paradise Lies at the Feet of Muslim Women," in Oduyoye and Kanyoro, *The Will to Arise*, 75.

59. Ibid.

60. Riffat Hassan, "An Islamic Perspective," in *Women, Religion, and Sexuality: Studies on the Impact of Religious Teachings on Women*, ed. Jeanne Beecher (Philadelphia: Trinity Press International, 1991), 117; and Asghar Ali Engineer, *The Rights of Women in Islam* (New York: St. Martin's Press, 1992), 21.

61. Abu-Sahlieh, *Male and Female Circumcision among Jews, Christians, and Muslims*, 112–13.

62. Ammah, "Paradise Lies at the Feet of Muslim Women," 79; and Engineer, *The Rights of Women in Islam*, 29.

63. Ammah, "Paradise Lies at the Feet of Muslim Women," 79.

64. Engineer, *The Rights of Women in Islam*, 22.

65. Leila Ahmed, *Women and Gender in Islam* (New Haven, CT: Yale Univ. Press, 1992), 63.

66. Ibid., 63, 67–69.

67. Ibid., 67.

68. Denise Lardner Carmody, *Women and World Religions*, 2nd ed. (Englewood Cliffs, NJ: Prentice-Hall, 1989), 197.

69. Wilhelmina Oduol, "Kenya Women's Movement: A Diagnosis of the Political Participation in Retrospect," in *The Women's Movement in Kenya*, ed. S. A. Khasiani and E. I. Njiro (Nairobi: AAWORD-Kenya, 1993), 24–26; and Tabitha Kanogo, "Kikuyu Women and the Politics of Protest: Mau Mau," in *Images of Women in Peace and War: Cross Cultural Historical Perspectives*, ed. Sharon MacDonald, Pat Holden, and Shirley Ardener (London: Macmillan, 1987), 78–79.

70. Kanogo, "Kikuyu Women and the Politics of Protest"; also discussed in Oduol, "Kenya Women's Movement."

71. Oduyoye, *Daughters of Anowa*, 91–96.

72. Hannah Kinoti, "Women and Spirit Possession," in *Groaning in Faith: African Women in the Household of God*, ed. Musimbi R. A. Kanyoro and Nyambura J. Njoroge (Nairobi: Acton Publishers, 1996), 231–32.

73. Vincent Crapanzano, "Introduction to Case Studies of Spirit Possession," in *Case Studies of Spirit Possession*, ed. Vincent Crapanzano and Vivian Garrison (New York: John Wesley, 1977), 10.

74. Janice Boddy, *Wombs and Alien Spirits: Women, Men, and the Zar Cult in Northern Sudan* (Madison: Univ. of Wisconsin Press, 1989), 133.

75. Kinoti, "Women and Spirit Possession," 239.

76. Ibid.

77. Nyambura J. Njoroge, "The Bible and African Christianity: A Curse or a Blessing?" in *Other Ways of Reading: African Women and the Bible*, ed. Musa W. Dube (Geneva: WCC Publications, 2001), 230.

Bibliography

BOOKS AND ARTICLES

Abu-Sahlieh, Sami Awad Aldeeb. *Male and Female Circumcision among Jews, Christians, and Muslims: Religious, Medical, Social, and Legal Debate*. Warren Center, PA: Shangri-La Publications, 2001.

Ahmadu, Fuambai. "Rites and Wrongs: An Insider/Outsider Reflects on Power and Excision." In *Female "Circumcision" in Africa: Culture, Controversy, and Change*, edited by Bettina Shell-Duncan and Ylva Herlund, 283-312. Boulder, CO: Lynne Rienner Publishers, 2000.

Ahmed, Leila. *Women and Gender in Islam*. New Haven, CT: Yale Univ. Press, 1992.

Amadiume, Ifi. *Daughters of the Goddess, Daughters of Imperialism: African Women Struggle for Culture, Power, and Democracy*. London: Zed Books, 2000.

Ammah, Rabiatu. "Paradise Lies at the Feet of Muslim Women." In *The Will to Arise: Women, Tradition, and the Church in Africa*, edited by Mercy Amba Oduyoye and Musimbi R. A. Kanyoro, 74-86. Maryknoll, NY: Orbis Books, 1992.

Amoah, Elizabeth. "Femaleness: Akan Concepts and Practices." In *Women, Religion and Sexuality: Studies on the Impact of Religious Teachings on Women*, edited by Jeanne Beecher, 128-53. Philadelphia: Trinity Press International, 1991.

——. "Violence and Women's Bodies in African Perspective." In *Women Resisting Violence: Spirituality for Life*, edited by Mary J. Mananzan, Mercy A. Oduyoye, Elsa Tamez, J. Shannon Clarkson, Mary C. Grey, and Letty Russell, 80-88. Maryknoll, NY: Orbis Books, 1996.

An-Na'im, Abdullahi Ahmed. "Human Rights in the Muslim World." In *International Human Rights in Context: Law, Politics, Morals*, edited by Henry J. Steiner and Philip Alston, 210-20. Oxford: Clarendon Press, 1996.

Anderson, W. B. "A History of the Kenya Churches." In *Kenya Churches Handbook: The Development of Kenyan Christianity 1498-1973*, edited by David Barrett, George K. Mambo, Janice McLaughlin, and Malcolm J. McVeigh, 29-34. Kisumu, Kenya: Evangel Publishing House, 1973.

Appiah-Kubi, Kofi. "Christology." In *A Reader on African Christian Theology*, edited by John Parratt, 69-81. London: SPCK, 1987.

Augustine, Saint. *The City of God.* Translated by Marcus Dods. New York: The Modern Library, 1950, 464-71.

Babatunde, Emmanuel. *Women's Rights Versus Women's Rites: A Study of Circumcision among the Ketu Yoruba of South Western Nigeria.* Trenton, NJ: Africa World Press, 1998.

Barrett, David B. "The Expansion of Christianity in Kenya AD 1900-2000." In *Kenya Churches Handbook: The Development of Kenyan Christianity 1498-1973,* edited by David B. Barrett, George K. Mambo, Janice McLaughlin, and Malcolm J. McVeigh, 157-91. Kisumu, Kenya: Evangel Publishing House, 1973.

Barrett, David B., George T. Kurian, and Todd M. Johnson, eds. *World Christian Encyclopedia: A Comparative Survey of Churches and Religions in the Modern World.* Oxford: Oxford Univ. Press, 2001.

Beckwith, Francis, and Gregory Koukl. *Relativism: Feet Firmly Planted in Mid-Air.* Grand Rapids, MI: Baker Books, 1998.

Beecher, Jeanne, ed. *Women, Religion and Sexuality: Studies on the Impact of Religious Teachings on Women.* Philadelphia: Trinity Press International, 1991.

Bell, Linda. *Rethinking Ethics in the Midst of Violence: A Feminist Approach to Freedom.* Lanham, MD: Rowman and Littlefield Publishers, 1993.

Berger, Peter. *The Sacred Canopy: Elements of a Sociological Theory of Religion.* New York: Anchor Books, 1990.

Boddy, Janice. *Wombs and Alien Spirits: Women, Men, and the Zar Cult in Northern Sudan.* Madison: Univ. of Wisconsin Press, 1989.

Boer, Jan Ham. *Missionary Messages of Liberation in a Colonial Context: A Case Study of Sudan United Mission.* Amsterdam: Rodop, 1979.

Bonvillain, Nancy. *Women and Men: Cultural Constructs of Gender.* 3d ed. Upper Saddle River, NJ: Prentice-Hall, 2000.

Bouldware-Miller, Kay. "Female Circumcision: Challenges to the Practice as Human Rights Violation." *Harvard Human Rights Journal* 8; *Women's Law Journal* (1985): 155-64.

Bujo, Bénézet. *Foundations of an African Ethic: Beyond the Universal Claims of Western Morality.* New York: Crossroad, 2001.

Bullough, Vern L. "A Historical Perspective." In *Theories of Human Sexuality,* edited by James H. Geer and William T. O'Donohue, 49-62. New York: Plenum Press, 1987.

Carmody, Denise Lardner. *Women and World Religions.* 2nd ed. Englewood Cliffs, NJ: Prentice Hall, 1989.

Carey, Margaret. *Myths and Legends of Africa.* New York: Hamlyn Publishing Group, 1970.

Central Intelligence Agency. *The World Factbook, 2003.*

———. *The World Factbook, 2006.* Available at http://www.cia.gov/cia/publications/factbook/geos/ke.html.

Cerny-Smith, Robyn S. "Female Circumcision: Bringing Women's Perspectives into the International Debate." *Southern California Law Review* 65, no. 5 (1992): 2470-2502.

"Charge Them with Murder," *Daily Nation Online*, December 7, 2004. Available online.

Chesaina, Ciarunji. "Images of Women in African Oral Literature: A Case Study of the Kalenjin and the Maasai Oral Narrative." In *Understanding Oral Literature*, edited by Austin Bukenya, Wanjiku Mukabi Kabira, and Okoth Okombo, 85-92. Nairobi: Nairobi Univ. Press, 1994.

Coquery-Vidrovitch, Catherine. *African Women: A Modern History*. Boulder, CO: Westview Press, 1997.

Crapanzano, Vincent. "Introduction to Case Studies of Spirit Possession." In *Case Studies of Spirit Possession*, edited by Vincent Crapanzano and Vivian Garrison, 1-39. New York: John Wesley, 1977.

Daly, Mary. *Gyn/Ecology: The Metaethics of Radical Feminism*. Boston: Beacon Press, 1978.

Davison, Jean. *Voices from Mutira: Change in the Lives of Rural Gikuyu Women, 1910-1995*, 2nd ed. Boulder, CO: Lynne Rienner Publishers, 1996.

DeLamater, John. "A Sociological Approach." In *Theories of Human Sexuality*, edited by James Geer and William F. O'Donohue, 237-53. New York: Plenum Press, 1987.

Desai, Ram, ed. *Christianity in Africa: As Seen by Africans*. Denver: Alan Swallow, 1962.

———. "Christianity in Danger." In *Christianity in Africa: As Seen by Africans*, edited by Ram Desai, 11-36. Denver: Alan Swallow, 1962.

Dorkenoo, Efua. *Cutting the Rose: Female Genital Mutilation: The Practice, and Its Prevention*. London: Minority Rights Publication, 1994.

———, and Scilla Elworthy, *Female Genital Mutilation: Proposals for Change*. Rev. ed. London: Minority Rights Group International, Report 92/3, Library West: GN484. F44 1992.

Durkheim, Emile. *The Elementary Forms of Religious Life*. Translated by Karen E. Fields. New York: The Free Press, 1995.

El Dareer, Asma. *Woman, Why Do You Weep? Circumcision and Its Consequences*. London: Zed Books, 1982.

Saadawi, Nawal El. *The Nawal El Saadawi Reader*. London: Zed Books, 1997.

Engineer, Asghar Ali. "Religion and Liberation." In *Religion and Liberation*, edited by Asghar Ali Engineer, 1-12. Jawahar Nagar Delhi: Ajanta Publications, 1989.

———. "Religion, Ideology, and Liberation Theology—An Islamic Point of View." In *Religion and Liberation*, edited by Asghar Ali Engineer, 135-48. Jawahar Nagar Delhi: Ajanta Publications, 1989.

———. *The Rights of Women in Islam*. New York: St. Martin's Press, 1992.

Flanagan, Jane. "Kenyan Sisters Win Judgment on Circumcision." *News Telegraph*, December 17, 2000.Available from www.telegraph.co.uk/news/main.jhtml?xml=/news/2000/12/17/wcirc17.xml

Freire, Paulo. "Conscientization as a Way of Liberating." In *Liberation Theology: A Documentary History*, edited by Alfred T. Hennelly, SJ, 5-13. Maryknoll, NY: Orbis Books, 1970.

———. *Education for Critical Consciousness*. New York: Continuum, 1987.

Friday, Nancy. *My Secret Garden*. New York: Pocket Books, 1973.

Gagnon, John H. "The Interaction of Gender Roles and Sexual Conduct." In *Human Sexuality: A Comparative and Developmental Perspective*, edited by Herant A. Katchadourian, 225-45. Berkeley and Los Angeles: Univ. of California Press, 1979.

Gamson, William, W. Bruce Fireman, and Steven Rytina. *Encounters with Unjust Authority*. Chicago: Dorsey Press, 1982.

Geertz, Clifford. *The Interpretation of Cultures*. New York: Basic Books, 1973.

Gifford, Euginie Anne. "The Courage to Blaspheme: Confronting Barriers to Resisting Female Genital Mutilation." *UCLA Women's Law Journal* 4 (1994): 329-64.

Githieya, Francis Kimani. *The Freedom of the Spirit: African Indigenous Churches in Kenya*. Atlanta, GA: Scholars Press, 1997.

———. "The Church of the Holy Spirit: Biblical Beliefs and Practices of the Arathi of Kenya, 1926-1950." In *East African Expressions of Christianity*, edited by Thomas Spear and Isaria N. Kimambo, 231-44. Nairobi: East African Educational Publishers, 1999.

Green, December. *Gender Violence in Africa: African Women's Response*. New York: St. Martin's Press, 1999.

Groothuis, Rebecca Merrill. *Good News for Women: A Biblical Picture of Gender Equality*. Grand Rapids, MI: Baker Books, 1997.

Gruenbaum, Ellen. *The Female Circumcision Controversy: An Anthropological Perspective*. Philadelphia: Univ. of Pennsylvania Press, 2001.

Gunning, Isabelle. "Arrogant Perception, World Traveling, and Multicultural Feminism: The Case of Female Genital Surgeries." *Columbia Human Rights Law Review* 23 (1992): 189-248.

Hackett, Rosalind I. J. "Women and New Religious Movements in Africa." In *Gender and Religion*, edited by Ursula King, 257-290. Oxford: Blackwell, 1994.

Hassan, Riffat. "An Islamic Perspective." In *Women, Religion, and Sexuality: Studies on the Impact of Religious Teachings on Women*, edited by Jeanne Beecher, 93-128. Philadelphia: Trinity Press International, 1991.

Hennelly, Alfred T., ed. *Liberation Theology: A Documentary History*. Maryknoll, NY: Orbis Books, 1990.

Hernlund, Ylva. "Cutting without Ritual and Ritual without Cutting: Female 'Circumcision' and the Re-ritualization of Initiation in the Gambia." In *Female "Circumcision" in Africa: Culture, Controversy, and Change*, edited by Bettina Shell-Duncan and Ylva Hernlund, 235-52, Boulder, CO: Lynne Rienner Publishers, 2000.

Hicks, Esther K. *Infibulation: Female Mutilation in Islamic Northeastern Africa*. London: Transactions Publishers, 1996.

Hinga, Teresia M. "Jesus Christ and the Liberation of Women in Africa." In *The Will to Arise: Women, Tradition, and the Church in Africa*, edited by Mercy Amba Oduyoye and Musimbi R. A. Kanyoro, 183-94. Maryknoll, NY: Orbis Books, 1992.

Hite, Shere. *The Hite Report: A Nationwide Study of Female Sexuality*. New York: Macmillan, 1976.

Hodgson, Dorothy L. *Once Warrior's Gender, Ethnicity, and the Cultural Politics of Maasai Development*. Bloomington: Indiana Univ. Press, 2001.

Holway, James D. "Islam in Kenya and Relations with the Churches." In *Kenya Churches Handbook: The Development of Kenyan Christianity 1498-1973*, edited by David B. Barrett, George K. Mambo, Janice McLaughlin, and Malcolm J. McVeigh, 295-301. Kisumu: Evangel Publishing House, 1973.

Holy, Ladislav. *Religion and Custom in a Muslim Society: The Berti of Sudan*. New York: Cambridge Univ. Press, 1991.

hooks, bell. *Feminist Theory: From Margin to Center*. Boston: South End Press, 2000.

Horowitz, C. R., and C. Jackson. "'Female Circumcision'": African Women Confront American Medicine." *Journal of General Internal Medicine* 12 (1997): 491-99.

Hosken, Fran P. *The Hosken Report: Genital and Sexual Mutilation of Females*. 4th ed. Lexington, MA: Women's International Network News, 1993.

Jackman, Mary R. "Gender, Violence, and Harassment." In *Handbook of the Sociology of Gender*, edited by Janet Saltzman Chafetz, 275-317. New York: Kluwer Academic Plenum Publishers, 1999.

James, Stanlie. "Listening to Other(ed) Voices: Reflections around Female Genital Cutting." In *Genital Cutting and Transnational Sisterhood: Disputing US Polemics*, edited by Stanlie M. James and Claire C. Robertson, 87-113. Urbana: Univ. of Illinois Press, 2002.

Kabira, Wanjiku Mukabi. "Images of Women in African Oral Literature: An Overview of Images of Women in Gikuyu Oral Narratives." In *Understanding Oral Literature*, edited by Austin Bukenya, Wanjiku Mukabi Kabira, and Okoth Okombo, 77-84. Nairobi: Nairobi Univ. Press, 1994.

Kahiga, Miriam. "One Rite, Too Many Wrongs," *Daily Nation*, April 1994.

Kanogo, Tabitha. "Kikuyu Women and the Politics of Protest: Mau Mau." In *Images of Women in Peace and War: Cross Cultural Historical Perspectives*, edited by Sharon MacDonald, Pat Holden, and Shirley Ardener, 78-99. London: Macmillan, 1987.

Kanyoro, Musimbi R. A. "Cultural Hermeneutics: An African Contribution." In *Other Ways of Reading African Women and the Bible*, edited by Musa W. Dube, 101-13. Geneva: WCC Publications, 2001.

———. *Introducing Feminist Cultural Hermeneutics: An African Perspective*. Cleveland: Pilgrim Press, 2002.

Kassindja, Fauziya. *Do They Hear You When You Cry?* New York: Delacorte Press, 1998.

Kemei, Kipchumba. "38 Girls Evade Circumcision." *East African Standard.* May 5, 2003. Available from *East African Standard*, www.eastandard.net/headlines/news0505200301.htm.

Kenyatta, Jomo. *Facing Mount Kenya: The Tribal Life of the Gikuyu.* New York: Vintage Books, 1962 (1938).

———. "Christianity and Clitoridectomy." In *Christianity in Africa: As Seen by Africans*, edited by Ram Desai, 84-88. Denver, CO: Alan Swallow, 1962.

Kinoti, Hannah. "Women and Spirit Possession." In *Groaning in Faith: African Women in the Household of God*, edited by Musimbi R. A. Kanyoro and Nyambura J. Njoroge, 230-41. Nairobi: Acton Publishers, 1996.

Kitzinger, Celia. "Problematizing Pleasure: Radical Feminist Deconstructions of Sexuality and Power." In *Power/Gender Social Relations in Theory and Practice*, edited by H. Lorraine Radtke and Hendrikusj Stam, 194-215. London: Sage Publications, 1994.

Knappert, Jan. *East Africa: Kenya, Tanzania and Uganda.* New Delhi: Vikas Publishing House, 1987.

Lacey, Mark. "Genital Cutting Shows Signs of Losing Favor in Africa." *The New York Times*, June 8, 2004. Available at http://www.nytimes.com/2004/06/08/international/africa/08cutt.html.

Lane, Sandra D., and Robert A. Rubinstein. "Judging the Other: Responding to Traditional Female Genital Mutilation Surgeries." *Hastings Center Report* 26, no. 3 (1996): 31-40.

Levine, Amy. "Sexuality." In *Encyclopedia of Women and World Religion*, vol. 2, edited by Serenity Young, 888-91. New York: Macmillan Reference, 1999.

Levinson, Pnina Nave. "Women and Sexuality: Traditions and Progress." In *Women, Religion and Sexuality: Studies on the Impact of Religious Teachings on Women*, edited by Jeanne Beecher, 45-63. Philadelphia: Trinity Press International, 1991.

Lewis, Hope. "Between Irua and 'Female Genital Mutilation,' Feminists Human Rights Discourse and the Cultural Divide." *Harvard Human Rights Journal* 8 (Spring 1995): 1-55.

Lightfoot-Klein, Hanny. *Prisoners of Ritual: An Odyssey into Female Genital Circumcision in Africa.* New York: Harrington Park, 1989.

———. "The Sexual Experience and Marital Adjustment of Genital Circumcised and Infibulated Females in the Sudan." *The Journal of Sex Research* 26, no. 3 (1989): 375-92.

Lingermann, Patricia Madoo, and Jill Niebrugge-Brantley. "Contemporary Feminist Theory." In *Sociological Theory*, 5th ed., edited by George Ritzer, 443-89. New York: McGraw Hill, 2000.

MacKinnon, Catharine A. "A Feminist/Political Approach: Pleasure under Patriarchy." In *Theories of Human Sexuality*, edited by James H. Geer and William T. O'Donohue, 65-90. New York: Plenum Press, 1987.

————. "Sexuality." In *Feminist Theory: A Reader*, edited by Wendy K. Kolmar and Frances Bartkowski, 437-49. Toronto: Mayfield Publishing Company, 2000.

Maendeleo Ya Wanawake Organization (MYWO). *Harmful Traditional Practices That Affect the Health of the Women and Their Children*. Nairobi: MYWO, 1993.

Makabila, Stephen. "Over 100 Girls Flee FGM, Hide in Churches." *East African Standard*, February 7, 2003.

Mann, Judy. "Torturing Girls Is Not a Cultural Right." *The Washington Post*, February 23, 1994.

Mashuq Ibn Ally, Muhammad. "Theology of Islamic Liberation." In *World Religions and Human Liberation*, edited by Daniel C. Cohn-Sherbok. Maryknoll, NY: Orbis Books, 1992.

Mbiti, John S. *African Religions and Philosophy*. London: Heinemann Educational Books, 1990.

————. *Concepts of God in Africa*. London: SPCK, 1970.

McLean, Scilla, ed. "Female Circumcision, Excision, and Infibulation: The Facts and Proposal for Change." Report 47/3. London: Minority Rights Group International, 1985.

McVeigh, Malcolm J. "Theological Issues Related to Kenyan Religious Independency." In *Kenya Churches Handbook: The Development of Kenyan Christianity 1498-1973*, edited by David B. Barrett, George K. Mambo, Janice McLaughlin, and Malcolm J. McVeigh, 135-45. Kisumu, Kenya: Evangel Publishing House, 1973.

"Meru Elders Reject Female Cut." *The Nation* (Nairobi), March 30, 1999. Available at http://www.hartford-hwp-com/archives/36/index-beaa.html.

"Missionaries Successful in Curbing Female Mutilation in Kenya." *Afrol News*, December 11, 2000. Available at http://www.afrol.com/html/Categories/Women/wom018_fgm_kenya.htm. Accessed June 19, 2004.

Moore, Henrietta L. *Space, Text, and Gender: An Anthropological Study of the Marakwet of Kenya*. London: Cambridge Univ. Press, 1986.

Morgan, Robin, and Gloria Steinem. "The International Crime of Genital Mutilation." In *Outrageous Acts and Everyday Rebellions*, edited by Gloria Steinem, 331-40. New York: Henry Holt and Company, 1983.

Morrow, Lance F. "Women in Sub-Saharan Africa." In *The Cross-Cultural Study of Women: A Comprehensive Guide*, edited by Margot I. Duley and Mary I. Edwards, 290-375. New York: The Feminist Press, 1986.

Mousette, Kris Ann. "Female Genital Mutilation and Refugee Status in the United States." *Boston College International and Comparative Law Review* 19, no. 2 (1999): 353-96.

Mugo, Micere Githae. "Elitist Anti-Circumcision Discourse as Mutilating and Anti-Feminist." *Case Western Reserve Law Review* 47, no. 2 (1997): 461-79.

Murray, Jocelyn M. "The Kikuyu Female Circumcision Controversy, with Special Reference to the Church Missionary Society's 'Sphere of Influence.'" Ph.D. dissertation. Los Angeles: UCLA; Ann Arbor, MI: UMI Library West: DT433.575.M7x, 1974.

Murray, John. "Varieties of Kikuyu Independent Churches." In *Kenya Churches Handbook: The Development of Kenyan Christianity 1498-1973*, edited by David Barrett, George K. Mambo, Janice McLaughlin, and Malcolm J. McVeigh, 128-34. Kisumu, Kenya: Evangel Publishing House, 1973.

Narayan, Uma. *Dislocating Cultures: Identities, Traditions, and Third-World Feminism*. New York: Routledge, 1997.

Nasimiyu-Wasike, Anne. "Christology and an African Woman's Experience." In *Faces of Jesus in Africa*, edited by Robert J. Schreiter, 70-84. Maryknoll, NY: Orbis Books, 1991.

Nasong'o, S. W. "Women and Economic Liberalization in Kenya: The Impact and Challenges of Globalization." In *Women in African Development: The Challenge of Globalization and Liberalization in the 21ˢᵗ Century*, edited by Sylvain Boko, Mina Baliamoune-Lutz, and Sitawa R. Kimuna, 37–64. Trenton, NJ: Africa World Press, 2005.

Nation Correspondent, "Teenager Dies in Hospital after Secret 'Cut' at Home." *Daily Nation* on the Web, December 9, 2003. Available at http://www.nationmedia.com/dailynation/oldarchives.asp?archive=True.

Nation Correspondent, "Girl Gets Ill after Being Circumcised," *Daily Nation Online*, October 1, 2004. Available at http://www.nationmeda.com.

Nelson, Harold D., ed. *Kenya: A Country Study*. Washington, DC: The American University, 1984.

Njoroge, Nyambura J. "The Bible and African Christianity: A Curse or a Blessing?" In *Other Ways of Reading: African Women and the Bible*, edited by Musa W. Dube, 207-36. Geneva: WCC Publications, 2001.

Norwegian Church Aid. "Women Rights as Human Rights: A Contradiction between Policy and Practice in Kenya." Occasional Paper Series No. 01/2004.

Nussbaum, Martha C. *Sex and Social Justice*. New York: Oxford Univ. Press, 1999.

Nyangweso, Mary. "Christ's Salvific Message and the Nandi Ritual of Female Circumcision." *Theological Studies* 63 (2002): 579-600.

Obermeyer, C. M. "Female Genital Surgeries: The Known, the Unknown, and the Unknowable." *Medical Anthropology Quarterly* 13 (1999): 79-106.

Obiora, L. Amede. "Bridges and Barricades: Rethinking Polemics and Intransigence in the Campaign against Female Circumcision." *Case Western Reserve Law Review* 47, no. 2 (1997): 275-378.

Oboler, Regina Smith. *Women, Power, and Economic Change*. Stanford, CA: Stanford Univ. Press, 1985.

Oduol, Wilhelmina. "Kenya Women's Movement: A Diagnosis of the Political Participation in Retrospect." In *The Women's Movement in Kenya*, edited by S. A. Khasiani and E. I. Njiro, 21-38. Nairobi: AAWORD-Kenya, 1993.

Oduyoye, Mercy Amba. *Daughters of Anowa: African Women and Patriarchy*. Maryknoll, NY: Orbis Books, 1999.

Okin, Susan Moller. *Women in Western Political Thought*. Princeton, NJ: Princeton Univ. Press, 1997.

Okoko, Tervil. "Kenya's No-Win War against Female Genital Mutilation." *Panafrican News Agency*, October 12, 2000. Available at http://www .hartford-hwp.com/archives/36/193.html.

Omosa, Mary. "Persistent Cultural Practices: A Review of the Status of Women in Kenya." In *From Strategies to Action: A Research Perspective*, edited by AAWORD, 61-87. Nairobi: AAWORD, 1995.

Ortner, Sherry B. "Introduction: Accounting for Sexual Meanings." In *Sexual Meanings: The Cultural Construction of Gender and Sexuality*, edited by Sherry B. Ortner and H. Whitehead, 1-27. Cambridge: Cambridge Univ. Press, 1981.

———. "Is Female to Male as Nature Is to Culture?" In *Woman, Culture and Society*, edited by M. Z. Rosaldo and L. Lamphere, 67-87. Stanford, CA: Stanford Univ. Press, 1974.

Parker, Melissa. "Rethinking Female Circumcision." *Africa* 65 (1995): 506-24.

Parrinder, Geoffrey. *Sex in the World's Religions*. New York: Oxford Univ. Press, 1980.

Rahman, Anika, and Nahid Toubia. *Female Genital Mutilation: A Practical Guide to Laws and Policies Worldwide*. New York: Zed Books, 2001.

RAINBO. *Female Circumcision and Women's Health*. New York: RAINBO, 1999.

———. Female *Circumcision: A Religious and Cultural Discussion*. New York: RAINBO, 1999.

———. *Female Circumcision: Federal and New York State Laws*. New York: RAINBO, 1999.

Reaves, Malik Stan. "Alternative Rite to Female Circumcision Spreading in Kenya." Africa News Service, November 1997. Accessed at *World History Archives*,-hartford Web Publishing http//www.hartford-hwp.com/ archives/36/index-beaa.html..

Ritzer, George. *Sociological Theory*, 5th edition. New York: McGraw Hill, 2000.

Robertson, Claire C. "Grass Roots in Kenya—Women's Genital Mutilation and 'Collective Action.'" In *Unspoken Rules: Sexual Orientation and Women's Human Rights*, edited by Rachel Rosenbloom. London: Cassell, 1996.

Rosberg, Carl G., and John Nottingham. *The Myth of "Mau Mau" Nationalism in Kenya*. London: Pall Mall Press, 1966.

Ruether, Rosemary Radford. *Sexism and God-Talk: Toward a Feminist Theology*. Boston: Beacon Press, 1993.

Salmon, Merrilee H. "Ethical Considerations in Anthropology and Archeology or Relativism and Justice for All?" *Journal of Anthropological Research* 53 (Spring 1997): 47-63

Schreiter, Robert J. *Constructing Local Theologies.* Maryknoll, NY: Orbis Books, 1997.

Schüssler Fiorenza, Elisabeth. *Bread Not Stone: The Challenge of Feminist Biblical Interpretation.* Boston: Beacon Press, 1984.

Schwartz, Pepper, and Virginia Rutter. *The Gender of Sexuality.* London: Pine Forge Press, 1998.

Segundo, Juan Luis. *The Liberation of Theology.* Maryknoll, NY: Orbis Books, 1976.

Shapiro, Judith. "Cross-Cultural Perspectives on Sexual Differentiation." In *Human Sexuality: A Comparative and Developmental Perspective,* edited by Herant A. Katchadourian, 269-308. Berkeley and Los Angeles: Univ. of California Press, 1979.

Shell-Duncan, Bettina, and Ylva Hernlund. "Female 'Circumcision' in Africa: Dimensions of the Practice and Debates." In *Female "Circumcision" in Africa: Culture, Controversy and Change,* edited by Bettina Shell-Duncan and Ylva Hernlund, 1-40. Boulder, CO: Lynne Rienner Publishers, 2000.

Shell-Duncan, Bettina, Walter Obungu Obiero, and Leunita Auko Muruli. "Women without Choices: The Debate over Medicalization of Female Genital Cutting and Its Impact on a Northern Kenyan Community." In *Female "Circumcision" in Africa: Culture, Controversy, and Change,* edited by Bettina Shell-Duncan and Ylva Hernlund, 109-28. Boulder, CO: Lynne Rienner Publishers, 2000.

Slack, Alison T. "Female Circumcision: A Critical Appraisal." *Human Rights Quarterly* 10 (1988): 437-86.

Smith, Christian. "Correcting a Curious Neglect or Bringing Religion Back In." In *Disruptive Religion: The Force of Faith in Social Movement Activism,* edited by Christian Smith, 1-25. New York: Routledge, 1996.

Smith, Dorothy. *Writing the Social Critique: Theory and Investigations.* London: Univ. of Toronto Press, 1999.

Spear, Thomas. "Toward the History of African Christianity." In *East African Expressions of Christianity,* edited by Thomas Spear and Isaria N. Kimambo, 3-25. Nairobi: East African Educational Publishers, 1999.

Steiner, Henry J., and Philip Alston. *International Human Rights in Context: Law, Politics, Morals.* Oxford: Clarendon Press, 1996.

Steward, Julian. "Comments on the Statement on Human Rights." *American Anthropology* 50, no. 2 (1948): 352-55.

Stowasser, Barbara Freyer. *Women in the Qur'an: Traditions and Interpretation.* New York: Oxford Univ. Press, 1994.

Strobel, Margaret. "Women in Religion and in Secular Ideology." In *African Women South of the Sahara,* edited by Margaret Jean Hay and Sharon Sticher, 87-102. London: Longman Group, 1984.

Telewa, Muliro, "Female Genital Mutilation Hospitalizes 21 Girls in Kenya." The British Broadcasting Company, October 31, 2001.

Temu, A. J. *British Protestant Missions*. London: Longman Group, 1972.

Thomas, Lynn. *"Ngaitana* (I Will Circumcise Myself): Lessons from Colonial Campaigns to Ban Excision in Meru, Kenya." In *Female "Circumcision" in Africa: Culture, Controversy, and Change*, edited by Bettina Shell-Duncan and Ylva Hernlund, 129-50. Boulder, CO: Lynne Rienner Publishers, 2000.

Toubia, Nahid. *Female Genital Mutilation: A Call for Global Action*. New York: RAINBO, 1995.

Umbima, Joyce K. "Kenya: Mothers in Action." In *Women, Violence, and Non-Violent Change*, edited by Aruna Gnanadason, Musimbi R. A. Kanyoro, and Lucia Ann McSpadden, 96-102. Geneva: WCC Publications, 1996.

United Nations. *Universal Declaration of Human Rights*, 1948.

———. *The United Nations Convention on the Rights of the Child*. 1990.

United Nations Development Program. *Human Development Report 1994*. New York: Oxford Univ. Press, 1994.

———. *Human Development Report 2003*. New York: Oxford Univ. Press, 2003.

Walker, Alice. *Possessing the Secret of Joy*. New York: Harcourt Brace Jovanovich, 1992.

———, and Pratibha Parmar. *Warrior Marks: Female Genital Mutilation and the Sexual Blinding of Women*. San Diego: Harcourt Brace and Co., 1993.

Walley, Christine. J. "Searching for 'Voices': Feminism, Anthropology, and the Global Debate over Female Genital Operations." In *Genital Cutting and Transnational Sisterhood: Disputing US Polemics*, edited by Stanlie M. James and Claire C. Robertson, 17-53. Urbana: Univ. of Illinois Press, 2002.

Washbourn, Penelope. "Process Thought and a Theology of Sexuality." In *God, Sex, and the Social Project*, edited by James H. Grace, 22-105. New York: Edwin Mellen Press, 1978.

Wasunna, Angela. "Towards Redirecting the Female Circumcision Debate: Legal, Ethical, and Cultural Considerations." *McGill Journal of Medicine* 5 (2002): 104-10.

Welbourn, F. B. *East African Rebels: A Study of Some Independent Churches*. London: SCM Press, 1961.

Welbourn, F. B., and B. A. Ogot. *A Place to Feel at Home: A Study of Two Independent Churches in Western Kenya*. Nairobi: Oxford Univ. Press, 1966.

West, Traci, C. *Wounds of the Spirit: Black Women, Violence, and Resistance Ethics*. New York: New York Univ. Press, 1999.

William, L., and T. Sobieszyzyk. "Attitudes surrounding the Continuation of Female Circumcision in the Sudan: Passing the Tradition to the Next Generation." *Journal of Marriage and the Family* 59 (1997): 966-81.

Wiredu, Kwasi. *Cultural Universals and Particulars: An African Perspective.* Bloomington: Indiana Univ. Press, 1996.

World Health Organization (WHO). "Female Genital Mutilation: Information Kit." Geneva: WHO, 1996.

————. "Female Genital Mutilation: World Health Assembly Calls for the Elimination of Harmful Traditional Practices." Press Release. May 12, 1993.

————. "Female Genital Mutilation: Information Pack," 1999. Available at http://www.who.int/frh-whd/FGM/infopack/English/fgm_infopack.htm.

————. "Female Genital Mutilation: Report of a WHO Technical Working Group." Geneva: WHO, 1996.

Wynter, Sylvia. "'Genital Mutilation' or 'Symbolic Birth?' Female Circumcision, Lost Origins, and the Aculturalism of Feminism/Western Thought." *Case Western Reserve Law Review* 47, no. 2 (1997): 501-53.

Young, Marion Iris. "Five Faces of Oppression." In *Rethinking Power*, SUNY Series in Radical Social and Political Theory, edited by Thomas E. Wartenberg, 174-95. Albany: State Univ. of New York Press, 1992.

FILMS

American Anthropological Association. *Rites.* 52 min. British Broadcasting Company, 1990.

Anenden, H. R. Omaar, et al. *The Road to Change.* 45 min. Geneva: World Health Organization, 1999.

The Angel Returns: Changing the Tradition of Female Circumcision. 50 min. Fatusch Productions, 2002. Available from Filmakers Library.

Changing Paths: Female Circumcision in Mali. 46 min. Fatusch Productions, 2003. Available from Filmakers Library.

Connell, M. C. Pearson, et al. *Africa's Children.* 58 min. Princeton, NJ: Films for the Humanities and Sciences, 2001.

Female Circumcision: Beliefs and Misbeliefs. 45 min. New York: RAINBO.

Folly, A. L., and Amour Production. *Femmes aux Yeux Ouverts* (Women with Open Eyes). 52 min. San Francisco: California News Reel, 1994.

Hoffman, Barbara G., and University of California System. *Womanhood and Circumcision: Three Maasai Women Have Their Say.* Berkeley and Los Angeles: Univ. of California, Extension Center for Media and Independent Learning, 2002.

Hunter-Gault, Charlayne. *Rights and Wrongs.* 30 min. New York: Global Vision, International Center for Global Communications Foundation, 1993.

————, and E. L. Ortiz. *Female Circumcision.* 27 min. Global Vision, International Center for Global Communications Foundation, 1993.

————, and Global Vision Inc. *Women's Rights: A Global Movement*. 50 min. Chip Taylor Communications, 1995.

————. *Genital Mutilation*. 27 min. Global Vision International Center for Global Communications Foundation, 1993.

In the Name of God: Changing Attitudes toward Mutilation. 29 min. National Women's Studies Association, 1997. Available from Filmakers Library.

Longinotto, Kim. *The Day I Will Never Forget*. 92 min. London: Women Make Movies, 2002.

Mathis, D. A. Samad, et al. *Healthy Behaviour: Female Genital Mutilation*. 33 min. AHEAD Inc, 2001. For information, see http://www.fgmnetwork.org/reference/biblio.html.

Mayer-Hohdahl, M. S. Thomas. *Female Circumcision: Human Rites*. 40 min. Princeton, NJ: Films for the Humanities and Sciences, 1998.

Mire, Soraya. *Fire Eyes*. 60 min. 1994. Available from Filmakers Library.

Nikiema B., and D. Kabore. *Ma Fille ne Sera Pas Excisée* (My Daughter Will Not Be Circumcised). 70 min. Brussels: Médiatheque des Trios Mondes, 1990.

Ousmane, Sembene. 2004. *Moolaade*. 124 min. New Yorker Films, 2004.

Panton, Louise. *Female Circumcision*. BBC Enterprises, 1983.

Radosh, P. *Cross Cultural Compassions*. 120 min. Western Illinois Univ. Board of Governors Univ., 1995. Available from RMI Media Distributor.

Rashad, Sara. *Tahara*. 18 min. From the Heart Productions, 2004.

Rights of Passage. 30 min. UNICEF, 1994. Available online from UNICEF.

Senegal: The Power to Change. 30 min. G. I. Polden for NRK, 2000. Available from Filmakers Library.

Shafik, Viola. *The Season of Planting of Girls: A Documentary*. 37 min. Mediahouse Productions, 1999.

Walker, Alice, and Pratibha Parmar. *Warrior Marks*. London: Women Make Movies, 1995.

WNET Thirteen, *Women under Attack*. Oakland, CA: Global Vision, 1993.

Yacoub, Z. M., et al. 1994. *Feminine Dilemma: Women Circumcision*. 22 min. Tele-Tchad (Chad Television Network), 1994.

Zirn J. P. *Des Lames et des Femmes*. 22 min. Brussels: Médiatheque des Trios Mondes, 1990.

ADDITIONAL REPORTS ON FEMALE CIRCUMCISION ON THE INTERNET

Bartoo, Vincent. "FGM: Rights Group, Parents Clash Over Missing Girls." January 30, 2004. Available from STOPFGM! The Media International Press Releases, *East African Standard*, Daily Newspaper, http://www.stopfgm.org/stopfgm/Media/scheda.jsp?idMedia=774&Mediatype=1.

Carnell, Brian. "Female Genital Mutilation Hospitalizes 21 Girls in Kenya." February 13, 2002. Available from Equityfeminism.com at http://www .equityfeminism.com/articles/2002/000023.html.

Gakunga, Agnes. "Muslims to Fight FGM," December 18, 2003. Available from *Kenya Times* at http://www.kentimes.com/18dec03/nwsstory/ news28.html.

"Girls Rescued from 'Cut' May Leave School." February 19, 2004. Available from STOPFGM! The Media International Releases, *Daily Newspaper*, http://www.stopfgm.org/stopfgm/media/scheda.jsp?idMedia=779 &mediatype=1.

Mathenge, Gakuu. "2500 Girls Undergo Female Rite." September 12, 2003, *Daily Nation*. Available at http://wwwnationmedia.com/Dailynation/ Oldarchives.asp?archive=True and http://www.stopfgm.org/stopfgm/ media/scheda.jsp?idmedia=611&Mediatype=1.

Mwangi, Susan. "Contrary to Expectations, FGM Flourishes Underground." *Daily Nation*, July 20, 2001. Available at http//www.nationmedia.com/ dailynation/oldarchives.asp?archive=True and www.nationaudio.com/ News/DailyNation/Today/Comment?Comment1.html.

Okoko, Tervil. "Teenage Girl Bleeds to Death after Ritual." *Panafrican News Agency*, December 11, 2000. Available at http://www.duei.deliak/show .php/de/content/archiv/fgm/AfrPresse.html.

Omanga, Beautah, and Bernard Kwalia. "Parents Defy Female Cut Ban." Available from *Daily Nation* (Nairobi), December 5, 2003. Available at http://www.nationmedia.com/dailynation?oldarchives.asp?archives=True and http://www.nationaudio.com/New/DailyNation/05/22003/ News05122003150.htm.

Panafrican News Agency, "Despite Campaigns, Female Circumcision Continues in Kenya." Available from *Somalia Watch*, March 23, 2000. Available at http://www.somaliawatch.org/archive/000323102.htm.

Reuters MSNBC News Online Media. 2003. "Kenyan Woman Circumcises Herself to Please In-laws." August 29, 2003. Available from STOPFGM! The Media International Releases. Available at http://www.stopfgm/ stopfgm/media/scheda.jsp?idmedia=607&mediatype=1.

Whiting, Kristin. "Reporter's Notebook: Female Circumcision in Africa," February 19, 2002. Available at http:news.nationalgeographic.com/news/ 2002/02/0220_020219_TVcircumcision.html.

Index